Smithsonian Folkways Recordings

AMERICAN
MUSICAL
TRADITIONS

Smithsonian Folkways Recordings

AMERICAN MUSICAL TRADITIONS

Volume

Native American Music

Jeff Todd Titon

Bob Carlin

SCHIRMER REFERENCE

GALE GROUP

THOMSON LEARNING

New York • Detroit • San Diego • San Francisco
Boston • New Haven, Conn. • Waterville, Maine
London • Munich

Schirmer Reference
1633 Broadway
New York, NY 10019

Gale Group
27500 Drake Rd.
Farmington Hills, MI 48331

Library of Congress Cataloging-in-Publication Data

    American musical traditions / [general editors] Jeff Todd Titon, Bob Carlin.
      P.   cm.
    "Published in collaboration with The Smithsonian Folkways Archive."
    Includes bibliographical references, discographies, videographies, and index.
    Contents: v. 1. Native American music—v. 2. African American music—v. 3. British Isles music—v. 4.
      European American music—v. 5. Latino and Asian American Music.
    ISBN 0-02-864624-X (set)
    1. Folk music—United States—History and criticism—Juvenile literature. 2. Music—United States-History and criticism
      —Juvenile literature. 3. Ethnomusicology—Juvenile literature. [1. Folk music—History and criticism. 2. Music—History
      and criticism.]
    I. Titon, Jeff Todd, 1943-   II. Carlin, Bob.

ML3551.A53 2001
781.62'00973-dc21

TABLE OF CONTENTS
VOLUME 1

TABLE OF CONTENTS
VOLUMES 2, 3, 4, AND 5

VOLUME 2: AFRICAN AMERICAN MUSIC

VOLUME 3: BRITISH ISLES MUSIC

VOLUME 4: EUROPEAN AMERICAN MUSIC

CENTRAL/SOUTHERN EUROPEAN—ACADIAN/FRENCH MUSIC

CENTRAL/SOUTHERN EUROPEAN—ITALIAN MUSIC

GERMAN/EASTERN EUROPEAN MUSIC

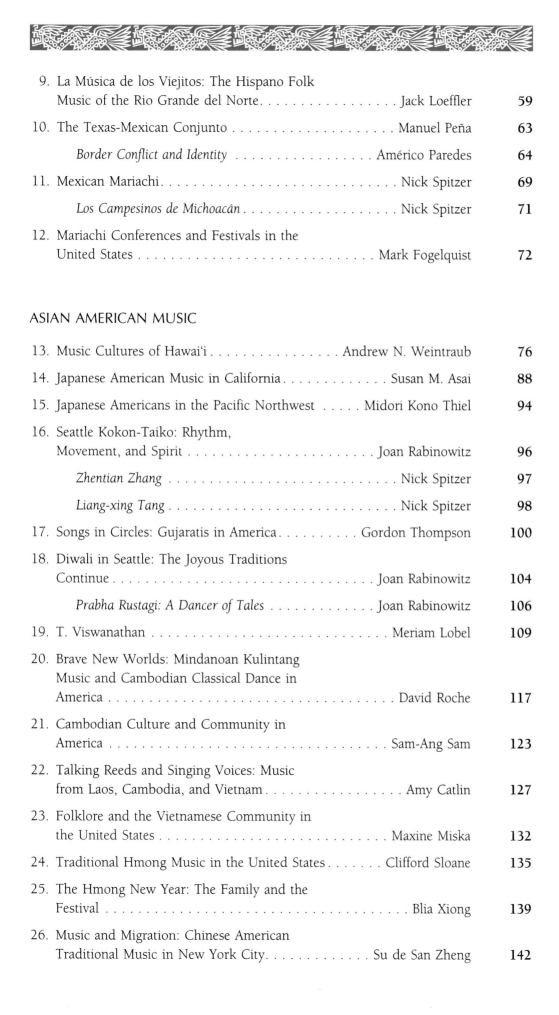

INTRODUCTION TO *AMERICAN MUSICAL TRADITIONS*

Jeff Todd Titon

This five-volume work presents an American musical mosaic. Folklorists and ethnomusicologists whose research centers on musical traditions in the United States wrote authoritative essays specifically for *American Musical Traditions*. We solicited additional materials from the Smithsonian Institution's Center for Folklife and Cultural Heritage, particularly from Smithsonian Folkways Recordings and the Smithsonian Folklife Festival. Keyed to musical examples and illustrations on both the Smithsonian Folkways website and the Brown University website (addresses below), *American Musical Traditions* presents a combination of words, sounds, and images so readers can hear, as well as read about, much of the music under discussion.

It goes without saying that at the start of the twenty-first century, every community in the United States has music. But this has been true for as long as the continent has been settled by humans; among the Native Americans, music (and dance) has always played an important role in ceremony and recreation.

My great-grandparents grew up in a world in which people who wanted to hear music had to learn to sing and play it themselves. Today televisions, videocassette recorders, radios, and compact disc players can be found in most American households, along with collections of recordings. All of these are products of the twentieth-century revolution in electromechanical musical reproduction, permitting anyone to hear music on demand without performing it.

In addition to the old methods of distributing music, a dizzying array of new digital formats and delivery methods, including mini-disc, CD-R, CD-RW, mp3, and DVD, along with the World Wide Web, are bringing music into the new century, while musical performance itself is being reconceived with the help of electronic equipment, sampling, and computers. Today, of course, music from all over the globe is available at the flip of a switch or movement of a computer mouse. But every community also has its live music makers. Music is taught and learned in the public schools, in music academies, and by private teachers. Community bands and orchestras, informal chamber music groups, singer-songwriters with guitars, basement or garage rock and country bands, singers of all stylistic persuasions—these music makers can be found in just about every community, large or small.

Outside the mainstream there is another kind of music, one that members of certain populations regard as their own. While contemporary popular music is set in the present and strives for novelty and sales, and while classical music looks to the future and strives for originality, this other music, which in this book we call "traditional," is almost always linked to the past and bounded in certain ways. The traditional music we have in mind usually arises in connection with ethnic or regional identity, and sometimes it is connected to an original homeland outside the United States. The groups that possess traditional music often

attach it to particular (named) people and places, with ties to an older generation of source musicians from whom it has been learned.

Traditional music has sometimes been called folk music, but in university circles today the word "folk" carries troublesome baggage (such as nationalism, purity, and noblesse oblige) and so the younger generation of scholars tends to avoid it. Today the word "traditional" often substitutes for "folk," but "tradition" can be a troublesome word as well. Scholars have shown that it is naive to consider traditions a set of ancient, sacred rules, like the American Constitution, that we must interpret reverentially. Traditions turn out to be far more flexible than we ever imagined. After all, traditions must adapt to the present moment or they will fail; and more than a few traditions turn out, on inspection, to be the invention of things we want to believe about the past but that have little or no basis in fact. For example, the contemporary sound of "Irish traditional music"—represented by popular Irish bands featuring uillean pipes, fiddles, wooden flutes, guitars, tin whistles, citterns, bouzoukis, and bodhrans, a sound that is marketed as "Celtic music" and is sometimes pictured with ancient mists and druidic artifacts on album covers—turns out to be only a few decades old. The periodic revival of Celtic culture seems to be a tradition itself, one that the poet William Butler Yeats invoked more than a hundred years ago in *The Celtic Twilight*.

Today it is easy to debunk invented traditions wherever an ancient pedigree is foolishly sought, and music seems particularly susceptible to this kind of search. Yet when the dust settles we see that all living traditions bend the past to the present in order to continue into the future. Regarded in the present as manifestations of the past, they are thought to carry some authority (or not carry it) by virtue of that association.

In the upper Midwest, for example, where Germans, Swedes, Finns, and Norwegians settled more than a hundred years ago, many communities have retained, and revived, and in so reviving further developed, musical traditions that are recogniz-ably their own. The same is true of other ethnic immigrant populations in different parts of the country. It is a mistake to think that traditions are rigid. Change, it seems, is built into most musical traditions. African Americans created music styles such as the blues, spirituals, jazz, and soul music, all featuring improvisation. Hip-hop, the most modern musical manifestation of this improvised cultural tradition, has its roots in the oral poetry of the African American "toast" (Jackson 1974) and in a lengthy tradition of vernacular dance. In African American musical traditions, innovation is the norm.

Geographical region, ethnic population, and musical style have guided most research into American vernacular musical traditions. This work reflects those boundaries. Volume 1 presents Native American music; Volume 2 offers African American music; Volume 3 concentrates on the music of the British Isles, including Ireland, in America. These are the three areas that have received the most attention from musical scholars. In the last thirty years or so, research has increasingly focused on the music of European and Asian immigrant ethnic groups. Volume 4 therefore presents music from European American immigrant communities, including those from France, Italy, Germany, Poland, Czechoslovakia, Hungary, Sweden, Norway, and Finland; and Volume 5 offers music from the Spanish-speaking communities as well as Asian American music. Readers who wish to learn more about how and where ethnic groups settled in the United States are referred to James Paul Allen and Eugene James Turner, *We the People: An Atlas of America's Ethnic Diversity,* and to the *Harvard Encyclopedia of American Ethnic Groups.*

Organizing these volumes according to ethnic groups must not leave the impression of a rigid, balkanized United States of tight-knit musical enclaves. Classical music is available to all. Few consider this Western art music to have ethnic boundaries. Popular music that comes from the media is also open to all. While many musical communities do take stewardship of music they identify as their own, their people also participate in the mainstream of America's popular

music styles that do not reflect the perspective of any single group. In addition, they may adopt practitioners who learn their traditional music but who did not grow up in their communities.

Although the Navajo, for example, continue to practice their traditional ceremonial and recreational music, they compose music in new modes reflecting influences from contemporary gospel music, Hollywood film music, acoustic guitar–based singer-songwriter music, and New Age music, among others. Yet the most popular music on the reservations is country music, and Navajos regularly form country and rock bands.

Nor should we think of traditional music as extending unchanged back through time. The accordion, a musical staple for several generations among Hispanic musicians on the Texas-Mexican border, was borrowed from German immigrants to that region. The guitar, regarded by some as the American folk instrument par excellence, gained its great popularity only in the twentieth century. And the five-string banjo, identified today with hillbillies and bluegrass musicians, derives from an African instrument that, along with the African American population, significantly changed the sound and style of vernacular dance music in the American South. Although this work emphasizes those styles of music that the various ethnic musical communities consider to be their own, we do not wish to claim that this is the only, or necessarily the principal, music with which the people in these communities are involved.

These volumes are not meant to cover each and every musical tradition. It would be impossible to do so; first because this work is not large enough, and second because the scholarship available is uneven in coverage. There are many more musical communities than scholars surveying the subject. We have selected representative communities and musical genres to give an idea of the range of traditional music in the United States. Some of this research is current, representing musical communities today; some is historical and represents musical communities in the past. The writing

includes two main perspectives: essays on communities and examples of their music, and interviews or profiles of particular musicians and musical groups. Although this is a large work, we do not claim to be comprehensive or definitive; thus we invite further research. Because each volume has an introductory essay describing its contents, in what follows I will discuss the origin and development of the project as a whole.

From the outset, this reference work was conceived to reflect recent research by folklorists and ethnomusicologists on the one hand, and the holdings of the Smithsonian Institution's Center for Folklife and Cultural Heritage on the other. Since the early 1970s, public-sector folklorists, ethnomusicologists, and their academic colleagues have surveyed ethnic and regional music-making in many communities across the United States. Often sponsored by arts councils, cultural organizations, and community initiatives, and in many cases underwritten by the Folk Arts Division of the National Endowment for the Arts, the American Folklife Center of the Library of Congress, and the Smithsonian's Center for Folklife and Cultural Heritage (formerly the Office of Folklife Programs), from about 1977 to 1995 folklorists could be found in nearly every one of the fifty states, surveying folklife and expressive culture (including music) and documenting and presenting the products of this research. Those products were unprecedented in number and quality. Fieldnotes, booklets, recordings, videos, festivals, tours, exhibits, and apprenticeships most often were targeted back into those communities rather than meant for archives or a central data bank.

Cutbacks and reorientation in public funding for the arts, however, coupled with the lack of formal, ongoing, institutional support, have redirected public-sector workers' efforts toward heritage and tourism. Thus, it seemed an appropriate moment to ask these fieldworkers and arts administrators to contribute essays to a project that would gather some of this work together. Accordingly, in 1995 I sent out a prospectus for this work along with invitations to all

the state folklorists and ethnomusicologists listed in the *Public Folklore Newsletter* as well as to numerous academic colleagues, inviting topics, entries, and proposals for additional contributors. It was a long process, but several people responded positively and the fruits of their labors are evident throughout these volumes, as their contributions make up a substantial proportion of this work. Obtaining them and guiding their direction was my main task. Co-editor Bob Carlin's primary job was to select materials from the Smithsonian Institution for these volumes.

Many contributors to this project also worked, at one time or another, for the Smithsonian Folklife Festival, formerly known as the Festival of American Folklife (FAF); and therefore we could draw upon that work for their contributions to this volume. The Smithsonian Folklife Festival is an ongoing, multicultural, international event, staged annually since 1967 in the nation's capital on the mall between the Lincoln Memorial and Washington Monument. It is the largest and by far the most expansive, longest-lasting folk festival in the United States. Typically it runs for two weeks during late June and early July and features a few hundred singers, musicians, dancers, storytellers, crafters, and other folk artists in an outdoor museum setting meant to celebrate the diverse folkways of the United States and other lands. The Festival presents these folk artists on stages, in tents, and in open-air locations where they perform and demonstrate for an audience of tourists amid a celebratory atmosphere. During the more than thirty years that the FAF has run, the staff has implemented a cultural policy that involves more than merely a demonstration and preservation theater. Theirs is a vision of a multicultural world living in harmony, celebrating mutuality while learning from different traditions.

From the outset, the festival planners understood the importance of documentation as well as presentation. Every event that took place on every stage was recorded by festival staff. Festival recordings and related materials are housed in the Ralph Rinzler

Folklife Archives and Collections at the Center for Folklife and Cultural Heritage, Smithsonian Institution. Each year an elaborate program booklet is prepared for the public. It contains essays introducing many of the individuals and the communities featured at the festival. Written by the folklorists and ethnomusicologists who had researched the music, crafts, and other expressions of folklife for the annual presentations, these essays are both authoritative and accessible. Often they are the best short introductions to the musics of particular ethnic and regional communities; we have drawn liberally on them for this volume. The Smithsonian's other contribution derives from the materials in Smithsonian Folkways Recordings.

Folkways Recordings, begun in 1948 by Moses Asch, reflected the very broad tastes of its founder. From the Folkways catalog you could hear everything from the demonstration collection of world music recorded at the turn of the twentieth century for the Berlin Archiv to the music of Leadbelly, Woody Guthrie, and Pete Seeger, as well as the famous Harry Smith *Anthology of American Folk Music,* recently reissued by Smithsonian Folkways.

But Asch did not stop there. Modern poetry in the voices of the authors, bird songs, and even the sounds of factory work fell within the recorded output of this eclectic operation. Folkways was one of very few record companies in the 1940s and 1950s publishing folk music from American communities, including Native American and European immigrants, along with the British American and African American music that collectors had been emphasizing throughout the twentieth century. Many, but not all, of these albums came with copious (and only lightly edited) documentation by the field researchers and other experts, in the form of notes slipped into the double-channeled Folkways album cover. Folkways recordings cost a little more than most, but they provided more, too; and in many instances they provided the only recordings available representing various populations on the planet. During the folk revival of the late 1950s and early 1960s, Folkways was the first to

present the traditional music of Roscoe Holcomb, Wade Ward, Doc Watson, and others from the southern Appalachian Mountains. Much of their material is of enormous historical value and, for that reason, we have preserved the original text that accompanied their works.

In 1987, the Smithsonian's Folklife division acquired Folkways Recordings and hired Anthony Seeger to direct the operation. (In 2001 Seeger was replaced by Daniel Sheehy, formerly the Director of the Folk Arts Program, National Endowment for the Arts.) Smithsonian Folkways kept all of the back catalog in print (it can be ordered at any time from their website), and they have produced more than a hundred new albums; we have drawn liberally on those with American subjects for this work. Finally, we have gone outside of commissioned articles and Smithsonian materials to obtain other well-documented descriptions of musical communities where they were needed to fill in gaps. We present the whole as a spicy stew, a mosaic, and a mix that we think will appeal and stimulate the reader's appetite for more.

LINKS TO WEBSITES

On occasion, the essays in *American Musical Traditions* discuss recordings that are part of the vast Smithsonian Folkways library, particularly those essays that were originally Smithsonian materials. The relevant Folkways catalog number for the recordings appears in each essay's headnote, when available, or elsewhere in the essay. Readers may then visit the Internet's World Wide Web to listen to those recordings; in many cases, they are available for direct purchase online after they have been previewed. The Smithsonian recordings, in both Liquid Audio and RealAudio format, may be downloaded from the Smithsonian Folkways website, which is found at http://www.si.edu/ folkways. There, readers should click on the "Liquid Audio" link to go directly to the Smithsonian's catalog of recordings.

In addition, I am building my own site at Brown University to house links to record-

ings and other materials that are not part of the Folkways collections. As *American Musical Traditions* was going to press, the site was still under construction, but content is being added. It can be located at http://www.stg.brown.edu/MusicAtlas.

VOLUME 1: NATIVE AMERICAN MUSIC

This first volume of *American Musical Traditions* brings together research on Native American music conducted since the mid-twentieth century. Some essays give a historical overview of the musical and dance styles practiced by the various tribes discussed here; some of these dance and musical styles may have changed or ceased to exist today. The volume is organized by tribes, moving from east to west across the United States. The two introductory essays comment on Native American music as a whole; at the end of the volume, there are two essays on modern adaptations that have occurred as Native American culture has mixed with diverse influences, from rock and roll to reggae.

GLOSSARY AND INDEX

Each volume of *American Musical Traditions* includes a glossary of terms used in that volume and an index that includes citations to all five volumes in the series. Throughout the essays and sidebars in each volume, certain terms appear in boldface, indicating that the term is fully defined in the glossary at the back of the book. The glossary also includes "See" and "See also" references to make locating the appropriate term easier. The index in each volume is comprehensive—that is, it includes citations to all five volumes of *AMT,* not just the individual volume. Numerals followed by a colon and then the page number are used to indicate in which volume a citation appears. In addition, page references in bold refer to a main essay or sidebar on that topic and page references in italics refer to photos; maps are

clearly indicated. Index sub-topics are indented beneath the main topic. For example, an index citation for drums might look like this:

Drums, 1:**23–28**, 2:54, 3: 125
   double-barreled drum, 2:76
   in Native American ceremonies, 1:48
   in calypso music, 5:35
   spread of across the Great Plains 1:98 (*map*)

ACKNOWLEDGMENTS

We gratefully acknowledge the assistance of the Smithsonian Institution's Folklife division, the National Endowment for the Arts' Folk Arts Program, the Scholarly Technology Group of Brown University, and Schirmer Reference in making this project possible. We thank the many artists and musicians who cooperated with the researchers who wrote the entries, as well as the researchers themselves who are named in this book as contributors. Special thanks to the authors of the introductions to each volume: Burt Feintuch, David Evans, Thomas Vennum, Philip Nusbaum, and Tom Van Buren. Thanks to Art Rosenbaum for his wonderful cover designs. In addition, we would like to thank Richard Carlin for overseeing this project and keeping it on track during his tenure at Schirmer. Thank you to Charlotte Heth for her expert review of the Native American volume. Finally, we are grateful to those in the Smithsonian Institution who helped with this project. Anthony Seeger and the staff of Smithsonian Folkways made their archives available to us. Diana Parker, director of the Smithsonian Folklife Festival, and Richard Kurin, head of the Smithsonian's Office of Folklife and Cultural Heritage, helped us obtain additional information related to the musical communities represented down through the years at the Festival.

We would also like to thank our editors including Deborah Gillan Straub, Stephen Wasserstein, and Brad Morgan, as well as the members of Gale's production and design staff, including Wendy Blurton, Evi Seoud, Mary Beth Trimper, Randy Bassett, Barb Yarrow, Pam Reed, Christine O'Bryan, Tracey Rowens, Cindy Baldwin, Margaret Chamberlain, and others who provided able assistance.

BIBLIOGRAPHY

Allen, James Paul; and Turner, Eugene James. (1988). *We the People: An Atlas of America's Ethnic Diversity.* New York: Macmillan.

Jackson, Bruce, compiler. (1974). *"Get Your Ass in the Water and Swim Like Me!": Narrative Poetry from the Black Oral Tradition.* Cambridge: Harvard University Press.

Thernstrom, Stephan. (1980). *Harvard Encyclopedia of American Ethnic Groups.* Cambridge: Harvard University Press.

INTRODUCTION

Thomas Vennum, Jr.

Thomas Vennum, Jr., is curator of the Native American music program at the Festival of American Folklife. He is senior ethnomusicologist in the Center for Folklife Programs and Cultural Studies and author of The Ojibwa Dance Drum: Its History and Construction *(1982) and* Wild Rice and the Ojibway People *(1988).*

The oldest body of music in North America is kept alive today by Indian tribes who survived the European colonization of the continent. The pervasiveness of Indian song and dance in nearly every Indian community testifies to the continuing central role of music in what these people recognize as their "traditional" culture. Despite their decimation through warfare and disease and centuries of cultural oppression by missionaries and government agents, Indian people have managed to maintain a tie, however tenuous, to their ancient past through their music. The survival of some old ceremonies and their song **repertoires** is attributable to their having been "hidden" from the authorities, as H. F. "Pete" Gregory asserts in his essay, "Music Holds the People Together."

Although a rich and varied corpus of music exists, as is evident in the essays in this book, it is still possible to make some generalizations about North American Indian music to distinguish it from, say, the tribal music of West Africa. To cite but one example: Both musics contain large repertoires of songs accompanied by percussion, but in Africa the drummers and singers may be grouped apart, whereas in North America, most singers provide *their own* percussion accompaniment. African singers often perform in **parallel thirds** (**harmony**) and the drummers may provide simultaneously more than one layer of beats (**polyrhythm**), whereas North American Indians, for the most part, sing and drum in **unison**.

Most Indian music consists of songs performed with rhythmic accompaniment meant to regulate the steps and choreography of dancers. Because traditional Indian music, at least until recently, is considered sacred in origin and purpose, participants consider dancing to it a form of prayer, a means of supplicating the spirits or expressing gratitude to them. The dancers are typically dressed in some sort of regalia that incorporate an assortment of symbolic decoration of beadwork, animal skins, bird

CHUKCHI SEA

ARCTIC OCEAN

BERING SEA

Bering Strait

BEAUFORT SEA

BAFFIN BAY

LABRADOR SEA

GULF OF ALASKA

HUDSON BAY

Yupik

Kutchin

U.S.A.
CANADA

PACIFIC OCEAN

Kwakiutl
Haida

CANADA
U.S.A.
Blackfoot
Flathead

Chippewa

Pawnee

Seneca

ATLANTIC OCEAN

Navajo
Pueblos
Yaqui
O'odham

Cherokee
Choctow

Cherokee
Creek

MEXICO

U.S.A.

GULF OF MEXICO

Arctic
Subarctic
Northwest Coast
Plateau
Great Basin
California
Southwest
Great Plains
Northeast
Southeast
Middle America
Caribbean Area

CARIBBEAN SEA

0   1000 Mi
0   1000 Km

Regional Overview of Native American Tribes in North America

feathers, or all of these. (The regard for the serious purpose of dance is clear: When, today, an Indian woman arrives at a social dance in street dress, as her token nod to tradition she will invariably borrow a shawl from a friend before entering the dance circle.) James S. Griffith gives a good description of dance regalia in his essay on the Yaqui Pascola/Deer Dance; Ann Fienup-Riordan does the same in her piece on Yupik dancing.

The basic unit of Indian music is the song, which may last only fifteen seconds or take several minutes to perform. Many tribes have arranged their briefer songs into **cycles**, so that they are performed continuously without interruption (for example, the Oklahoma Cherokee **hymn** cycles, as described by Charlotte Heth). The song may be performed by a soloist or a group singing in unison. Most singers are male, but the repertoire includes **genres** typically sung by females, such as love songs.

Songs are composed by individuals recognized within their community for their talent, although ritual song composition by group is occasionally found—Pueblo musicians in their kivas, for instance. Given the sacred nature of song, their creators may receive them in dreams or through visions, the normal sphere of song composition. There are certain restrictions as to their use; considered the personal property of their recipients, they may be bought and sold or exchanged with other tribes. (As Gene Weltfish relates in her essay, the Pawnee Kind Warrior in the early 1800s returned to his people after three years among the Wichita, bringing back with him their Deer Dance and its songs; for Haida ownership and song exchange, see Ida Halpern's essay.) Upon the owner's death their ownership may revert to a close relative or even be added to the tribal repertoire. Use restrictions may also impose taboos on their performance; some songs can be performed only in certain seasons, or may be specified by gender as to who may sing them. Thus, as Michael Kline tells us, the Cherokee Medicine song is meant to be performed only at sunrise to protect oneself from witchcraft, and singing Eagle Dance

songs in summer would bring undesired cold weather.

Lacking musical notation, Indian people have handed down their songs orally, sometimes through generations. Indian children are exposed to music frequently at an early age; as they grow they may begin to sing with their elders, thus ensuring accurate transmittal. According to Mary Frances Riemer, this is how the Seneca Avery Jimerson learned, by accompanying his father to the longhouse ceremonies, and he in turn taught the repertoire at the local high school. Making a mistake while performing a song or dance can have severe consequences. Ida Halpern describes the intense training required of the young Kwakiutl Christine Twice to avoid mistakes during a potlatch.

North American Indian songs may contain meaningful words in the native language (or English) or in lexically meaningless syllables called **vocables**, but they usually feature some combination of the two. The texts (except for lengthy ritual cycles) are normally brief, and their meaning—even if intelligible—is usually obscured by archaic language and oblique references to spiritual matters. Many of the more sacred songs contain texts whose meaning is known only to their owner.

As Indian languages began their decline (hastened in part by government boarding schools, where children were prevented from using them), the proportion of texted songs greatly decreased, and songs were performed increasingly in vocables, albeit in strict, fixed sequences. Linguists have debated whether vocables are in fact vestiges of meaningful but archaic words. In any case, it is rare nowadays in social contexts to hear any meaningful words in a song, although in communities where the language is making a comeback, even young singing groups may request elders to "put words" into their songs. (Halpern describes the use of vocables in the Kwakiutl hamatsa songs, while Mary Jo Ruggles does the same for Plains Indians.)

Like other tribal musics in the world, Indian music is, for the most part, utilitarian—

that is, each song has a specified use within the culture. The O'odham, for example, have songs used only in the context of some village saint's feast day; earlier they had songs connected to raids on their enemy, the Apache, or in conjunction with salt pilgrimages to the Bay of California, according to Griffith. Thus songs can be identified as to genre: songs accompanying communal labor (Pueblo ditch-cleaning songs, Navajo corn-grinding songs), various aspects of warfare (protective songs, recruiting songs, homecoming songs, scalp dance songs, death songs), gift-giving songs, and the myriad songs accompanying every movement and dance within some lengthy sacred ceremony (the various Navajo curative "ways" such as Enemy Way and Blessing Way), to cite just some of the many examples. Stylistically, these genres differ in their accompaniment patterns, styles of vocal production, forms of the song, and so on. Consequently an Indian may need only hear a brief snatch of a song to recognize, if not the very song itself, at least what genre it is ("Oh, that's a Rabbit Dance song!").

The vocal style of North American Indian music is distinctive. Singers usually perform at full volume, using slightly nasal, high-pitched tones. Styles vary by tribe, as Bruno Nettl demonstrated in his landmark study, *North American Indian Styles* (1954). Reviewing nearly everything published about the music or recorded, he was able to define six major musical culture areas in North America based on tribal sharings of certain stylistic elements. Vocal style was one of his defining criteria; thus his "Plains–Pueblo" area is characterized by group unison singing at great volume and with much evident tension in the singers' faces and necks, whereas his Great Basin vocal style, by contrast, is considerably more relaxed.

Song form was another feature. Singers on the Plains tend to use almost exclusively a standard incomplete repetition form, ABC/BC. Navajo and Apache music, on the other hand, feature AABB/CCCC/AABB verse/refrain structures. Progressive call/response forms (AA, BB, CC, DD, etc.) char-

See glossary for definition of boldfaced terms

acterize southeastern **stomp dances** songs as described by Gregory.

Because song is usually accompanied by some iterative percussion pattern provided by the singer(s), an enormously rich inventory of **membranophones** (drums) and idiophones (**rattles**, **rasps**, etc.) is found in North America. Rattle types alone comprise the most varied array in the world. Performers used almost anything that could serve as a container, filling **gourds**, animal horns, large moth cocoons, turtle carapaces, wooden and bark cylinders, and even baking powder cans with lead shot, pebbles, corn kernels, or BBs. (Gregory gives a good description of the variety of Choctaw percussion **instruments**.) The **rhythmic pattern** performed with these was also a genre identifier. War songs, for instance, used a simple repeated sequence of two beats of equal duration and intensity; scalp and **round dance** songs, by contrast, used heavy accentuations on alternate beats.

Beginning with the arrival of Europeans in North America, it was inevitable that hybrid types of music would emerge. Craig Mishler describes the emergence of indigenous Gwich'in **square dancing** as a hybrid of Native American and European dance styles. That this happened almost immediately upon contact and continues to unfold is testament to the great talent Indian people have for adaptation. I describe these many cross-influences in my essay on the changing "soundscape" of Indian music; Heth similarly shows the mix of cultures in Cherokee hymn singing. Still, as young Indian musicians venture into new areas of performance style, they observe a strict separation between their tribe's traditional repertoire and their own more individual expressions in music, as many of these authors show.

Much of what we know today about Indian song and dance can be credited to the work of pioneer musicologists around the turn of the century. (Today they would be called **ethnomusicologists**.) During the 1890s, for example, Alice C. Fletcher collected whatever Omaha songs she could while lying sick in a tipi. Frances Densmore, undaunted by the wilderness, carted heavy recording equipment in leaky birch bark canoes to reach the music of the Chippewa. Without the efforts of these pioneers and others like them it would be difficult for scholars to trace the histories of tribal musics on this continent. (Bruno Nettl offers a useful historical chronology of the fieldwork and recording of Blackfoot music in his essay.) Although the number of ethnomusicologists specializing in North American Indian music is small compared to those who study, say, classical repertoires of the Far East, they have nevertheless done enough work and collecting to enable many of them to become specialists in the music of one particular tribe or area—for instance, Bruno Nettl on the Blackfoot, Alan Merriam on the Flathead, David McAllester and Charlotte Frisbie on the Navajo, William Powers on the Lakota, Charlotte Heth on the Cherokee, Ida Halpern on the Northwest Coast, Victoria Lindsay-Levine on the Choctaw, Beverly Diamond on the Northeast, Thomas Vennum on the Ojibwa, and Judith Vander on the Shoshone. Many of these area specialists have contributed to this book.

Early pioneers in the study of Indian music (such as Densmore) were relatively few in number. In the absence of any widespread appreciation of Indian music on its own merits, it was inevitable that stereotypes and misunderstandings would emerge among the general public. One common misperception about Indian musical practice involves instruments. For instance, although Native Americans use a wide variety of musical instruments, the general impression is that there is but one: the **tom-tom**. The word itself is not derived from any North American native language, as many assume, but is probably of Hindustani origin and has been used deprecatingly by English speakers worldwide to describe drums of any "uncivilized" people that produce a "monotonous" sound. The stereotypical tom-tom is usually a commercially made child's toy with two rubber heads laced together. While some tribes use drums resembling these (but with animal-skin heads), others rely on a wide variety of different drum types. They vary from tribe to tribe and even within a single tribe,

depending upon their use. The Ojibwe, for example, traditionally use a single-headed **water drum** for religious ceremonies, a large **double-headed dance drum** for social occasions, a variety of small hand drums or **drum-rattles** for doctoring, and a large **tambourine**-like drum for the moccasin game.

Nor is the drum the only instrument used to provide rhythmic background for Indian song and dance. Most people know little about the many rattles or special percussion instruments such as the rasp, a notched stick scraped rhythmically by the Utes in a spring dance to imitate the sound of the bear, by the Pueblo in the Basket Dance, or by the Yaqui in their Deer Dance (see Griffith).

Crow singer/drummer, photographed c. 1880. He holds a frame drum, which he beats with a stick that appears to be wrapped with twine. This is a typical type of drum used to accompany songs. *Photograph courtesy Smithsonian Institution, National Anthropological Archives.*

Native American chief with his wife, holding a large frame drum and beater, *c.* 1910. Early pictures like this one helped establish the common stereotypes for Indian costumes and head dress.
Photograph courtesy Smithsonian Institution, National Anthropological Archives.

Another almost universal misconception is that the standard Indian drum accompaniment consists of a pattern of four beats of equal duration, with the first heavily accented: BOOM–boom–boom–boom, BOOM–boom–boom–boom. This rhythmic pattern has been so thoroughly exploited by the media that it has become a cliché. The mere introduction of it in the musical score of a Western film signals that an Indian ambush is imminent. The pattern has also been used to impart an "Indian" flavor to radio and television commercials and to popular team fight songs heard at athletic events. The rhythm invariably appears in children's piano pieces wherever the word *Indian* is found in the title.

While this particular percussion pattern is not totally absent from Native American music, it is one of the least typical. Even where it can be found—in the accompaniment for the San Juan Pueblo Buffalo Dance, for example—it occurs only momentarily as part of an elaborate chain of different rhythmic patterns. Native Americans even joke among themselves about this stereotypical beat; it is said that Indians across the continent use the pattern as a sort of drum message to signal the arrival of Europeans, the drum warning, "WHITE–man–com–ing, WHITE–man–com–ing."

Despite the persistence of stereotypes, increasing numbers of young ethnomusicologists are taking a fresh look at the music and addressing tribal musics that have hitherto been overlooked. Decades after the completion of Densmore's landmark study, *The Chippewa* (1910), the tribe's music is still very much alive. Although acculturation has had drastic effects on all other aspects of tribal life, the music has remained relatively intact. What changes have occurred reflect the effects of acculturation in general; as the number of Indians who speak their own language has diminished, so has the proportion of songs containing meaningful texts. As the traditional source of spiritual power—the boy's vision quest—was abandoned, so vanished most of the dream songs.

Many of the song genres that Densmore recorded are nearly extinct or have disappeared entirely. Pipe Dance songs and Begging Dance songs are now part of the historical past. Only a handful of the members of the oldest generation recall the love songs. Moccasin game songs, once considered sacred, had already become **secular** by the time Densmore collected them. When the government prohibited gambling on some Ojibwe reservations in the early 1920s, it hastened the game song's decline. (The same happened to the Blackfoot, as Nettl observes.) By mid-

century the songs had been forgotten, although a drum still accompanied the game in the few places where it was played.

Despite such changes, the substance of Indian music has not been radically affected and continues to be virtually uninfluenced by Western music. Although Indian musicians had begun to venture in some remarkably different directions by the mid–twentieth century, traditional singers continued to use many of the same vocal techniques, tonal patterns, and song forms that ethnomusicologists recorded on wax cylinders at the beginning of the century. Singers still observe distinctions between drumbeat patterns for various genres, and the melodies of many old songs have survived in variant versions.

Indian song and dance today serve as focal points in renewing pride in tribal cultural heritage—witness the proliferation of annual summer **powwows**. But whether tribal musics will remain stylistically different in the future is uncertain. Distinctions between tribal styles are increasingly blurred, due primarily to increased mobility and the advent of inexpensive recording equipment. The powwow circuit each summer takes singers by car to the celebrations of neighboring tribes, where, in addition to performing, they collect songs from the other tribal groups using cassette tape recorders. They take the tapes home, learn the new songs, and then teach them to others. As tribal repertoires merge in this way, their distinguishing features are certain to be lost. That this has been happening for some time in the evolution of the powwow in Oklahoma is evident in Gloria A. Young's essay. At the same time, encouraging efforts are underway to revive old ceremonies and reinstall lost traditional repertoires by tribes divorced geographically by history, such as the Eastern and Oklahoma Cherokee, as described by Kline, or the Oklahoma and Mississippi Choctaw, as noted by Gregory.

MUSIC HOLDS THE PEOPLE TOGETHER

H. F. "Pete" Gregory

H. F. "Pete" Gregory is a professor of anthropology at Northwestern State University at Natchitoches, Louisiana. He is highly regarded by both the academic community and southeastern Indian peoples for his vast knowledge of southeastern expressive culture and for his participation in tribal preservation programs. This essay originally appeared in Remaining Ourselves: Music and Tribal Memory—Traditional Music in Contemporary Communities, *edited by Dayna Bowker Lee, published in 1995 by the State Arts Council of Oklahoma.*

Like the winds whirling across the earth, tying all things and places together, music and dance hold the southeastern Native Americans together. Past and present, men and women, living and dead, young and old, all come together in dance and song. Music is the integral element for the whole region.

In the nineteenth century when the tribes were forced to relocate, they picked up their sacred fires and moved them to new ceremonial grounds in the West. Dance and song then began to renew the people, to purify their new homes as they had their ancient places. Tribes that somehow escaped the removal, in whole or part, clung desperately to what they had. Often living in poverty, in fear of removal or worse, constantly pressured by Euro-Americans to change their cultures, these people went to extreme measures to keep their music traditions. In isolated places like the Florida Everglades and the Big Thicket of east Texas, they sang their songs, danced, and prayed. Their music and dance, like their traditional religions and arts, managed to survive.

Descriptions of tribal music and dance were some of the first things Europeans wrote about Native Americans. Southeastern cultures such as the Timucua, Creek, Cherokee, Natchez, and others were all noted as dancers and singers. It is beyond this effort to summarize these early accounts. Still, it must be said that these dances and songs can still be heard from Oklahoma to the Atlantic seaboard as people have struggled to hold on to their traditions. So there is a continuum; and if one community drops something, others exist as a template for renewal. At Yellow Hills Dance Ground in Oklahoma, for example, traditional Choctaw music has experienced a revival among the Tennessee Choctaw and their Oklahoma counterparts. People in Oklahoma still speak of their "birth grounds" with deep reverence, knowing their lives are tied to the homelands of their people. Indian people today save vacation or

sick leave and travel great distances to participate in their shared obligations.

So the ancient music still sounds across the Southeast. Drums, **rattles**, rhythm sticks, and voices all combine to echo songs and prayers, to regulate dances, and blend it all into community participation. The sacred fire, corn, thunder, and wind are all intertwined in southeastern Native American religions and, thereby, are connected to one of the most elaborate musical traditions on this continent. In most southeastern Indian cultures, the **secular** and the sacred are part of the continuum, not separate entities as is the case in Western culture. Sacred elements, such as the commemoration of warriors past and present in the Caddo Turkey Dance, end with the women inviting people to their social dance **cycle**. Similarly, the dancing and singing of the other tribes—Creek, Seminole, Yuchi, Choctaw, Cherokee, Tunica-Biloxi, and others—glide from sacred to social and back again.

When Christianity was introduced, it was modified to serve the same functions in Native American cultures as native religions had in the past. The all-night sings, with egg and wild-onion suppers, have moved to the churches in large cities like Oklahoma City and Tulsa. **A cappella** choirs, singing in English and/or their various Indian languages, have added a new dimension to Native music. But at the churches, the drum and rattles dropped out; the missionaries seemed to know how really sacred these instruments were. Banning them was a destructive act.

The sacred/profane dichotomy in Euro-American music likely made the drum and rattles a threat to early missionaries, who tended to see all Native American music as profane. The drum, rattle, and percussion sticks were as potentially evil as the European **fiddles** were in their own homelands. Secular dances and songs were, after all, temptations of the flesh.

Tribal locations in the American Southeast in the seventeenth century.

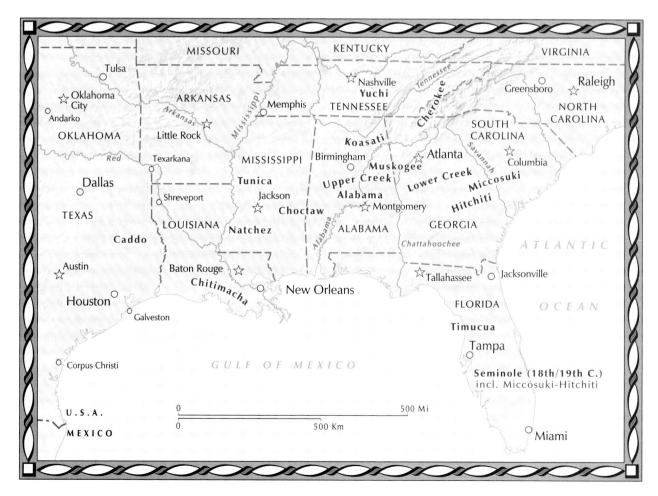

All across the Southeast (including eastern Oklahoma), people hid their traditional music at sacred grounds while developing their own Christian music at community churches. They even played their fiddles with sinful non–Indian neighbors at their dances.

The call-response music was typical for most southern tribes. It was strongest on the sacred ceremonial grounds of the Creek, Yuchi, Seminole, and Cherokee. It certainly has enjoyed a continuous life of its own. These shellshaking traditions, especially among the Muscogee Creek and their neighbors, seem most deeply rooted in their cultures and share broader connections. **Pantribally**, women take an active role in both song and dance. While the drum and percussion sticks were men's tools for making rhythm, the "turtle shells" or "cans" were tied to the women's foot and leg movements, and the dance music was metered by them. Among other tribes, women responded vocally and were sometimes **chanters** or

singers; hand rattles often accompanied their songs. Among the Caddo, the women always started the dancing. Traditionally, a head woman dancer of the Caddo tribe carried a sacred staff, a special symbol of authority, and it was her job to encourage others to participate. (So important was her role that she even shared the power of a chief.) As in other areas of life, music and dance, again interrelated with an obligation to keep harmony between the oppositional forces of the universe, were and are the duty of all tribal people.

Among the last vestiges of traditional culture to be weakened by white contact, songs and dances were kept by even highly acculturated tribal groups. In Louisiana, the Choctaw, Koasati, and Tunica-Biloxi maintained their traditional music. The Tunica-Biloxi songs and dances survived even after those languages were abandoned in favor of French or English. Local Cajun French populations learned traditional Native American music and sports. When Creole teams played

Tribal locations in the American Southeast in the twentieth century.

racquette, a Louisiana French version of the Native American game of stickball, they continued making up ball songs in the French language. Cajun dances often had Native American fiddlers, and the old Scottish-**Celtic** drone tunings of the fiddle found a refuge in the bows and fiddles of Native American musicians who always respected old ways of doing things. In the 1980s, a Coushatta (Koasati) fiddler, Deo Langley, actually won the Cajun fiddle contest held in southwest Louisiana! So even the European music of the Southeast came to be influenced and expanded by Indian music in many cases. The popular country tune "Cherokee Fiddle" was but a recent tip of the Anglo-American hat in that direction. "Seminole Wind" has carried that connection further, with the video actually showing a Seminole dance.

There were numbers of regional and tribal variations in southeastern Indian music, but some things seem to cut directly across geographic, linguistic, and political boundaries. Instrumentation was one of those. The drum, percussion sticks, the varied rattles, and the **flageolet** or flute were universal.

Kinds, styles, and modes of drumming varied, but the drum itself was sacred. Many were **water drums** made from hides stretched over cypress knees, clay vessels,

and, later, crocks or iron kettles. The late Choctaw ethnologist Claude Medford, Jr., noted, "These were filled with four mouthfuls of water, enough to keep them wet." Tunica Chief Joseph Pierite always placed a piece of potsherd and a lump of charcoal in his drums—water, earth, fire, and thunder were all tied together in one instrument! Most of the tribes had a single drummer. In southeastern tradition the drummer/chanter stood at the side of the dancers who circled the fire. The Caddo, the westernmost southeastern culture, used a drum carried by four drummers accompanied by singers; again, the drum circled the fire and opened the dances—the symbol of unity and the world.

"Dry" drums were made of logs, cypress knees, and, eventually, cedar buckets. The Bayou LaCombe Choctaw in Louisiana used a unique wooden or vine strip around the drumhead to tighten it. That sole feature seems similar to African drum traditions, possibly a borrowing from the *Place Congo* African drumming in nearby New Orleans. After the War of 1812, the northern Choctaw borrowed the European **snare drum**, stretching a taut cord across the bottom of their cedar bucket drums to give them the "snap" of European drums. Despite such variations, the tribal musicians played the drum with only a single stick. The drums

were not allowed to touch the earth and were never drummed with the hand. Today virtually every tribe has a traditional drummer, and those who do not have one treasure tape recordings of their last drummers.

Rattles vary more than drums. Early rattles were turtle shells or **gourds** filled with selected pebbles or, later, glass beads. Cured or tuned gourds were used and, once dried or baked, were placed on handles and filled with small pebbles. Later, two styles became more widespread: a larger, heavier rattle that seems to reflect an older style, and a lighter bottle gourd "top," similar to those used in peyote ceremonies of the Native American Church, that seems to be a more recent introduction.

The shells of the land terrapin have long been a popular rattle in the Southeast. Loaded carefully with white quartz pebbles, these rattles can be handheld by a leather thong or mounted on a wooden handle. Among the prehistoric examples are even copper copies of turtle shells. These are clearly a continuation of very ancient religion and music. The use of rattles echoes today in the "cans" that often replace turtle shells worn by women dancers on the stomp grounds.

Shells and cans are worn on leather legging-like pieces attached to the women's lower legs. These turtle shells may also be attached to cowboy boot tops, replacing earlier deerskin or leather leggings. Over the years, evaporated milk cans have gradually become as popular as the turtles of earlier **shellshakers**. (Old craftspeople increasingly fear that one day they will not be able to obtain the turtle shells they need to make rattles.) The Seminole, Muscogee, Miccosuki, and Hitchiti seem to have had the strongest shellshaker traditions. The Yuchi and Cherokee also continue to use the "shackles" or "turtles" in their dances. It is this shellshaking tradition that is tied to the "**stomp dance**," a term used for both the secular and sacred dances where the dancing women's feet provide the music. Shellshaking actually replaces the drum, especially in "stomps." In most cases, these turtles are still ritually prepared and carefully "sunned" from time to time because turtles need the sun. Some tribes have integrated drums and shells, but the women complain that those sounds confuse the dancers.

Among the Choctaw, rhythm sticks—actually two hardwood sticks or the handles of stickball rackets—are struck together by the chanter, providing the musical time for the dancers. They serve as a substitute for both the rattle and the drum.

While all these represent traditional musical instruments and styles, some others are barely recognized. Among the Koasati, Chitimacha, and other tribes, four women usually pounded corn in **unison** while singing, the beat set by the pestles striking the log mortars. River cane flutes were also common and have begun to make a comeback in modern times. The Delaware folded a dried deer hide that was beaten drum-style to accompany their songs. In prehistoric Louisiana, pairs of engraved Whistler Swan leg bones were made into flutes, and sets of copper tubes were played as **panpipes**. Also dating back to the prehistoric era was a **whistle** or caller made from an antler. In all this music, the beat was the dominant element; song **scales** were mainly **pentatonic**.

Call-response songs dominated dance music, and dancing was most often commu-

Hopi women perform a circular dance in this photograph taken in 1879 in Oraibi, Arizona. Circular dances like this one are very common among many Native American tribes.
Photograph © CORBIS.

nal. Circles of hand-holding dancers were common in all the southeastern tribes. These circles rotated clockwise around the fire or the drum; others reversed motion and went counterclockwise. Singers or chanters were highly regarded, and most tribes had both men and women who sang. Often, as among the Mississippi Choctaw or the Alabama in east Texas, a woman would respond to a male chanter's lead. Individuals also sang solos. Love songs, curing songs, and ballgame songs were the most common forms. The Tunica-Biloxi men had a Run Dance that ballplayers sang as a group while running to a ball ground. Once at the ball field, each man had his own song that he sang at the goalposts as a counter to witchcraft or as a dare to the other team.

Old people sang songs at dawn (most likely prayer songs), but much of this pre-Christian music has been lost. The calumet ceremony, sung with the presentation of the sacred pipe in a number of Native communities throughout the South, is also lost, but the feather wands carried in Creek and Cherokee dance seem to be its lineal descendant. The plaintive "Long Cry" of the Oklahoma Creek and Yuchi square grounds, like the newer, Christian **shape-note** singing of the Cherokee church choirs, carry forward strong sacred music traditions often dating back to ancient times.

Rock groups such as the Choctaw Shamrocks of northern Mississippi carry the Native American musicians past powwows and even Forty-nine dances (special social dances performed mostly by young people after powwows). Still, the **Two-step**, Stirrup Dance, and Stealing Partners dances are as prime a set of social forces as one could hope to find anywhere in North America. Secular music stretches from smoke shops and casinos to tribal dance grounds. Caddo and Delaware singers and drummers have been on the airways from Anadarko, Oklahoma, for a long time.

Old men still hear their Drunk Dances and Tom Cat songs and remember the all-night dancing and the horseback rides home across the grass or through the woods. Among the Tunica-Biloxi, they still speak of their ghost chief, "all dressed in silver," who is seen returning home from an all-night dance. The Mobilian phrase, *Tali hata pisa achokma*, "silver looking good," refers to the full moon in their old songs. Younger people think of school dances, church singing, and riding around the countryside. They may stop and develop an impromptu dance, using a car for a drum. A modern Forty-nine dance may then develop. Powwows are universal from the Atlantic to Oklahoma and Texas.

Somehow it has all come together. Some things are transposed; others lost or replaced, and some are still being invented. Nevertheless, the Indians of the Southeast cling to their music, making new forms while preserving older ones. **Jazz** musicians, cowboy quartets, rock groups, and church choirs crowd in on the "old ways." Still, it is good to remember that the old music has survived. Like much of Native American tradition, it has preserved the best of the old, and that contributes to the new. The cultures are alive!

BIBLIOGRAPHY

Adair, James. (1775). *The History of the American Indians.* Long. Bushnell, David L. (1909). "The Choctaw of Bayou Lacombe, St. Tammany Parish, Louisiana." *Bureau of American Ethnology Bulletin* 46. Washington, D.C.: U.S. Government Printing Office.

Densmore, Frances. (1937). "The Alabama Indians and Their Music." *Publication of the Texas Folklore Society* 13:270–93.

———. (1942). "A Search for Songs Among the Chitimacha Indians in Louisiana." *Bureau of American Ethnology Bulletin* 133, Anthropological Papers 19. Washington, D.C.: U.S. Government Printing Office.

———. (1943). "Choctaw Music." *Bureau of American Ethnology Bulletin* 136, Anthropological Papers No. 28. Washington, D.C.: U.S. Government Printing Office.

———. (1956). "Seminole Music." *Bureau of American Ethnology Bulletin* 161. Smithsonian Institution. Washington, D.C.: U.S. Government Printing Office.

Haas, Mary. (1935). *Tunica Grammar.* Berkeley: University of California Press.

Heth, Charlotte. (1992). *Native American Dance: Ceremonies and Social Traditions.* Washington, D.C.: Museum of the American Indian. Smithsonian Institution.

———. (1994). "Music." In *Native Americans in the Twentieth Century,* ed. Mary Davis. New York: Garland Press.

Howard, James. (1981). *Shawnee! The Ceremonialism of a Native American Tribe and Its Cultural Background.* Athens: Ohio University Press.

Howard, James, and Levine, Victoria Lindsay. (1990). *Choctaw Music and Dance.* Norman: University of Oklahoma Press.

Lena, Willie, and Howard, James. (1984). *Oklahoma Seminoles: Medicine, Magic and Religion.* Norman: University of Oklahoma Press.

Newkumet, Vynola, and Meredith, Howard L. (1988). *Hasinai: A Traditional History of the Caddo Confederacy.* College Station: Texas A & M Press.

Smyth, Willie, ed. (1989). *Songs of Indian Territory: Native American Music Traditions of Oklahoma.* Oklahoma City: Center of the American Indian.

Speck, Frank C. (1911). "Ceremonial Songs of the Creek and Seminole." *Museum of Anthropology Publication* 1(2). University of Pennsylvania.

WHERE THE RAVENS ROOST: SONGS AND CEREMONIES OF BIG COVE

Michael Kline

At the time this essay was first published, Michael Kline was a staff folklorist at the Mountain Heritage Center of Western Carolina University in Cullowhee, North Carolina. There he produced a cassette tape of ceremonial songs performed by Walker Calhoun that is still available through the Mountain Heritage Center. Kline now resides in Elkins, West Virginia, where he directs "Talking Across the Lines: Worldwide Conversations," a folkloric communications collective, and also continues to produce folk music and audio-history CDs. The following essay originally appeared in the fall 1990 issue of the Old Time Herald *and was revised for publication in* American Musical Traditions.*

As Walker Calhoun raised his **gourd rattle** and began to sing ancient Cherokee **verses** in a soft, clear voice to the shaking rhythms, a hush fell over the campfire. Walker then stood to lead 150 children in the Friendship Dance, concluding a daylong gathering of the Cherokee Challenge, a scouting program for boys and girls held throughout the summer months in Birdtown, North Carolina.

The high, lonesome strains of Walker's haunting dance song soon had the children on their feet, snaking single file around the fire. Rhythms from Walker's gourd rattle connected them with a long tradition of dancing and singing that has bonded their people with one another and with this place for centuries.

As we sat under a shade tree at the gathering, enjoying fry bread and getting acquainted, Walker explained that his half-uncle, the venerable Will West Long, had passed the songs along to him when he was just a boy attending dances in his home community of Big Cove. A medicine man with a vast knowledge of Cherokee culture, history, letters and language, Will West Long died in 1947 at age seventy-seven. His elders were men and women who had hidden from the soldiers during the Cherokee removal to Oklahoma in 1838. At the time of West Long's childhood, two generations later, the tiny Big Cove community was still traumatized by that upheaval, as were Native American communities throughout the southeastern states.

By 1891 the Bureau of Indian Affairs had assumed responsibility for Indian education and launched programs of aggressive acculturation. Cherokee children were punished for speaking their own language in local government schools. With the great chestnut blight and the deepening depression of the mid-1930s, traditional hill-farming among the Cherokee gave way to dependency on economic programs administered by white bureaucrats. In addition, the foundations were being laid for a tourist industry that

would commercialize and distort Cherokee culture. Traditional values, language, and song fell by the wayside at an alarming rate.

The pervasive influence of Christian mission churches and ten years at white boarding schools could not rid Will West Long of traditional Cherokee beliefs and ancient customs centering on the supernatural. The ceremonies he brought virtually single-handedly into the twentieth century were chanted litanies and dances of thanks honoring the animal life that sustained fragile native communities. And though Cherokee people no longer depend on the flesh and the hides of the beaver and bear for sustenance, their dances honoring these animals satisfy hungers for a sense of identity and connection with the past. The **rattle**, song, and dance have sustained Cherokee people through succeeding waves of difficult change.

Will West Long was the good shaman, leader of his people, and driver of the dance.

A hillside farmer and medicine man, he conjured for Big Cove stickball games and preached peace and love among neighbors. So strong was his gentle leadership that his death in 1947 left a vacuum that resulted in the decline of many ceremonies. Lloyd Sequoyah and Walker's older brother, Lawrence Calhoun, both now deceased, were among the practitioners who followed. Somehow the ceremonies persisted, though they did not always flourish.

Walker's father, Morgan Calhoun, kept an old factory-made **banjo** around the house, probably ordered from a Sears catalog. (Other Big Cove families had banjos, too, and played mostly from house to house.) His favorite tune was "Shoo Fly," and Walker can dimly remember the **drop-thumb** style his dad picked.

When Walker was nine his father died, and the banjo passed to his older brothers, Lawrence, Henry, and Lawyer. Henry was

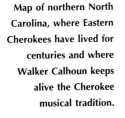

Map of northern North Carolina, where Eastern Cherokees have lived for centuries and where Walker Calhoun keeps alive the Cherokee musical tradition.

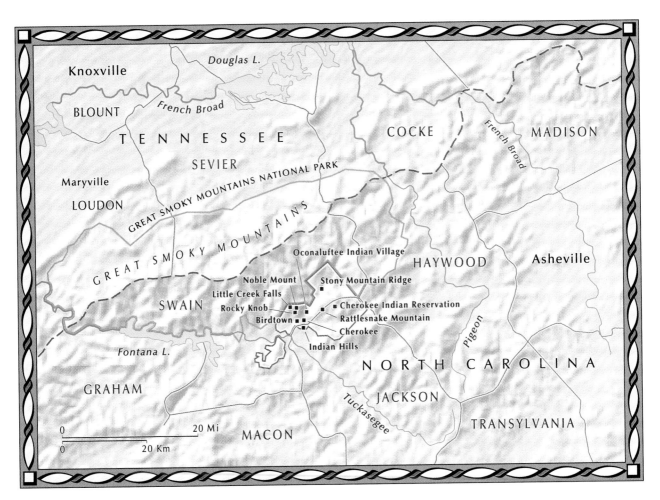

the best banjo-picker in the community. The banjo hung on the wall out of Walker's reach. The younger children (there were ten in all) were not permitted to play it. As soon as the older boys were gone, Walker was up on a chair practicing chords without taking down the banjo. "I could play it, and it hanging right there on the wall," he recalls with a smile. By 1930 the family had a **guitar**, and Walker joined in playing standards like "Redwing," "Down Yonder," and "Down in the Willow Garden." He subsequently developed a modified **three-finger picking style**, sometimes using metal finger picks, but is also comfortable with the drop-thumb rapping style he remembers from his father.

Sometimes when he was alone, Walker would quietly pick some of the Cherokee melodies he knew from his song mentor, Will West Long, but he never played these for anyone else. Walker seldom sings the old mountain **ballads**, preferring the ancient ceremonial dance songs in his own language that honor the bear, beaver, quail, and eagle. He also sings the "Horse Dance Song," which the Cherokee made when Spanish explorer Hernando de Soto brought the horse in 1540. "That's not such an old song," Walker reflects. "The rest of them are *old*."

The Calhoun family lives high on a hillside overlooking the Raven's Fork River, where Will West Long once led dances around sacred embers of a ceremonial fire built in the center of the cove. Walker Calhoun, whose first language is Cherokee, has been heir to these traditions of thought and song. In 1984, at the first gathering of the Eastern and Western bands of the Cherokee, on the Cherokee fairgrounds, Walker was drafted by a local performing dance group to sing the old songs he remembered from his youth in Big Cove. His first public performance before that assembly launched his career as a ceremonial singer.

He has also kept alive practices of folk medicine locked within the Big Cove community. His wisdom and humility have a charismatic effect, drawing people of all ages to him. Walker's children and grandchildren, raised in the dance traditions of Big

Noted Native American singer Walker Calhoun of Cherokee, North Carolina.
Photograph by Jeff Todd Titon.

Cove, were charter members of the Raven Rock Dancers, named in honor of a huge outcropping on the mountain high above their home, where ravens once roosted and nurtured their young. The ensemble has fully outfitted itself in traditional regalia and now performs at a number of festivals and **powwows** around the southeastern states. Members of the community believe the Raven Rock Dancers present the most authentic renditions of traditional Cherokee song and dance.

In recognition of his efforts to perpetuate Cherokee culture and customs, Walker received the first Sequoyah Award (created especially to honor him) at a gathering of the Eastern and Western bands at the Cherokee Fall Festival in October 1988. Less than six months later, in June 1989, he received the North Carolina Folk Heritage Award recognizing a lifetime of community cultural achievement. And in 1990, the Folk Arts Division of the National Endowment for the Arts presented Walker Calhoun with a National Heritage Fellowship Award.

New friends and admirers from the Western Band of the Cherokee in Oklahoma have initiated an informal exchange with Walker and his family. The Calhouns have gone to Oklahoma to visit and attend **stomp**

dances, and an Oklahoma contingent has traveled to Big Cove to encourage the Calhoun family in its quest to revive the stomp-dance religion. Working together, they have been clearing weeds from the old dance grounds once cherished by Will West Long. Scattered ashes dug from ancient ceremonial fires around the region have been used to resanctify the Big Cove dance grounds. Oklahoma friends will return to join in the renewal of the stomp dance and share ancient customs surviving in both communities despite more than 150 years of separation.

Spiritual leader Walker Calhoun and his family of dancers symbolize the determined survival of old songs and dances that have brought people together within the hidden beauty of Big Cove for generations. Walker is the last link between the legacy of Will West Long and the cultural development of his own children and grandchildren. His quiet commitment to these traditions assures their place in the lives of those who will come after him.

Afterword: In the decade since this article was published, Walker's sixteen-year-old grandson, Patrick Smith, has begun growing into a songleader and often leads the cere-monial dances with his grandfather's encouragement. The dance grounds are now located in a tiny meadow near the Calhoun home, overlooking Big Cove. Walker, now eighty-three, is the Keeper of the Fires for the Stomp Dance ceremonies each month and teaches a class in Cherokee language for his family and neighbors each week. He and his family of dancers have also been featured at folk music festivals and powwows throughout the region and were scheduled to appear at the Smithsonian Institution's 2001 Festival of American Folklife, held on the Mall in Washington, D.C.

BIBLIOGRAPHY

Speck, Frank G., and Broom, Lenord. (1983). *Cherokee Dance and Drama.* Norman: University of Oklahoma Press.

Where the Ravens Roost: Ceremonial Dance Songs of Big Cove. 1991. Walker Calhoun singing with rattle and drum. Recorded by Michael Kline. Cullowhee, NC: Western Carolina University.

Woodside, Jane Harris. (1989). "The Cherokee: Hungry for the Dance." *Now and Then: Center for Appalachian Studies* 6 (3).

SENECA SOCIAL DANCE MUSIC

Mary Frances Riemer

Mary Frances Riemer was a folklorist who specialized in the music of Native American tribes in upstate New York. In 1980 she produced a recording entitled Seneca Social Dance Music *(Folkways 4072); the annotations she wrote to accompany that recording provide the basis for this essay.*

The Seneca ("people of the big hill") were the largest of the original five tribes of the Iroquois Confederacy founded during the sixteenth century. The Confederacy, which occupied most of present-day upper New York State, also included the Mohawk, Oneida, Onondaga, and Cayuga tribes. After 1715, the Tuscaroras were admitted as the sixth nation and given a portion of the Oneida territory. As the most western of the Iroquois, the Senecas were designated as the Keepers of the Western Door. Today the Senecas of New York State live on three reservations: Tonawanda, Cattaraugus, and Allegany, each named for the streams along which they are located. The Allegany Reservation stretches for forty-two miles along the Allegheny River (literally "beautiful river"). Located in Cattaraugus County in the southwestern corner of New York State, the reservation lies in a beautiful region of thickly forested hills and valleys.

This land, which included 30,469 acres, was granted to the Senecas under the Pickering Treaty of 1794. Signed by George Washington, it was the first treaty made by the United States as a nation and guaranteed that "the U.S. will never claim the same, nor disturb the Seneka Nation...in the free use and enjoyment thereof." During the nineteenth century, with help from the Society of Friends, the Senecas became farmers, laborers, and businessmen and established their own republican government in 1848, complete with elected president, legislative council, and judiciary. (Only the Allegany and Cattaraugus Senecas are included in the Seneca Nation; the Tonawanda Band of Seneca Indians remains a separate political entity.) The Senecas of Allegany also leased land of their reservation for railways, highways, and towns occupied mostly by whites. Salamanca, with a population of approximately 7,500, is the largest of these.

In 1941, despite the assurances of the Pickering Treaty, the Senecas found their reservation lands threatened by plans—which had already been authorized by Congress—to

build a dam at Kinzua, fifteen miles south of the Allegany Reservation in Pennsylvania. The stated purpose of the Kinzua Dam project was flood control on the Allegheny River, but other writers have also pointed to the use of reservoir water for the Pittsburgh steel mills (Fenton 1967, p.7; Wilson 1959, p.195). Although the Senecas carried the issue to the Supreme Court, the power of Congress to condemn the land required for the project was upheld in 1959. Construction by the Army Corps of Engineers began almost immediately, and by 1965 the dam was complete. The project flooded over 9,000 acres of the best bottom lands (almost one-third of the reservation); caused the dispossession of 130 Seneca families from their homes at Red House, Coldspring, Quaker Bridge, and Onoville; and forced the removal of the Longhouse from Coldspring to Steamburg. The Seneca Nation, again with assistance from Quakers, fought for compensation for their lands and homes lost to the reservoir. A total of $15,000,573 was appropriated by Congress "to provide for the relocation, rehabilitation, social, and economic development of the members of the Seneca Nation." Part of this money was used to create the two new suburban-like developments of Jimersontown and Steamburg, ten miles apart, and the displaced Seneca families were relocated to ranch-type homes on three-acre plots at these settlements. Improvements such as community buildings, the newly opened Iroquois museum, and library have also come from the relocation fund. However, the general sentiment among the Senecas is that no amount of compensation can replace their flooded lands.

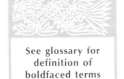

See glossary for definition of boldfaced terms

THE MUSIC
OCCASIONS

The Senecas possess an extraordinary amount of music associated with their Longhouse religion. The followers of Handsome Lake perform a calendrical cycle of Thanksgiving ceremonies in which they sing and dance rituals addressed to the Creator and to the Food Spirits. The numerous medicine societies also have their own ritual songs. However, all of this ceremonial music is held sacred by the Longhouse faithful and, in complying with the wishes of Avery and Fidelia Jimerson (one of the Seneca families relocated to Jimersontown in 1965) that this music not be "let out," it has not been recorded. Social dance music, while still associated with the Longhouse, is much more in the public and **secular** sphere and is for everyone's enjoyment. Thus, these songs have been recorded.

Occasions for social dance music are numerous. During ceremonials such as the Green Corn and the Midwinter, which last several days, social dances may be held at the Longhouse in the evening. Prior to the moving of the Coldspring Longhouse in 1965, "socials," with music and dancing, were held there every Sunday evening. A dinner was given beforehand and the evening's proceeds used for Longhouse needs. Today socials are occasionally given at the new gymnasium (part of the community building) at Steamburg, but it is not considered a good space for singing and, consequently, there is no social dancing. Parties, formerly held in the cookhouse next to the old Coldspring Longhouse to honor a person on a particular occasion, provide further opportunities for social dancing. "Sings" at private homes feature social dance music but no dancing, and are usually associated with meetings of the Singing Society. Finally, replacing the old Sunday evening socials of the Longhouse are "singouts," usually held on the weekends of major Christian holidays such as Thanksgiving, Christmas, and Easter, or national holidays such as the Fourth of July. Not associated with the Longhouse, they are now held in the community building at Steamburg and are sponsored by the Singing Society, which tries to have new songs for the event.

GENERAL CHARACTERISTICS

The Senecas share a musical style that is common to all the Indian tribes of the Eastern Woodlands. Their songs are relatively short: some are as brief as fifteen seconds, but

usually they will last about one to one and a half minutes. Songs (usually about seven) of a similar **genre** are often sung consecutively, with little pause between each, thus forming a "set" or "cycle." For some of the newer imported songs, singers do not generally possess a large enough **repertoire** to enable them to sing as many as seven but, since these non–Seneca songs tend to be longer, the end result is a set of appropriate length.

The melodies of these songs generally have an **undulating contour** but with slightly more descent than ascent overall. Iroquois scales are mainly **pentatonic** (i.e., five tones); **major** seconds and **minor** thirds are the most important **intervals**. **Octave** leaps are fairly frequent, especially in the new Ladies' Dance songs, where they begin the songs.

Songs usually have a **range** of one octave, with the **tonic** (or base tone) often being the lowest, or next to lowest, tone of the scale. Other notes that receive special emphasis are the **fifth**, **third**, and octave above the base tone.

Rhythmic organization is relatively symmetrical and simple, with two or three **note values** per song being most commonly used. Other rhythmic figures are occasionally introduced for interest and variety. Rhythmic accompaniment, provided by the **water drum** and various types of **rattles** (see below), is most often a simple **duple beat** that coincides with the basic pulse of the melody. **Tremolo** effects are also produced on the drum and rattle. In the dance songs, alterations in rhythmic accompaniment signal choreographic changes in the dance.

The structure of individual songs can be fairly complex. Each song is composed of several short sections, which can be ordered and repeated in various combinations. A formula commonly used is AABAB. As mentioned earlier, songs are grouped together to form a set or cycle.

Song structure becomes further involved through the use of an **antiphonal** (or **call-and-response**) technique, which is a

An upper New York state Iroquois Indian dancing outside of a reconstructed Iroquois longhouse in 1973. The Seneca longhouse would have resembled this structure, as would the costume.
Photograph © Nathan Benn/CORBIS.

The Young Nation Singers performing at a longhouse powwow. Formed in the mid-'80s, this group performs both at traditional longhouse ceremonies and at intertribal powwows across the country. Photograph courtesy of J. J. Foxx.

distinctive feature of Eastern musical style. This type of singing requires either two individuals or, more commonly, a **leader** plus group. The leader begins by singing a single **phrase**, which is then repeated (possibly with minor **variation**) by the group. The call-and-response pattern occurs at beginnings and endings of many songs and is the sole structural device of the **Stomp Dance**.

Iroquois vocal technique has several of the features generally associated with Indian singing style: a moderate amount of tension in the throat, **pulsation** on sustained notes, downward **glides**, and **grace notes**.

The majority of social dance songs have meaningless syllable (vocable) texts; however, the **vocables** used in any given song are fixed and are repeated the same way each time the song is performed. (This is not the case with the religious songs, which often contain meaningful texts in the form of prayers and thanksgivings.) The vocables are usually set syllabically; i.e., one vocable is sung to one note. Meaningful texts, when they occur in social dance music, are found most often in the newly composed Ladies' Dance songs and, within the song set, in the initial and the final songs.

INSTRUMENTS

The only instruments used to accompany the social dances are the water drum (whose Indian name literally means "covered keg") and cow horn rattle, although there are several others with specific functions in Longhouse rituals. (For a comprehensive discussion of Seneca "singing tools," see Conklin/Sturtevant 1953).

The water drum is a small, round, wooden vessel about five to six inches in diameter, covered with a soft-tanned hide stretched and held in place by a cloth-wrapped wooden hoop. Water is introduced into the drum through a hole in its side, and, before playing, the head is thoroughly soaked and tightened until the characteristic high "pinging" sound is obtained. The player

holds the drum in his left hand and strikes the drum skin with a small wooden beater.

The cowhorn rattle is made from a conical piece of cowhorn mounted on a wooden handle. The horn contains steel pellets and is closed at the top with a wooden plug. Its overall length is usually about nine to twelve inches. Only one water drum is used at a social dance and is played by the lead singer. His assistants each shake a cowhorn rattle.

An enumeration of the various types of social dance currently performed on the Allegany Reservation presents one with a complicated list of names and associations. In the past, writers on Iroquois music (see Kurath 1951, 1964, 1968) have organized the traditional Seneca dances according to the two basic dance steps used: the stomp-type and fish-type. This grouping remains useful and workable if, added to it, are the **shuffle step** of the new Ladies' Dance and the numerous imported dances that have reached Allegany since the early 1960s.

The stomp-type of social dance involves a simple forward trotting step in which the right foot shuffles forward and the left is brought up to meet it. This is the most recurrent step in Iroquois social dancing and is performed by both men and women. The social dances using this step include:

1. Trotting Dance—also called Standing Quiver or Stomp Dance—is the paradigm of stomp-type dances;
2. Corn Dance;
3. Bean Dance, also called Hand-in-Hand or Linking-Arms Dance;
4. Squash Dance, also called Shaking-the-Pumpkin or Shaking-the-Jug.

The Corn, Bean, and Squash are essentially Food Spirit dances performed at the food-spirit festivals and, therefore, belong more in the religious sphere. Only the Corn Dance appears on social dance programs at Allegany.

5. Pigeon Dance;
6. Duck Dance;
7. Robin Dance.

The Pigeon, Duck, and Robin dances possibly were part of a former spring ritual giving thanks for the return of wild birds. All are performed as social dances at Allegany.

8. Alligator Dance;
9. Fishing Dance, stomp dance, not to be confused with the Fish Dance, which uses the fish-type step;
10. Garters Dance;
11. Shaking-the-Bush, also called Naked Dance. This is danced with a variation of the stomp-type step.

The fish-type of social dance is often compared to the Charleston, but the Seneca version, being centuries old, obviously predates it. The sequence of the fairly complicated fish step is: start with both feet turned out, right foot slightly in front. With a sharp movement, turn both feet in, the right foot brushing to the side. Both feet are now turned in, with the right foot slightly behind. With another sharp movement, turn both feet out, the left foot brushing to the side but remaining in front of right. From this position the sequence is repeated with the left foot stepping backwards.

Although not as ubiquitous as the stomp, the fish step (also danced by both men and women) is used in several dances:

1. Old Moccasin Dance, also called the Fish Dance, is the paradigm of fish-type dances;
2. Raccoon Dance;
3. Sharpening-the-Stick;
4. Choose-a-Partner;
5. Chicken Dance. This dance includes both the fish-type and the women's shuffle step that is used, in social dancing, only here and in the Women's Shuffle (or Ladies') Dance. As the name implies, it is only danced by women. The step is essentially a shuffling twist of the feet. With feet together, put weight on the balls of feet, raise heels slightly, and twist them to the right. Heels should hit the floor on the beat. With feet still together and weight on the heels, raise toes and twist them to the right. Front of feet should hit the floor on the beat. Repeat whole sequence and continue moving to the right. On

Seneca Long-house Songs

Ceremonial and Public Traditions of the Seneca Indians

Nick Spitzer is a folklorist widely known for his work on Creole cultures and cultural policy and as a public radio broadcaster. Artistic director and host of the "Folk Masters" concert series from 1990–1997 at Carnegie Hall and Wolf Trap, he also served as senior folklife specialist for the Smithsonian Institution and as the first Louisiana State Folklorist. In addition, Spitzer hosts American Routes, *the nationally broadcast weekly public radio music series. He is professor of cultural conservation and urban studies at the University of New Orleans. This essay originally appeared in the program guide for the 1993 Folk Masters concert series, held March 5–April 10 at the Barns of Wolf Trap in Vienna, Virginia.*

The Seneca are prehistorically linked to the Iroquois Confederacy, referred to as Six Nations, each with territories and settlements in what is now New York and Canada. The Seneca Reservation in Tonawanda, New York, has nearly 600 people, descendants of those who resettled there after 1812 from the Buffalo Creeks area. The Haudenosaunee or "people of the Longhouse" traditions of the Seneca are linked to the other Six Nations tribes: Cayuga, Oneida, Onondaga, Mohawk, and Tuscarora. Each group has a role in a shared ceremonial Longhouse tradition. The Seneca are considered the "Keepers of the Western Door" and the "Older Brother" in relation to the other tribes.

There are two types of Longhouse songs: private ceremonial songs that are for curing and thanking the Creator and other life forces for providing what is needed to live; and social dance songs that are for fun but that also show concern for how to live well and honor what the Creator provides. The ceremonial songs are not shared outside the Longhouse. The social songs and dances may be presented to the public. Indeed, some of the ceremonial and curing songs are not fully shared outside the Longhouse, even within the tribe, and younger men in the Longhouse must come to the knowledge.

The Longhouse today is usually a long, narrow rectangular frame building painted white. It is at the heart of traditional social events in the community, such as group dinners and "tea meetings," as well as weddings, birthdays, and anniversaries. Men and women enter through their own doors and sit on opposite sides. One elder will announce the dances while another will stand and give a

each beat, the knees flex to give the body a slight bouncing movement.

The typical Seneca social dance is performed in a counterclockwise circle, single or double file, around a centrally located singers' bench. (If there are several singers, two benches are used and the singers sit facing each other). Men usually start the dance and, after two or three songs, the women join, placing themselves at the end of the line or alternating with the men, depending upon the dance. In double-file dances (e.g., the Duck Dance), the pairs are composed of two women or two men. The pairing of dancers of opposite sex, linking arms or holding hands, are features of the imported dances and, at Allegany, were resisted on moral grounds and were slow to gain acceptance.

Imported dances, introduced to Allegany over the past twenty years, include:

1. Cherokee Stomp Dance, also called Snake Dance. The step is essentially like the Seneca Stomp Dance but ends with the single file of dancers following a serpentine line and closing into a spiral;
2. Delaware Feather Dance, also called the Delaware Stick, or Skin Beating Dance. For the slow introductory songs, the stomp step is used. With the increase of **tempo**, experimental and improvised steps are performed, as the dance is still new and the form not yet fixed;
3. Friendship Dance;
4. **Two-Step** Dance.

The Friendship and Two-Step are examples of pan-Indian dances that are beginning to arrive at Allegany.

5. **Round Dance**;
6. Rabbit Dance;

"Thanksgiving Address" recounting tribal history and philosophy—showing respect for all the natural and spiritual forces "from the earth to beyond the sky" that help humanity survive. An initial song in some traditions is the "Standing Quiver," also known as a "**stomp dance**." It is done by men moving from their fireplace area in a counterclockwise direction, singing without **instruments**.

Most dances are done with wood and cowhorn rattles and the timekeeping of a larger, handheld **water drum**. The instruments are played by men seated on benches in the center of the Longhouse as the dancers move around them. In an evening, **sets** of as many as twenty songs are performed in **antiphonal** style with a lead singer beginning each song, and with a short **phrase** of **vocables** (sounds without referential meaning) followed by an answering phrase. Dances include the Moccasin Dance, Rabbit Dance, Fish Dance, and Robin Dance. There are at least thirty different social dance sets, some with thirty or more songs in each. Some are danced with couples, others single file, each with characteristic **melody**, rhythm, and steps, as well as accompanying knowledge about the origins of the dance.

The Young Nation Singers participate privately in Longhouse ceremonials and social dances at home and with other Six Nations tribes. However, they also participate nationally on the pan-Indian **powwow** circuit. Group leader Gary Parker explains:

> Longhouse is not for competition or show. It is for the people to dance and for the Creator. That's who we are trying to please. Powwow was adapted from Western peoples like the Sioux. We use the big drum. It is usually a competition for money using more contemporary songs.

> The powwow dances and songs are called "intertribals" and may include competition songs, Grass Dance, Jingle Dress Dance, and special men's and women's dances.

The Young Nation Singers were formed in the mid-1980s and have since become known as one of the best "drums" in the East. They bring their own style, songs, and Seneca language to the powwow. Parker is concerned that the Seneca are losing their dances, languages, and singers. The Young Nation Singers reflect this interest in the future of Seneca culture.

Nick Spitzer

7. Eskimo Dance, also called Cold Dance, Dance of the North, Mohawk Dance;
8. Smoke Dance.

BIBLIOGRAPHY

Bartlett, Charles E. (1955). "Some Seneca Songs from Tonawanda Reservation." *Bulletin of the New York State Archaeological Association* 5:8–16.

Chafe, William L. (1963). "Handbook of the Seneca Language." *New York State Museum and Science Service Bulletin* 388. Albany, NY: University of the State of New York.

Conklin, Harold C., and Sturtevant, William C. (1953). "Seneca Indian Singing Tools at Coldspring Longhouse: Musical Instruments of the Modern Iroquois." *Proceedings of the American Philosophical Society* 97 (3).

Fenton, William H. (1942). "Songs from the Iroquois Longhouse: Program Notes for an Album of American Indian Music from the Eastern Woodlands." Archive of American Folk Song, Library of Congress, Album 6. Washington, D.C.: U.S. Government Printing Office.

———. (1948). "Seneca Songs from Coldspring Longhouse." Chauncey Johnny John and Albert Jones. Archive of American Folk Song, Library of Congress, Album 17. Washington D.C.: U.S. Government Printing Office.

———. (1967). "From Longhouse to Ranch-type House: The Second Housing Revolution of the Seneca Nation." In *Iroquois Culture, History and Prehistory: Proceedings of the 1965 Conference on Iroquois Research,* ed. Elisabeth Tooker. Albany, NY: New York State Museum and Science Service.

Gaus, Dorothy Shipley. (1967). "Change in Social Dance Song Style at Allegany Reservation, 1962–73: The Rabbit Dance." 2 vols. Diss. Catholic University of America.

Hogan, Thomas E. (1974). "City in a Quandary: Salamanca and the Allegany Leases," *Salamanca Republican Press,* 6.

Iroquois Social Dances. 1969. William Guy Spittal. Iroqrafts Records QC 727–729.

Kurath, Gertrude P. (1951). "Local Diversity in Iroquois Music and Davis." In *Symposium on Local Diversity in Iroquois Culture,* ed. William N. Fenton. *Bureau of American Ethnology Bulletin* 149. Washington, D.C.: U.S. Government Printing Office.

———. (1956a). "Antiphonal Songs of Eastern Woodland Indians." *Musical Quarterly* 42:520–26.

———. (1956b). *Songs and Dances of Great Lakes Indians.* NY: Ethnic Folkways Library P 1003. Record album.

———. (1964). "Iroquois Music and Dance: Ceremonial Arts of Two Seneca Longhouses." *Bureau of American Ethnology Bulletin* 187. Washington, D.C.: U.S. Government Printing Office.

———. (1968). "Dance and Song Rituals of Six Nations Reserve, Ontario." *National Museum of Canada Bulletin* 220, Folklore Series No. 4. Ottawa, Canada: Roger Duhamel.

Morgan, Arthur E. (1971). *Dams and Other Disasters: A Century of the Army Corps of Engineers in Civil Works.* Boston: Peter Sargent.

Morgan, Lewis Henry. (1962). *League of the Ho-de-no-sau-nee or Iroquois.* 1851. Reprint, Secaucus, NJ: Citadel Press.

Nettl, Bruno. (1954). *North American Indian Musical Styles.* Vol. 45 of *Memoirs of the American Folklore Society.* Philadelphia: American Folklore Society.

Sturtevant, William C. (1961). "Comment on Gertrude P. Kurath's 'Effects of Environment on Cherokee-Iroquois Ceremonialism, Music, and Dance.'" In *Symposium on Cherokee and Iroquois Culture,* ed. William N. Fenton and John Gullick. *Bureau of American Ethnology Bulletin* 180. Washington, D.C.: U.S. Government Printing Office.

Trigger, Bruce G., ed. (1978). *Handbook of North American Indians.* Vol. 15, *Northeast.* Washington, D.C.: Smithsonian Institution.

U.S. Congress. Senate. Committee on Interior and Insular Affairs. *Kinzua Dam (Seneca Indian relocation).* 88th Cong., 2nd sess., 1964. Washington, D.C.: U.S. Government Printing Office.

Wilson, Edmund. (1959). *Apologies to the Iroquois.* Bound with a study of *The Mohawks in High Steel* by Joseph Mitchell. NY: Vintage.

PUEBLO MUSICAL COMMUNITIES

Brenda M. Romero

Brenda M. Romero is an associate professor on the musicology faculty at the University of Colorado in Boulder. She received a Ph.D. in ethnomusicology at the University of California, Los Angeles (focusing on indigenous and Hispano traditions of New Mexico), as well as bachelor's and master's degrees in music theory and composition at the University of New Mexico. She performed the violin for the Pueblo of Jemez Matachina Dance for nine years, aiding the tradition's ability to continue until a local player could take over.

The Pueblos belong to the Southwest culture area that centers on Arizona and New Mexico and includes the Athapaskan-speaking Dineh (Navajo and Apache) tribes. The Pueblos, whose roots in this area are ancient, were already advanced agricultural peoples who built multiple-storied apartments of adobe and stone masonry and had developed their religions and native arts to a high degree when the Spanish arrived in 1598. (The word "pueblo" has subsequently taken on two meanings; besides describing specific groups of Native Americans who live in the southwestern United States, it is also the word used to refer to their villages.)

The Pueblos maintained a kind of governance, based on the abundance of corn, that resembles more the city-states of the groups in Mexico and not so much the North American Plains model of portable living, following the buffalo. Nineteen pueblos survive in New Mexico today, subdivided into northern Tanoan-speaking groups mostly on the Rio Grande and Jemez rivers, the western Keres-speaking groups, and the Zuni of western New Mexico, whose language is related to indigenous groups in Mexico. In addition, the Hopi, of a Uto-Aztecan, Shoshonean linguistic family, live in Arizona adjacent to Navajo reservations (as are the Zuni in New Mexico). The Hopi and Zuni have preserved their masked ceremonials that were suppressed by the Spanish and almost disappeared in the northern and western pueblos. They are centers of the kachina spiritual practice, in which effigies of mythical characters carved of cottonwood are honored daily. The kachinas, in their various guises, appear in person during ritual observances, the center of traditional musical life in all the Pueblos.

The majority of Puebloans today commute to urban centers and engage in a wide variety of employment. Sometimes problems arise when the ceremonial calendar requires individuals to take time off to attend a Pueblo event. They also face demands on their time as they prepare for feast days

while trying to maintain jobs outside the community.

MUSIC

It is rare to see a complete musical **ethnography** on a Pueblo community. A great deal of secrecy still surrounds the traditional belief systems, and since traditional music contexts revolve around religious ceremonials, this poses significant limitations for fieldwork. Christian missionaries have long established an Hispano Catholic church **repertoire** and newer, Protestant worship musics in English are being disseminated. The **Matachina** is a Dance of Conquest introduced by the Spanish to the Pueblos, where it has taken on its own character and meaning. (For more information, see Volume 5 of *American Musical Traditions* for the entry on Latino musical communities in New Mexico and Colorado.)

The Matachina remains the only Pueblo ceremonial to use European **instruments** (violin and **guitar**), although some Pueblos have a version that uses only the drum and a male **chorus**, and the ceremonial dress has been reinterpreted to conform to traditional formats. The tradition of "borrowing" or "receiving" ceremonies from outside groups is a longstanding practice that underscores the importance placed on the power of ritual as the basis for survival. New contexts in which one hears music in the Pueblos have been added, so that it is not uncommon to hear Pueblo rock bands. In Hopi an annual Sunsplash features famous **reggae** musicians like Ziggy Marley. The Hopi are also receptive to bringing performances by other indigenous peoples around the world, including Australian Aboriginal and Peruvian groups.

TRADITIONAL FORMATS

The most intensive part of the ritual calendar is during the winter months, when fresh food is least available. Food sharing is a regular aspect of both public and private communal ceremonies. In the pueblo of Jemez, a syncretism of Pueblo and Spanish-Mexican ideas of food sharing and posada, or shelter, has led to a tradition in which the household that has the Infant Jesus (usually made of porcelain) receives and feeds anyone at any time except between the hours of 2:00 A.M. and 5:00 A.M., for the two weeks starting on December 24 and ending January 6. The "Infant's House" is draped in brilliantly colorful rugs, tapestries, scarves, shawls, tinsel, and artworks, lending the ambience a magical quality. During this time the house becomes the center for a variety of music, dance, and dance/drama performances in honor of the Holy Child, whose shrine is placed in a corner of the room for all to see and worship. It is common to see female burlesques of Matachina and other dances in the Infant's House, when humor is especially

Pueblo Music of New Mexico.

given a free reign, as well as shortened versions of traditional dances that might take place during other times of the year.

The ritual calendar is typically divided into summer (turquoise) and winter (pumpkin or squash) ceremonials. Among the Tewa the summer moiety is responsible for the summer ceremonials, such as the communal rain and corn dances. The winter moiety, whose leader is called the Hunt Chief, is primarily responsible for hunting ceremonies, such as the Deer Dance. (When a tribe becomes too large for a single organization, its members typically divide into two subgroups, each of which is known as a moiety.) In contrast, among the Jemez and many of the Keres-speaking groups, both Turquoise and Pumpkin kivas (literally the Pueblo sacred ceremonial meeting chambers) prepare dances for the same communal celebrations, including the Catholic feast days. The pueblo of Jemez is unique in that the Turquoise kiva dances the "Spanish" version Matachina with violin and guitar, and the Pumpkin kiva dances the drum/chorus version immediately following (or vice versa). The Pueblos have many dances to honor animals. Most, if not all of the Pueblos, have eagle and buffalo dances, the latter said to have been brought to the Pueblos by Plains tribes such as the Kiowa. The male Tewas in San Juan Pueblo are obligated to dance the Turtle Dance on December 26, and those not participating are roped into the dance in their street clothes by two frightening kachinas. The Bow and Arrow Dance songs of Tesuque Pueblo refer to the songs of birds in the springtime. For nearly a hundred years, Taos Pueblo has encouraged its younger dancers to learn the virtuosic Hoop Dance, which requires the dancer to dance through complicated arrangements of hoops at a very fast **tempo**.

Most of the public music and dance ceremonies in the Pueblos are male-dominated, although women are responsible for seeing that food giveaways and feasting are well organized. Everyone, including men, women, and children, is obligated to dance in the communal dances, such as the annual corn dances, which are often danced barefoot in the blazing sun.

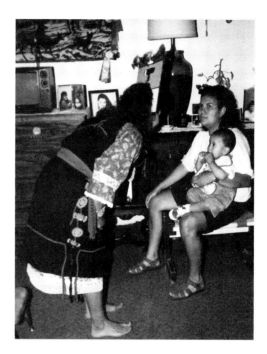

Nora Padilla of the Pueblo of Jemez takes a break in-between Corn Dances to visit with her daughter and grandson. *Photograph by Brenda M. Romero.*

FORM

Pueblo musical **forms** are among the more complicated formal structures used by indigenous peoples in the Americas. It is common to hear a brief introduction to a song, which in some cases, such as the Tewa Turtle Dance, also connotes the ceremony to which the song belongs. Long **verses** follow, usually including a contrasting section or sections. The words are carefully crafted poetic images that emphasize the Pueblo presence in harmony with the natural world and its forces. Care is taken to give texts sympathetic prayer magic, and entire songs are repeated ritualistically; four times is necessary to engage the unseen forces of the four cardinal directions. The drama of the multiple, somber, low-ranging voices and the dance they accompany is **ornamented** by sudden shifts from **duple** to **triple time**, and immediately back to duple, often simply pausing to hear the **syncopation** in the drum on the third beat then continuing. The Tewa refer to this technique as *taí* or pause, and it is heard across pueblos from Taos to Hopi.

HISTORY

The Pueblos are somewhat unique in contrast with other American Indian tribes in

North America, in that they were able to launch a successful revolt against the Spanish colonists in 1680. When the Spanish returned, they were never again to control the innermost workings of the Pueblo societies they continued to dominate. For this reason the Pueblos were able to maintain a more traditional core of ceremonial music culture that provided for music complexes with a wide variety of ritual and healing functions. The Pueblos are unique in an open, evolved male choral sound with rich, low **timbres**. They learned Spanish **polyphony** well but later abandoned it. The vestiges of this tradition are in the female-dominated church **hymn** and folk liturgical **genres** that have replaced the polyphonic music of the early church.

BIBLIOGRAPHY

American Indian Dance Theater: Finding the Circle. (1989). WNET/Thirteen in association with Tatge/Lasseur Productions, Inc. 59 min. New York: Great Performances. VHS videotape. Includes some traditional Zuni dances shot on location.

Discovering American Indian Music. 1971. Bernard Wilets for Barr Films. 23 min. Chatsworth, CA: AIMS Multimedia. VHS videotape. Part of the "Discovering Music" Series. Includes footage of some Pueblo dances and their meanings, including the Tesuque Bow and Arrow Dance and the Taos Hoop Dance.

Music of New Mexico: Native American Traditions. 1992. Notes by Edward Wapp Wahpeconiah. Smithsonian Folkways CD SF 40408. Indigenous music of the Southwest, including examples from Pueblo, Navajo, and Apache cultures.

Romero, Brenda M. (1993). "The Matachines Music and Dance in San Juan Pueblo and Alcalde, New Mexico: Contexts and Meanings." Ph.D. diss. University of California, Los Angeles.

Sweet, Jill. (1985). *Dances of the Tewa Pueblo Indians.* Santa Fe: School of American Research Press.

YAQUI MUSIC

James S. Griffith

James S. Griffith retired in March 1998 as coordinator of the University of Arizona's Southwest Folklore Center and subsequently became a research associate at the Southwest Studies Center of the University of Arizona. He has published extensively on the folklore, folklife, and folk arts of the various peoples of southern Arizona and northern Sonora, Mexico.

The Yaquis ("the people" in their own language) are of Uto-Aztecan language stock. Most of the 5,000 or more Yaquis in Arizona are descended from refugees who fled their homeland in Sonora, Mexico, around the turn of the century when the government of Porfirio Díaz attempted to free up Yaqui lands for large-scale agriculture by killing or deporting the inhabitants. Large numbers of Yaquis fled across the border into Arizona at that time; their descendants eventually came to occupy four communities in the Tucson area and one in the town of Guadalupe, near Phoenix.

HISTORY

The earliest contact between Yaquis and Europeans took place in 1533, when a Spanish slave-raiding expedition heading up the west coast of Mexico was met and repulsed by a group of armed Yaquis who were apparently defending the integrity of their land. This pattern of Spanish incursion and Yaqui defense continued into the seventeenth century, at which time the Yaquis followed yet another Spanish defeat with a request for missionaries unaccompanied by soldiers. In 1619, two Jesuits arrived in Yaqui country, along the banks of the Rio Yaqui, in what later became Sonora.

Their arrival ushered in a period of relatively stable, directed culture change, during which the Jesuits exposed the Yaquis to a new religious system as well as new crops, domesticated animals, and technologies. During this period Yaqui country was for the most part isolated from the incursions of secular Spanish miners, *hacendados* (farmers and ranchers), and others. As pressures on Yaqui land increased after the mid-eighteenth century, so did Yaqui resistance. Following the expulsion of all Jesuits from Spain's American colonies in 1767 (an act based on European power and politics rather than on any issues specifically related to the New World), most Yaquis spent several decades more or less

isolated from Catholic clergy. It seems to have been during this time that Yaqui native-Christian ceremonialism took its present form.

Yaqui resistance to pressures on the sacred land continued through the nineteenth century, culminating in a concerted attempt at Yaqui genocide on the part of the Mexican government under the dictatorship of Porfirio Díaz. During this program, which took place around the turn of the century, Yaquis were rounded up and shipped off to the henequin plantations in Yucatan. Others fled northwards, crossing the border into the United States. It is for the most part the descendants of these Yaqui refugees who make up Arizona's Yaqui population.

THE MUSIC
RITUAL MUSIC AND DANCE

By far the most important body of traditional Yaqui music and song has been preserved in the context of native Christian ceremonialism. Of the ritual performers who carry on these sacred traditions, the most ubiquitous is the *pascola* (the Spanish pronunciation of the Yaqui term *pahko o'ola,* or "Old Man of the Fiesta.") Pascolas are solo dancers who open and close the religious **fiesta** with prayers and orations, and who act as a focal point for the fiesta activity. At least one pascola and his accompanying musicians must be present at any religious fiesta.

The pascola is bare to the waist and wears breeches of light blanketing material. His hair is pulled up into a topknot decorated with a paper flower. He wears a small wooden mask with white eyebrows and beard on the back or side of his head. Around his waist is a leather belt from which hang metal hawks-bells *(koyolim)*, and thrust into the belt he carries a wooden, sistrum-like **rattle** *(senasom)*. His feet are bare; wrapped around his ankles and lower legs are long strings of dried cocoons *(teneboim)*

Map showing where the Yaquis tribe settled in Arizona when it fled Mexico at around the end of the nineteenth century.

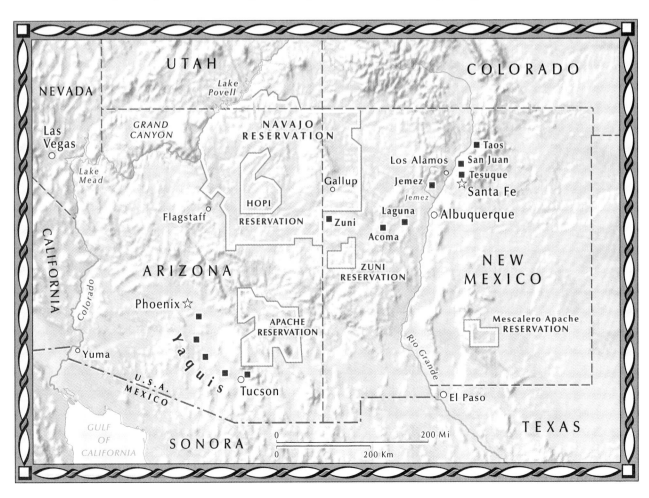

of the giant silk moth (*Rothschildia Jorulla*). The koyolim sound whenever the pascola moves; the teneboim accentuate his dance steps with a dry, rustling sound.

The pascola dances to two different kinds of music during the course of a typical fiesta. To the sound of the violin and harp he performs a complicated step dance, beating out the rhythm with his feet (and accentuating it with the teneboim). When each pascola has danced in turn, from youngest to oldest, another musician—the tampoleo—takes over. He is seated on the ground, leaning against a wooden backrest. He plays a cane flute with his left hand. With a small stick held in his right hand, he plays a small, **two-headed drum** that he holds between his thigh and his left elbow. When the tampoleo starts playing, the pascola pulls his wooden mask over his face, goes into a half-crouch, and performs a dance that involves little footwork but highly complex play with his senasom, which he holds in his right hand and plays against his cupped left hand.

At many larger fiestas the pascolas are joined by a deer dancer (*maso*) and his three singer-musicians. The deer dancer performs bare to the waist, with a dark rebozo (a long scarf) or shawl hanging from his waist. Around his waist is a leather belt with many pendant deer hooves; around his lower legs are teneboim. He holds a **gourd rattle** in each hand. Two of his singers play long wooden **rasping sticks** against half-gourd **resonators**; the third beats a waxed half-gourd floating in a pan of water. His beating stick is wrapped with corn shucks. The deer songs are sung in an archaic and formal Yaqui, and they present images of "our little brother" the deer as he moves through an enchanted world filled with flowers and other birds and animals.

The setting for all this fiesta activity is a special *ramada* or bower that is divided into two parts. On the left side is an altar, to which the appropriate saint's image or images have been carried. On the right side is a space for the pascola and deer dancers and

Los Matachines, traditional Matachin dancers, performing in front a pueblo building in New Mexico. Although wearing traditional masks, they sport Western-style clothing.
Photograph by Philippa Jackson, courtesy of the Smithsonian/Folkways Archives.

A Yaqui Matachin dancer, photographed in traditional headdress, in Tucson, Arizona, in 1951.
Photograph © Bettman/CORBIS.

their musicians. The back and sides of the ramada are walled; spectators crowd around the front to watch the ritual dancers.

The fiesta altar is the focus for two more kinds of musical performance. A group of women—*kopariam*—sit in chairs or on the ground in front of the altar and sing responsorial chants in Spanish, Latin, and Yaqui. They are led by the *maehto* or maestro, a Yaqui lay prayer leader. (Other than the kopariam, all the musicians, dancers, and singers involved in the fiesta arts are male.)

Finally, the *matachines,* a group of men and boys dedicated as soldiers of the Virgin of Guadalupe, perform contradances in the plaza in front of the ramada altar. They wear crowns with ribbons on them and carry a trident and a gourd rattle in their hands. They dance to the music of **guitars** and violins. On certain occasions such as Easter Sunday, the matachines braid and unbraid a maypole as part of their dance.

The matachines' dance and its attendant music are distributed widely over northern Mexico and the Southwestern United States. Indian and Hispanic communities in northern New Mexico perform it, as do mestizos (people of mixed European and Native American ancestry) all through the border states. Yaqui matachines are considered especially sacred, however, to the extent that they may not dance on **secular** occasions, and, according to Yaqui belief, ground that has been danced over by matachines has been blessed until the end of time. Although pascola and deer performers are also religiously dedicated, it is possible for them to appear on secular occasions such as civic and cultural festivals.

SECULAR MUSIC

There is a body of song in Yaqui called **corridos**, the same word that is used for Mexican **narrative folksongs**. Men perform these unaccompanied or to the music of a guitar, often while informally socializing; the songs deal with characters and events remembered by Yaqis. Finally, Arizona Yaqis on occasion form **mariachi** and **norteño** bands. These tend to play the standard **repertoires** of their **genres**, with the addition of a few regionally popular songs in the Yaqui language.

YAQUI MUSIC BEYOND YAQUI CULTURE

Yaqui music was widely recorded in both Mexico and the United States from 1940–1980. Many of these recordings have been issued commercially. A representative LP is *Yaqui Ritual and Festive Music* (1976), which contains pascola and deer performances, as well as a few secular corridos. Yaqui musicians and dancers have also traveled to larger venues such as the Smithsonian Festival of American Folklife and the National Folk Festival. The outlook for many of the ritual forms looks promising as well; young children are learning the traditional **instruments**, songs, and dances in increasing numbers.

BIBLIOGRAPHY

Evers, Larry, and Molina, Felipe S. (1987). *Yaqui Deer Songs/Maso Bwikam: A Native American Poetry.* Vol. 14 of the Sun Tracks Series. Tucson: University of Arizona Press.

Griffith, James S., and Molina, Felipe S. (1980). *Old Men of the Fiesta: An Introduction to the Pascola Arts.* Phoenix: Heard Museum.

Seyewailo, the Flower World: Yaqui Deer Songs. 1978. Larry Evers, Felipe S. Molina, and Denny Carr. Tucson: University of Arizona Radio-TV-Film Bureau. VHS videotape.

Spicer, Edward H. (1980). *The Yaquis: A Cultural History.* Tucson: University of Arizona Press.

Yaqui Ritual and Festive Music. 1976. Robert Nuss. Phoenix, Arizona: Canyon Records C–8001. Audiocassette and CD.

O'ODHAM MUSIC

James S. Griffith

Please see Chapter 5 in this volume for biographical information on James S. Griffith.

When the Spanish empire expanded into what are now the Arizona-Sonora borderlands, its soldiers and missionaries encountered native peoples who called themselves O'odham or "the People." Due to an apparent misunderstanding, the Spaniards assigned to them the name "Pima," which seems to be derived from an O'odham word meaning "I don't know." The descendants of these people still live in the Arizona portion of their traditional range and are divided into two main related cultural and linguistic groups: the Akimel O'odham or "River People," often called "Pimas" by Anglo-Americans, and the Tohono O'odham or "Desert People," formerly called "Papagos." Although this essay will deal with the musical traditions of both groups, it will start with the Tohono O'odham.

The Tohono O'odham occupy the second largest reservation in the United States, the Navajo Reservation being the largest. It stretches in southern Arizona from a point west of Tucson almost to the mining town of Ajo, and from the United States–Mexico border north almost to Interstate 10. As recently as the eighteenth century, there were many Tohono O'odham in what is now the Mexican state of Sonora; northward migrations to the United States began in the nineteenth century and continued well into the twentieth century, leaving only a handful of O'odham in their Sonoran homeland.

Traditionally, singing was a major means by which the O'odham connected with the world of power. Song **cycles** accompanied the major and minor ceremonies of the year and were important parts of extraordinary events such as raids against the Apache enemy and salt pilgrimages to the Gulf of California. Curers used song in the healing process; it was an important means by which disturbed balances were restored and health of all kinds was maintained. (A fine collection of various kinds of song texts appears in Underhill 1973.) Songs could be solo or group efforts and were accompanied

by **gourd rattles** and a drum made from a large, overturned basket.

This song tradition continues for curing, for those native religious ceremonies that are still performed, and to accompany group dancing. Two dances that persist are the *keihina* or "circle dance" and the *chelkona* or "skipping and scraping dance." From the evidence of painted pottery, the keihina seems to have been a part of desert life for at least 800 years. It is performed by both men and women holding hands in a circle. They sing a given song four times. The first two times the dancers walk in a counterclockwise direction to the sound of voices and **rattles**; when the basket drum accompanies the last two repetitions of the song, the dancers perform a hopping step, bringing their feet down on the ground "hard, so as to bring in the rain clouds." The chelkona is one of the dances that O'odham children still learn, and it is frequently performed in public at cultural festivals. (A selection of songs used during the 1970s may be heard on *An Anthology of Papago Traditional Music,* Volume 1, 1972.)

The O'odham traditionally learned songs for the keihina, chelkona, and other dances from the Spirit World. There are still those who receive songs in this way. Once received, the songs become the property of their composers.

Missionaries probably introduced European **instruments** such as violins, **guitars**, and military-style drums to the O'odham when the region was a part of New Spain. Assuming this to be the case, the skills necessary to play these instruments were already in place by the mid–nineteenth century when Anglos and others brought new tunes, rhythms, and dances into the desert country.

By the late 1860s, O'odham bands from nearby San Xavier Mission were playing **waltzes**, **polkas**, **schottisches**, and other dance rhythms at the annual San Agustín **Fi-**

The O'odham Indians, which translates as "the People," occupy the second largest reservation in the United States.

esta in Tucson. The makeup of the band may well have been that of old-time **fiddle** bands: two or more violinists, one or more guitarists, and two drummers (one on the bass drum and the other on the **snare drum**). Bands such as this, playing what the O'odham call *waila* music (from the Spanish word *baile* or "social dance") exist among both Tohono and Akimel O'odham.

The old-time O'odham fiddler's **repertoire** extends past the nineteenth-century couple dances to three other kinds of tunes. The *pácola* or *pascola* dance is a solo ritual dance the O'odham learned from the Yaquis. It is regularly performed at religious feasts, especially in the western portions of the Tohono O'odham Nation. O'odham pacolas dance to the music of a violin and a guitar. Also probably learned from Yaqui sources is the *matachines* dance, a ritual contradance done by men and boys and accompanied by violins and guitars. Finally, Tohono O'odham play and dance the *kwariya* ("cuadrilla" or "**quadrille**"). This is similar to what is known as the Appalachian **Big Circle**, with couples performing evolutions such as "Grand Chain" and "Promenade" from a large circle, and then splitting into two-couple **sets** for figures like "Duck for the Oyster" and "Four Hand Star." The route by which this dance and its music entered the O'odham

repertoire is unknown. Kwariya tunes are in 6/8 time and include the well-known Anglo-European song, "Flop-Eared Mule."

Since the 1950s, the older, violin-based waila bands have been largely replaced among the O'odham by ensembles featuring **accordion** and saxophone leads and rhythm provided by **electric guitar**, **bass** guitar, and full drum set. This music is also called waila, although some prefer the informal term "**Chicken Scratch**." Said to be derived from some of the dance steps used to the music, this name is most commonly used among Anglos and Akimel O'odham. Many Tohono O'odham find it derogatory and prefer "waila."

Although contemporary waila music obviously owes quite a bit to *la música norteña* of the United States–Mexico border region, it is not simply an Indian version of **norteño**. In the first place, waila is, with only one or two exceptions, instrumental music. Waltzes and **corridos**, so important in the norteño repertoire, are not played by waila bands. There are other, more subtle stylistic differences as well. Waila tunes may come from the Mexican ("Maquina 501," "Jalisco") or American ("Turkey in the Straw," "San Antonio Rose,") repertoires, or they may be O'odham compositions.

One major context for waila music is the village saint's day feast, an occasion that takes place in most O'odham villages every year or once every two years. A typical feast begins with Mass conducted by a Catholic priest in the village chapel. After Mass a procession leaves the chapel and, often accompanied by music, walks out to the cross that stands somewhere to the south or east of the chapel. Individuals in the procession carry all the holy pictures and statues that normally occupy the chapel altar. Once at the cross, the saint-bearers kneel while other villagers go from saint to saint, reestablishing a personal relationship with the images. The procession then re-enters the chapel.

At this time the feasting begins in a communal dining area attached to an open-air kitchen near the chapel. All comers to the

feast are served in shifts with red chile and beef stew, beef and vegetable stew, beans, freshly baked bread, wheat flour tortillas, potato salad, some sort of packaged fruit punch, coffee, and cake. As dark falls, the waila band starts playing beside a dance floor set near the chapel door. Traditionally, the band plays until dawn, alternating polkas, **two-steps**, and *cumbias* throughout the night. All ages participate in the dancing, and couples may consist of a man and a woman or two women. The basic steps are simple, with considerable economy of motion. Like the keihina dancers, waila dancers move in a counterclockwise direction.

Waila music has been available on record since 1973. The primary recorder and distributor is Canyon Records, a Phoenix, Arizona–based company specializing in all types of Native American music from across the United States and northwest Mexico. A large number of bands, both Tohono and Akimel O'odham, have recorded for Canyon over the years, and many of their records, cassettes, and CDs are still available. In addition, waila bands have played at such regional and national festivals as the San Diego Folk Festival, Tucson Meet Yourself, the National Folk Festival, and the Smithsonian Festival of American Folklife. An old-time fiddle band attended the Festival of American Fiddle Tunes in Port Townsend, Washington, in the early 1990s. Since 1987 an annual Waila Festival has been held in late spring at the Arizona Historical Society Museum in Tucson.

Since the 1980s, other musical forms have entered O'odham culture. The pan-Indian **powwow** movement has brought its own music, and O'odham drums have taken part in performances. A Tohono O'odham **blues** band was performing in the mid-1980s, and O'odham play various kinds of rock music. None of these forms, however, have been integrated into O'odham culture in the way the waila has.

BIBLIOGRAPHY

An Anthology of Papago Traditional Music. Richard Haefer. 1972. Canyon Records C–6084. LP record.

Chicken Scratch Fiesta. 1981. Canyon Records CR–8055. Audiocassette.

Gu-Achi Fiddlers: Old Time O'odham Fiddle Music. 1988. Canyon Records CR–8082. Audiocassette and CD.

Underhill, Ruth. (1973). *Singing for Power: The Song Poetry of the Papago Indians.* New York: Ballantine Books.

NAVAJO SONGS, DRUMS, AND FIDDLES

Nick Spitzer

Please see the sidebar accompanying Chapter 3 for biographical information on Nick Spitzer. This essay originally appeared in the program guide for the 1994 Folk Masters concert series, held March 11–April 16 at the Barns of Wolf Trap in Vienna, Virginia.

Native American music shows enormous diversity based on tribe, culture, and region. At the same time there is a deep similarity, due in many cases to the group-focused nature of performance and the ritual and festival settings in which it occurs. A more recent factor that favors unity of style is the pan-Indian influence that has produced **powwow** music based largely in the "big drum" format associated with the Great Plains. An equally significant force for individual diversity has been the emergence in the last two decades of many solo performers who have moved from traditional to pop and country music or avant-garde. Yet a balance remains between traditionalists and more transformed performance styles. Our program covers some of these many musical and cultural possibilities, drawing from southwestern and northern tribal music traditions. Included are Navajo, Mohican, and Métis. The range of performance practice runs from solo drumming, song, and flute-playing to **guitar**-accompanied singing

and fiddling, to powwow chanting and drumming.

The Navajo are the largest tribe in the United States, with about 190,000 people on their vast reservation that covers 25,000 square miles of Arizona, Utah, and New Mexico. They have resided in this land of desert, mountains, canyons, and forests since between A.D. 1000 and 1525, and the terrain is often mentioned in songs that refer to sacred locations and events that happened in particular places. The Navajo Nation is a mix of rural sheep farmers, professional artists, tribal administrators, forestry workers, ranchers, and many others. The Navajo performers come from the small settlements of Ganado and Steamboat, Arizona, about fifty miles west of Window Rock and the nearby border with New Mexico.

The desert area near these towns is composed of rolling hills, rock mesas, canyons, and massive vistas of rising terrain that seem to defy gravity. At small crossroads stores, one sees signs for country music shows and

powwows. The radios in stores and gas stations are set to KTNN, the voice of the Navajo Nation, which broadcasts from Window Rock in both Navajo and English, and is as likely to play Merle Haggard as the songs of our featured singer, Davis Mitchell.

Waiting to meet Davis one afternoon in Ganado, I stood around talking with older Navajo men who wore cowboy hats, dark green shades, and gold in their teeth. In contrast, the women wore long dresses, scarves over their heads, and abundant turquoise jewelry. Davis Mitchell—medicine man, singer, and rodeo cowboy—showed up around sundown. His wife and four children were in tow.

Davis, who is currently the hottest solo singer and drummer on the reservation, is also a sandpainter. It's something he began doing around 1982. The paintings are traditionally the work of medicine men. Davis obtains sand for colors—red, yellow, orange, black, turquoise, purple—by going to the Painted Desert, to craft shops, and also to brickyards where fine-grained red dust may be found. He says:

> The sandpaintings started from medicine men. And medicine men use the sun, father of the sun, or mother earth, or many types of designs like snake, like horses, bear, and corn. I don't reveal or sell the traditional designs because later on down in the future you can be hurt by it. That's what our medicine men believe.

Mitchell has been pulled in varied directions in his life, between following the medicine path of his father and uncle, and trying to gain success as a rodeo cowboy and country singer. Singing Navajo songs of his own making to entertain in the Indian community allows him to exist somewhat in both worlds. Navajo ceremonial life is quite active and music is often used to help restore good health, balance, and serenity (hózhó, or "harmonious conditions"). In his own life he has been part of ceremonials where his health has been sung over all night while he was piled under blankets. Receiving a **rattle**

as part of the ceremonial confirmed his role as a medicine man who could similarly heal others and bring them into balance.

Mitchell recalls his life at that time:

> I was a bull rider before. That's how I started, late in my high school days, in junior rodeo. After I got out of high school I bought me a membership card in Rodeo Cowboy Association. And I got in there for four years, I got hurt bad. The bull really hurt me, stepped on me, and kind of pulled me around for awhile. And then the doctor told me to stay off. And I was off for maybe seven months or six months and then I really thought that I didn't

Map showing the reservation of the Navajo tribe, which spans Arizona, Utah, and New Mexico.

Hopi Music

A Hopi in Two Musical Worlds

Jacob Coin, composer and musician, is a member of the Tobacco Clan, Hopi Nation, from Kykotsmovi Village, Third Mesa. He also represents Hopi interests in Washington, D.C. In 2000, after serving first as executive director of the Arizona Gaming Association and then as executive director of the National Indian Gaming Association, Coin assumed the post of executive director of the California Nations Indian Gaming Association. The following essay was originally published in the 1992 Smithsonian Festival of American Folklife program guide.

When our people first emerged onto this, the Fourth World, they came upon Massau, guardian of this world. Our people asked to live here and were given permission to do so with certain conditions. Massau instructed that to live here we must adopt four basic guides for our lives. First, we must have *na wakinpi* (prayer), a way of communicating with our Creator. Second, we must have *tup 'tseuni* (a religion) for spiritual guidance. Third, Massau said we must have *ka 'tsi* (a culture), a way of life that distinguishes us from others. Finally, Massau said we must have *navo'ti* (prophecy) to guide our people into the future.

Massau might also have instructed the people that to live in balance in the Fourth World, we must have music and song as a vehicle for integrating the four basic guides into our lives. As long as humanity has been here, music and song have been a primary means of teaching and learning the ways of the Fourth World.

As a young boy, I came to expect songs of the kachina to be a vehicle for learning the ways of the Hopi. (The kachina are god-like ancestral spirit beings who figure significantly in the ritual ceremonies of the Hopi and other Pueblo peoples.) Their songs told of the virtues of waking before sunrise and giving prayers, of having a

A traditional Hopi buffalo dancer, holding a symbollic lightning bolt, photographed in 1946. Traditions like these are preserved, while newer influences have also been felt.
Photograph © Bettmann/CORBIS.

good heart and respect for the environment and all living things. We understand that these virtues and others are basic to the Hopi way. At a young age all Hopi learn that teaching is one of the many roles music and song have in traditional Hopi life.

Universally among Indians, music is a part of the social environment, a medium for teaching the ways of tribal life, and a means of passing tribal and clan histories from one generation to the next. It is an instrument for learning the natural order of the world and of the universe and for understanding humanity's relationship with the earth and other living things. Indian people use music and song as a guide and a gauge for social conscience; music and song keep tribal

really care what doctor told me, and I just went back in and started again. And then late that year I really hit the ground, and I got knocked out. And that's the time I got sick again. And they told me, and the doctor told me, that time, you're going to die young, if you don't believe me, just take it.

After a difficult passage, Davis' dying father convinced him to follow the medicine way to look out for his family and the future of the Navajos. He predicted that through his music and medicine Davis would be widely known among the Navajos.

Navajo music is generally divided between sacred forms and popular styles, though some of the latter may also be used

mores and social expectations visible for all of the people. Music has certainly always been a key to spiritual growth among Indian and Native peoples. Above all, music is an invaluable entertainment medium and food for the heart and soul for all mankind.

For the most part, contemporary Indian and other Native musicians and songwriters accept and remain true to the traditional roles of music. For the contemporary Native musician, music is more than simply entertainment. Like their ancestors, today's Native artists agree that a commitment to music in its role as teacher is an important responsibility to be upheld.

Being a Hopi Indian and a musician/songwriter, I find guidance and inspiration for my music in traditional Hopi roots. I experiment with a matrix of techniques in using traditional Native musical forms and styles to create contemporary songs. In the end, I believe that traditional music and contemporary music are extensions of each other. The primary challenge is to bridge the gap between traditional and modern music effectively.

I have tried to do this by three methods. First, I pull the meaning of a traditional song into a contemporary piece by translating the song's lyrics into English and then composing a **melody** and defining a beat that conveys the meaning of the song as it was originally intended by the traditional composer. This is perhaps the easiest method, since it amounts to composing new music for existing lyrics without having to be faithful to the all-important original melody.

Second, I score a traditional song in its entirety for Western instrumentation, including **guitar**, piano, vocals, and the like. In this process I try to be faithful to the original melody, which is often difficult because traditional songs are composed solely for voice, and instrumentation often cannot exactly replicate notes produced by the human voice.

Third, I weave traditional songs together with contemporary musical forms, allowing both to express themselves in the composition. This practice is most innovative—and preferred—since it allows an artist complete freedom to create new music and new songs utilizing both influences.

For the most part, the drum was the primary instrument for Native music. Over time, drums were supplemented with flutes and **rattles** of various kinds. As the use of these **instruments** evolved, so did traditional music. The pattern of this evolution is created by traditional music's continual reaching out to embrace its developing contemporary relative.

Other instruments besides the drum have become accepted vehicles for the musical thoughts of Native artists. Guitar and other stringed instruments, flutes, and various percussion instruments have become the norm in the orchestration of contemporary Native songs.

What would really rock (and shock!) our ancestors would be the revolution brought by electrified instruments and electronic special effects. Of all Native musicians and songwriters, Keith Secola (Ojibwa) of Phoenix, Arizona, and Buddy Red Bow (Oglala Sioux) of Pine Ridge, South Dakota, have been most successful in maintaining the integrity of Native sound patterns while expanding on them with electric instrumentation and special effects.

Ronald Smith of Minneapolis, Minnesota, a Mandan/Hidatsa traditional singer/composer with the Eagle Whistle Drum, suggests that the inevitable evolution of music, both Native and contemporary, is a good reflection of social change at any given time. Without judging it, Ron describes contemporary music as a snapshot of society. According to Ron, the evolution of Indian music reflects the dynamism of Indian peoples. "We are not a people even close to extinction," he says.

(Continued on the next page)

for ceremonials. The sacred music is usually composed of long narrative texts dealing with creation, morality, and philosophical topics accompanied by group **chorus**, rattles, and drumming. The popular styles, which may be recorded and performed in public, are often for personal use to accompany herding, corn grinding, and other work or play activities. They may also be about people, patriotism, and parts of such ritualized events as the Squaw Dance or Nightway and Enemyway ceremonials.

Davis Mitchell's song style includes **vocables** (untranslatable syllables) and words linked together by **falsetto** leaps and steady chanting. He plays a small **water drum** and sings self-composed songs that may be honor songs, flag songs, or birthday songs.

(Continued from the previous page)

Has traditional music changed? It has really evolved. Traditional music has reached out and touched the twenty-first century. The fortunate result for both worlds is that Native musicians still understand and value the many social roles of music. Native musicians will continue to compose songs that have meaning, that have their genesis in traditional ideas and inspirations. Native musicians are to be recognized, just as their ancient predecessors have been, as teachers of thought conveyed through music and song.

Massau surely knew the importance of music in the Fourth World. He would never have insisted on people having Prayer, Religion, Culture, and Prophecy without assuming music as a medium for carrying them forward. Good for us, music continues to fill our hearts and minds with the good things of the Fourth World.

Jacob Coin

Some love songs, with titles like "Beautiful Girl from Afar" and "I'll Be There Unexpectedly" have earned him the title "The Navajo George Strait." Davis warms to the comparison, and enjoys his ability to be a singer in two worlds: "I dress up country all the time. Especially when I'm going to go entertain. I wear my trophy buckle, I wear my hat, and I walk out. I entertain, and maybe some people come around, 'Hey, help us,' they say, 'you're a medicine man.' Okay, I take off my belt, my buckle, my hat, put on the moccasin, and get a Pendleton blanket (for a healing ceremonial), there it is, being an Indian."

As is true throughout the country, big drum powwow style is popular in the Navajo Nation. Davis Mitchell is a member of a powwow group called Black Star Nation. To reach the homes of most of its singers one travels a few miles from the small settlement of Steamboat until a canyon veers off to the north at a jagged angle. At the entrance to the canyon is a wedge-shaped field of corn, waiting for rain. A maze of dusty trails leads back to a series of houses. Most are the traditional *hogans,* eight-sided and of log or board construction plastered with wattle and daub. Most are colored brown or salmon with thatched roofs and, occasionally, tarpaper.

I meet Jackson Gorman, the leader of the Navajo powwow group Black Star Nation Singers, near his house. His wife Orlinda and nephew Emmett Shorty are also part of the group. They are waiting for other nephews to return from a sweat lodge ceremonial and are all readying for a Squaw Dance that will be held tomorrow in the next canyon over. Drinking coffee and watching babies crawl around in the plywood house, Emmett Shorty says:

> We pray to Black Star, and that's where we got our name from. Our old people, like our grandpas and our parents, when they pray to the stars, they say Black Star is our traditional name, so that's what we call our drum singing group. The reason why I do that is because I respect my elderlies and my great-grandparents and my father's side and my mom's side. That's the way I am.

As the sky overhead fills with stars, we move outside into a little yard fenced for dogs, sheep, and goats, with a pigeon roost at the back. Dominant on one side of the compound is a large metal satellite dish—currently inoperable—that is a sign of status and allows the incongruity of seeing local television from the world over in this modest house in a remote canyon. As the various nieces and nephews assemble for singing, Jackson Gorman says, "We sing what we call fancy songs. We compose them ourselves, in Navajo. One describes a nice way of dancing to please Mother Earth."

Gathering about the big drum, they also sing of the Navajo captivity at Fort Sumner in 1864 and then move on to love songs, including those of Davis Mitchell, who has chosen to dignify the occasion by wearing a tuxedo T-shirt. After a break for sodas in the dusty air, Emmett, Jackson, and Davis stand up to sing together with handheld octagonal

Master singer/drummer Davis Mitchell, holding a small water drum under his arm.
Photograph by Nick Spitzer.

drums. These are used for the Owl Dance and **Round Dance** in ceremonials, but now they are singing a new love song called "Who's Been Holding You Tight?"

Jackson Gorman became interested in powwow in the mid-1980s. He had been dancing to the various regional styles when he was encouraged one day to start singing and beating the drum. Black Star Nation, made up of his wife, friends, nieces, and nephews, is the group he formed as a result of his interest. He has also worked with the widely respected Cathedral Lake Singers. Much of the year for Gorman is spent as a section gang worker for the Santa Fe Railroad. During the warmer weather he travels from Chicago to Los Angeles to Amarillo with an all-Navajo crew that replaces and straightens track, repairing switches or whatever needs doing.

SONGS OF THE PEOPLES OF THE NORTH AMERICAN PLAINS

Mary Jo Ruggles

Mary Jo Ruggles is an ethnomusicologist who served as professor of music at the University of Oklahoma prior to her retirement in 1994. She has worked extensively with the tribal music of the southern plains. In a show of great respect, the Cheyenne people have allowed Ruggles to record songs associated with the Sun Dance. This essay originally appeared in Remaining Ourselves: Music and Tribal Memory—Traditional Music in Contemporary Communities, *edited by Dayna Bowker Lee, published in 1995 by the State Arts Council of Oklahoma.*

The core of Native American musical expression is found in its songs. The use of the term "music" is not strong enough to describe the importance of song in Indian cultures, causing a loss of perspective and appreciation in regard to the spirit of personal expression. Songs of American Indian people, when learned in context, offer a window through which we may begin to comprehend many vital lessons from the culture of the people. The song matrix encompasses the name of the tribe, the singer, the maker of the song, the purpose of the song, and the proper time to sing the song.

Many Native American singers close their eyes when they sing, especially personal songs, spiritual songs, memorial songs, or any song that embodies a heightened emotion. They sing from within with the intensity of joy, sadness, love, and knowledge of their Creator. They sing for fun and to promote laughter and good humor. They sing for themselves and they sing for all beings, for all the creatures of the earth. They sing for the earth itself, clouds, water, air, fire, and for all creation.

The songs of the plains tribes are as expansive and diverse as the area known as the plains. There are songs made for all things that are important in the lifeways of the people. The plains of North America have been described as the area contained by the Missouri River on the east and the Rocky Mountains on the west, and by southern west-central Canada on the north and the southern border of Texas on the south. They comprise a vast area of grass prairies, tall grass in the north and shorter grass in the south, with few trees, most of which are willow and cottonwood—an area perfect for the growth of herds of North American bison or what we in Plains Indian Country call the buffalo. One of my favorite descriptions of the plains is found in Scott Momaday's book *On the Way to Rainy Mountain:*

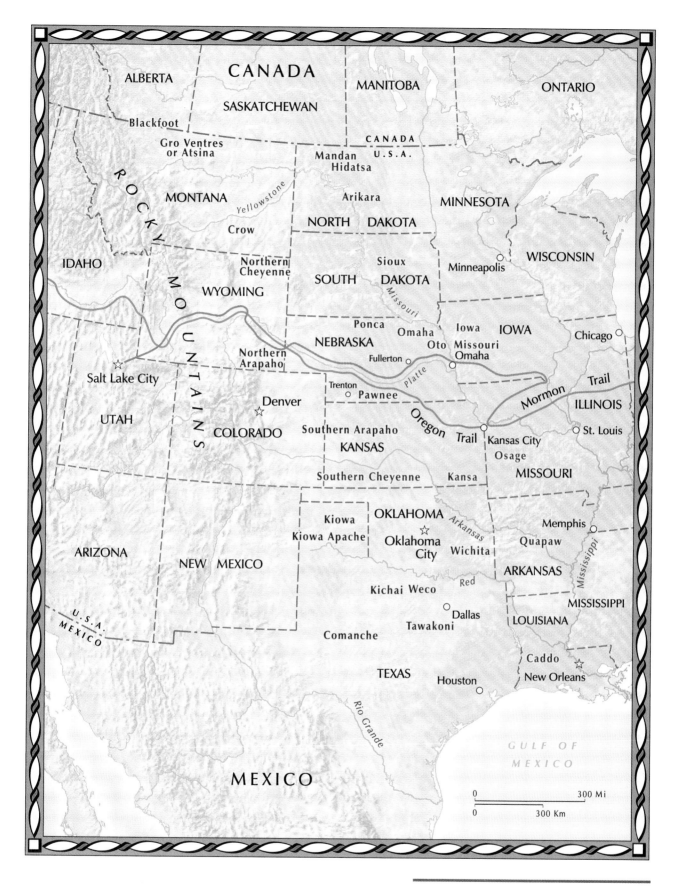

Tribal Music of the Plains (Tribal locations c. mid–nineteenth century)

The earth unfolds and the limit of the land recedes. Clusters of trees, and animals grazing far in the distance, cause the vision to reach away and wonder to build upon the mind. The sun follows a longer course in the day, and the sky is immense beyond all comparison. The great billowing clouds that sail upon it are shadows that move upon the grain like water, dividing light....The sun is at home on the plains. Precisely there does it have the certain character of a god.[1]

Most of the tribes we now consider to be plains people migrated to the plains from the eastern, southern, western, and northern parts of North America and Canada as necessities of life or tribal wars made it undesirable to continue to live in their places of origin. Many of the tribes now associated with the plains area were not originally nomadic hunters of buffalo but lived in villages near rivers where small game, fish, berries, and other edible plants were available. Some of these tribes were also cultivators of crops, especially corn. As is the way with Indian people, they embraced the changes necessary to continue to live and enjoy family and the earth. After the arrival of the horse (1659–1775),[2] a plains culture developed that included traditions from the past, traditions borrowed, and new ways of life.

The songs of these people of the plains reflect reverence for the Creator, who is known by many different tribal names. This reverence extends to the earth, sky, wind, rain, and all the elements of creation, and to the human and animal families of the earth. Songs also profess loyalty to family and tribe, thanksgiving for the spirit and the earthly manifestation of the buffalo and the horse, and good humor for a peaceful and loving existence. A wonderful attribute of Native culture is that everyone can be a singer if they choose, and most choose to sing either privately or with a group. The singers and singer-drummers learn the appropriateness of performance as they learn the song. As with all tribal peoples, songs are intertwined within the layers of lifeways and ceremonial

See glossary for definition of boldfaced terms

traditions. To learn a song is also to learn about private ownership, family songs, tribally associated songs, ceremonial songs, and songs for all the competition dances. The number of song **genres** (types) are numerous, and songs within a genre are beyond counting. This great body of songs includes songs of joy and sorrow, courage, love, celebrations, ceremonies, animal songs, personal spiritual songs, church songs, songs for dancing, honoring the earth, honoring each other, social songs, and so on.

The style of songs stretches from reverent prayer chants to wide-ranging melodies expressing joy and excitement. Personal and family songs include tender and funny baby songs and songs of gratitude for love and families. There are also exuberant, raucous songs unbounded by convention, and songs of friendship and gathering together. The songs come to singers in a vision or a dream, on the wind, from the simple need to express joy or sadness, or in the emotion of a moment when nothing else but song would suffice. Songs are embellished, as the spirit moves the singer, with exclamations and ululations or **lulus**.

Songs of native North Americans are born with a purpose—to fill a specific need in the life of the singer, his family, or his/her tribe. Songs are for singing and all that it implies. A single person offers living breath to express deep emotions. Singing can be either individual or collective, but songs are, from inspiration to first utterance, a gift from the Creator, and always individual. Although songs are an individual expression, they are often shared to become collective expressions. Individual expressions are sometimes kept in individual or family ownership, an ownership that may descend through many generations. As a song is received as a gift from God, it is sometimes given as a gift to another singer or friend as an offering of honor, love, or respect. When a gift of song is given, it is usually given without fanfare and kept only in the memory of those who receive the gift. This exchange represents the value of the song as well as the personal generosity of the giver. When a song is made for a special occasion, in honor of a person or event, the gift is even greater.

The most prominent text used in a large percentage of songs, in addition to tribal languages, is that of the vocable. In her comments about "Oklahoma Two-Step," Charlotte Heth states that "it should be emphasized that these untranslatable syllables (**vocables**) are not chosen arbitrarily, and that in many cases songs can be identified by their vocable texts as well as by their melodies."[3] Vocables are nonlexical syllables that perhaps were once word parts of a tribal language or abbreviations of words no longer in use. It is my opinion that vocables used throughout the plains are made up of the primary vowels used in tribal languages. Thus, tribal people from different language groups within the plains use different vowels as the vocables in their songs. These language groups of the plains are Siouan (Crow, Mandan, Quapaw, Omaha Ponca, Osage, Missouri, Kansa, Iowa-Oto, and Hidatsa), Algonquian (Blackfoot, Cheyenne, Arapaho, and Gros Ventre), Caddoan (Caddo, Wichita, Pawnee, and Arikara), Uto-Aztecan (Comanche), Athapaskan (Kiowa-Apache), and Kiowa-Tanoan (Kiowa).[4]

Vocables are also used in conjunction with tribal language and sometimes act as introductory and closing parts with tribal language text in the middle. Vocables are also added to **phrases** of tribal language text to finish a melodic or, more often, a rhythmic gesture.

Although the human voice is the most used **instrument** of song, it is not the only one. Instruments such as drums, **rattles**, flutes, and **whistles** accompany the voice at appropriate times. The drum is the major instrument of the Plains people. It is said to be a home for the spirit of the Creator as manifested by the spirits of the elements that gave up their existence to become the spirit of the drum. Its musical offering stretches from the rolling sound of thunder or buffalo hooves to the somber and respectful cadence of Flag and Memorial songs, from the incessant pulse of a Gourd Dance song to the welcoming and friendly beat of the **Round Dance** song. Perhaps the most familiar sound to urban America is the exciting sound of War Dance songs used for competition dancing.

The rattle, found in so many forms and used for many different purposes, is often a personal accompaniment to singing. Made from such diverse elements as **gourds** or aluminum cans, they are often decorated with beadwork that has been constructed with a prayer on every bead or, as used for hand game, with a dazzling tassel made for distracting the guesser for the other side. There are loud, high-pitched rattles, soft-sounding rattles made of gourds and natural seeds, and gentle-sounding rattles made of deer toes. Each of these instruments is special to the person who has ownership for as long as he or she needs it. The rattle may have been made by the person using it or given to that person as an honor by a friend or a member of the family.

The instrument called the plains flute has had a place in plains culture for hundreds, even thousands, of years. Its origin is still the subject of much individual and academic speculation. The plains flute, most scholars agree, originated as a courting flute and a personal companion on long journeys. Since the 1970s, this flute has experienced a flowering of renewed popularity. Most of the flute songs heard on radio, cassettes, and compact discs are not in the style of the traditional flute song. The use and sound of the flute has been borrowed by contemporary musicians, both Indian and non–Indian, to create peaceful, serene, and tranquil melodies. Acoustic flute sounds are enhanced by electronics, by the use of several sizes of larger flutes, and aboriginal flutes from other peoples around the world. The flute, once a companion on journeys, is now used by many people for another kind of journey—a journey in an automobile during which it is used to bring a little peace to drivers in a world going too fast and out of control. Through the magic of electronics, it is still used as a courting instrument for both Indian and non–Indian people. Traditional flute songs may still be heard at cultural exhibitions and at native ceremonial and social gatherings and by request from some flute players who remain in touch with the old ways and old songs.

This is a story or afterthought, as a way to synthesize the act of creation, performance, and gift of song:

Not long ago a friend and colleague made a surprise visit to my classroom to give me (and the students in my class) a gift, a gift of himself. He talked about how he felt about songs, and what they meant in his life. He does not sing on a regular basis with a drum group but sings with his people as he joins them on social and sacred occasions. He sang songs in two tribal languages and others with vocables. His story reminded me of how the need to voice an emotion rises within a person and demands expression. He related a time when he made a song. He was riding alone in a pickup truck in northern New Mexico headed for the mountains when the need to express his feelings brought forth a song—a song about the human spirit, first; about the travail of being a human being, second; and, last of all, to voice renewed understanding that all is well under God. His feeling was of a renewed faith caught from the overwhelming display of God's creation. All of these sentiments were expressed with vocables as the human spirit transcended the human being and the song was born on breath from the Creator. Thank you, Phil, for sharing.

NOTES

1. Momaday, N. Scott. (1969). *On the Way to Rainy Mountain.* Albuquerque: University of New Mexico Press, pp. 7–12.

2. Kehoe, Alice Beck. (1982). *North American Indians: A Comprehensive Account.* Englewood Cliffs, NJ: Prentice-Hall Press, pp. 297–98.

3. Heth, Charlotte. (1976). *Songs of Earth, Water, Fire and Sky.* New York: New World Records NW 246. Side two, band four.

4. Hollow, Robert C., and Parks, Douglas R. (1980). "Studies in Plains Linguistics." In *Anthropology on the Great Plains.* Ed. W. Raymond Wood and Margot Liberty. Lincoln: University of Nebraska Press, p. 75.

BIBLIOGRAPHY

Densmore, Frances. (1936). "Cheyenne and Arapaho Music." In *Southwest Museum Papers* No. 10. Los Angeles: Southwest Museum.

Bancroft-Hunt, Norman. (1992). *The Indians of the Great Plains.* Reprint of original 1981 edition. Norman: University of Oklahoma Press.

Hofmann, Charles, ed. (1968). *Frances Densmore and American Indian Music. A Memorial Volume.* New York: Museum of the American Indian, Heye Foundation.

Kehoe, Alice Beck. (1992). *North American Indians: A Comprehensive Account,* 2nd ed. Englewood Cliffs, NJ: Prentice-Hall.

Schlesier, Karl H., ed. (1994). *Plains Indians, A.D. 500–1500: The Archaeological Past of Historic Groups.* Norman: University of Oklahoma Press.

Waldman, Karl. (1985). *Atlas of the North American Indian.* New York: Facts on File.

MUSIC OF THE PAWNEE

Gene Weltfish

Gene Weltfish taught anthropology at Columbia University and was the author of The Lost Universe, *a study of Pawnee life and culture. During the late 1920s and 1930s, she actively collected the music of the Pawnee, mostly working with the Pawnee tribesman Mark Evarts. The recordings she made in the mid-1930s were issued in 1965 on Folkways album 4334, entitled* Music of the Pawnee. *This essay is derived from the notes that accompany the album.*

Under the great dome of the sky in the western plains lived the Pawnee people. Three rivers flow eastward from the foothills of the Rockies to the Missouri, crossing Nebraska and northern Kansas, and along their middle courses the Pawnee villages were clustered. Overhead the sky was their major deity and First Cause, and the stars were its minions, and each man was born under a star that watched over him throughout his life. For 600 years, from 1250 to 1876, life ran its course and through this time the Pawnee developed into a nation. Then history began to press in upon them. First the dispossessed Sioux from the Lakes region to the east and then other tribes were moved onto their lands and their hunting grounds and finally came the Oregon Trail, The Mormon Trail, the Gold Rush, and white settlement. At last they could remain no longer, and they tried to find a refuge to the south, leaving their ancestral lands behind.

Their substantial houses of timbers, thatch, and earth, circular in shape with a high domed roof, were grouped into villages along the high banks of the Loup and Platte, with their cornfields in the bottomlands. Each village had a heredity chief and braves who were his administrative assistants. These were federated into four major Bands—the *Skidi* or Wolf; *Kitkehaxki,* Little Earth Lodge Village; *Tsawi'i,* Begging the Big Game Hunter for Meat; *Pita-hawirats,* Man-Going Eastward or Downstream. There was a major division between the Skidi and the other three, which were called "South Bands" because of their location: the division was noted on an historical map at least as early as 1701, and it was apparent in a minor variation in the spoken language. In historic times the Skidi were the most highly organized of the four bands, with an integrated theology and an official priesthood of five priests as well as an established association of combined Doctor Cults that held an elaborate thirty-day Grand Opera after the harvest in the fall.

According to their theology, after Heaven had created the Universe in a series of pri-

A Pawnee family photographed in front of their family lodge in Loup, Nebraska, in 1873. The lodge is a typically elaborate structure that is made of wood and thatch with a circular roof.
Photograph by William H. Jackson, © CORBIS.

mordial storms over many eons, he created the stars that were to create Mankind. In the western skies he placed the Evening Star, a beautiful woman, goddess of night and fruitfulness and her helper, the moon and in the eastern skies, the Morning Star, god of light, war and fire, born of hot meteors and a hot bed of flint. Between their realms ran the Milky Way. Assisting Morning Star was his younger brother, the sun.

For the Pawnee, the dome of the house was the dome of the sky in miniature, and life kept flowing through from the stars to the people inside at all times. The circular walls of the house were like the larger horizon outside where the earth meets the sky all around them on the Great Plains. The house was always entered from the east through a long vestibule, and as the Morning Star rose in the eastern sky, it entered the house and touched the fireplace, creating life anew each day when the fire was kindled.

In her western realm, the Evening Star kept her cultivated gardens of food crops and her servants, the Winds, the Clouds, the Lightnings, and the Storms that were given her by Heaven itself at the Creation. Then Morning Star waged a war upon her, invading the western skies to bring light into the world and life. At the invasion, Evening Star transformed her four servants into fierce an-

imals in the four semicardinal quarters of the Universe—the winds in wild oat form in the southwest; the clouds as wolf in the southeast; lightning as mountain lion in the northwest; and the bear in the northeast. All these the Morning Star had to conquer through many trials, and at last he destroyed, with a meteor stone, the vaginal teeth that shielded the goddess from mating. From their union the first human being, a girl, was born, and a whirlwind carried her to earth. From the mating of their respective assistants, the Sun and the Moon, the first boy was born and also carried to earth. And so the human race—at least of the Pawnee, began.

But man had to pay for his life, for the Morning Star demanded the life of a young girl who was captured from an enemy tribe every year and sacrificed at planting time, so that all life could go on and the crops mature. The girl was sacrificed as she stood tied to a scaffold, shot with an arrow through the heart by a warrior impersonating the Wolf, god of death—the southeast star, Sirius. At the base of the scaffold was the oblong pit lined with white downy feathers symbolizing the Garden of the Evening Star, the *kusaru,* or bed. A number of features of Pawnee theology, particularly of the Skidi, are reminiscent of classical Mexican religion, and a direct analogy for the sacrifice is sug-

gested by Herbert J. Spinden and Clark Wissler (*American Museum Journal* XVI, No. 1, January 1916, p. 54) in the mode of human sacrifice of the Ciucatecan tribe of the State of Guerrero, Mexico, illustrated in the Codex Porfirio Díaz now preserved in the National Museum in Mexico City. Other evidence prompts the authors to attribute the time of the diffusion of this custom between 1506 and 1519, when the victory of Cortés ended their communication. When news of this dramatic rite first reached the eastern seaboard of the United States, in 1820–21, it created something of a sensation—especially in the light of the obvious Mexican analogies.

In 1816 an Ietan girl was captured by a Skidi warrior in preparation for sacrifice to the Morning Star in the spring of 1817. The chief of the Skidi at this time was Knife Chief (*ritsi-risaru*) of Pumpkin Village. In 1811 he had been on a delegation to see William Clark in St. Louis, who was then Superintendent of Indian Affairs for the region. They had a long and serious talk in which Clark impressed Knife Chief with the fact that white people were coming in ever-increasing numbers "like the waves of the ocean—in, in, in . . . It's coming. Every year more people come over here," and the Pawnee must prepare themselves.

Knife Chief, impressed with the validity of this, tried to get the people to abandon the custom of human sacrifice, but the warriors and priests, always suspicious of the political motives of the chiefs, were hostile and defiant. The ceremonies were continued and on the appointed day, the young girl was led out and tied to the sacrificial scaffold. On his trip to see William Clark, Knife Chief was accompanied by his son (or nephew) Man Chief, *pita-risaru,* an outstanding warrior in his early twenties and universally respected by all the people.

With the crowd gathered and the warrior ready to shoot the fatal arrow, Man Chief rode before them and told them his father disapproved of what they were about to do and he had come to rescue the girl or die right there. By Skidi belief, anyone who touched the con-secrated girl during her captivity would soon die, for they would be taken by the Morning Star in her stead. Thus all could see that Man Chief was offering his life as a forfeit for the girl. The crowd held off in awe while Man Chief cut the girl down, placed her on a horse, and sent her south where she was able to rejoin her own people.

By 1820–21, the story of the conduct of Knife Chief and his son, Man Chief, had come to the attention of Edwin James and Jedidiah Morse and through them it became known. An expedition of Pawnee chiefs from each of the four bands, including Man Chief, was called to Washington in 1821, led by Major O'Fallon. There, in the light of his bold rescue, the girls at "Miss White's Select Female Seminary" collected enough money to have a large silver medal cast to present to the handsome young Pawnee hero at a public ceremony. It bore the inscription: "To the Bravest of the Brave."

Man Chief was now a young man of about twenty-five. In his acceptance speech, Man Chief said when he did this thing, he did not know he was brave, but had acted according to his feelings, but now that they had called him brave and had given him this medal, he thanked them and would always remember them. His portrait was painted by Charles Bird King and appears in the Thomas L. McKenny and Hall volumes on Indian tribes. The medal was excavated near Fullerton, Nebraska, by Alonzo Thompson.

The Pawnee are historically credited by other tribes as the source of the main features of the Calumet or Peace Pipe Ceremony noted by the explorer Marquette as early as 1672, when he traveled down the Mississippi under its protection. This elaborate and beautiful ceremony was actually a ceremony of peaceful trade. The initiator of the expedition was a man of substance and influence, and for at least a year he enlisted his friends and associates in the accumulation of a quantity of valuable manufactured goods and preserved foods that they would carry as "gifts" to another tribe or politically distant band within the Pawnee group. When these preparations had been arranged

for, the leader sent a messenger to make the necessary diplomatic contact with the other group, particularly with a person of comparable status, wealth, and social influence to the leader. With this notification, this man would enlist the pledges of his friends and associates within his tribe or Band for contributions of horses to be given as return gifts to the visiting leader on behalf of his party. (Possibly in the past, the visiting party brought manufactured goods and dried crops and received dried buffalo meat as a return gift). Such a "Pipe Dance" expedition often included a hundred people.

These mundane aspects were almost unrecognizably embedded in an elaborate metaphor and ceremonial procedure. The visiting expedition included under the leader, a number of chiefs, braves, priests and medicine men, exemplifying the main personages of Pawnee officialdom. In addition to the goods as gifts, they carried with them the best in tents, camping equipment, utensils, and food, enough for the entire expedition, including the entertainment of the people they were to visit. These would be left behind as part of their offering.

They assisted their hosts in horticulture and other work so that they would be free to participate in the ceremony. The host, on his part, provided a large earth lodge in which the main ceremony could be performed, lodging in his home for the leader, and adequate camping facilities for the rest of the party. When the ceremony was over, the contributed horses were turned over to the leader of the visiting party, who would later distribute them among those who had contributed or participated in the expedition.

The visiting party came as "Fathers," the host being referred to as "Sons" or "Children." The "Father" was bringing and communicating all that he valued to his "Child." The pipe comprised two elaborately decorated pipe stems, one signifying the female eagle and the values of the home, and the other the male eagle, hovering about outside and protecting it from attack. The female pipe stem was decorated with a fan-shaped pendant of ten tail feathers of the brown or

See glossary for definition of boldfaced terms

golden eagle, and the male pipe stem with a fan-shaped pendant of seven tail feathers of the white eagle. Among the Pawnee, the symbolism of the pipe stem is basic; it signifies the windpipe, the breath, life, voice, speech, the soul, and the way of communication with the heavenly powers through the smoke of the tobacco, which rises to the Heavens.

The ceremony itself represented in a sense, a synopsis of Pawnee ceremonial and religious themes. A Pipe Dance Song "Baby Stop Crying—Look Upward at Father Sky" is described by its singer in these words: "They want the baby to stop crying and look up at the feathers at the end of the pipe stem, which is pointing with the mouthpiece upward (so that Heaven may smoke), and thence he will look up at Father Sky." The meaning is that Father Sky is the ultimate source of all their well-being, and it is in this direction that the child should look for his security. After the ceremony, a considerable number of horses, highly decorated for the occasion, are presented by the "Child" to the "Father." The "Father" leaves with the "Child" in addition to the other gifts, the sacred pipe stems, and all ceremonial paraphernalia. For a year or more at least, there will be peace between their two groups.

In my ethnological account, when the Pawnee villages were attacked by the Sioux, Eagle Chief took the decorated pipe stems and said to his wives, "Dear wives, it is said that this pipe is beloved of Heaven," and so he rode out holding the pipe stem aloft and as he approached, the enemy lined up, turned around, and rode away when they saw the pipe.

In addition to the interrelationship of the four bands of Pawnee, united in language as well as custom, were more distantly related people who spoke the kindred languages of the Caddoan language family. These people were distributed in a north-south "corridor" west of the Mississippi River in the midcourses of the rivers that flowed into it from the foothills of the Rockies. The Arikara, the northernmost of the Caddoan peoples, were in North Dakota, then the Pawnee in Nebraska and Kansas, the Wichita

to the south of them in Kansas and Oklahoma, and the Caddo, from whom the language stock is named, still further south toward the Gulf in Louisiana and Texas.

There was a tendency for each of these groups to look for certain kinds of cultural stimuli toward the group south of it. It would appear that in times past, individuals from among the Arikara would spend several years among the Pawnee to gain ceremonial knowledge, while from among the Pawnee in their turn, some men went south to the Wichita and apprenticed themselves to the leader of a religious cult for some years in order to learn the ceremonies, the songs, and ideas.

Sometime during the early part of the 1800s, a man named Kind Warrior went from the Pawnee among the Wichita and stayed for three years, returning with many new songs and religious ideas. He brought with him the knowledge of the *raris-ta*, Deer-Dance, a ceremony concerning the increase of the deer and their life on the plains and in the timber. The symbolic elements have a decidedly southern flavor, rather than one essentially native to the Pawnee habitat. They included the green sage, which symbolized the fresh odors of spring and with which the floor of the ceremonial house was covered, the mescal bean, smearing with white clay to symbolize its seeds, and the rattlesnake. The Pawnee Doctor Cults, for example, were concerned with Bear, the Buffalo, the Otter, the Beaver, the Wolf, willows, cottonwoods, and other trees of the area, as well as ducks, geese, loons, etc.

The raris-ta shared many important features with the Pawnee Doctor Cults, among them an intensive practice of legerdemain and various degrees of trance, interpersonal suggestion, and hypnotism. There was some difference in primary emphasis, the traditional association of the Pawnee Doctor Cults having as their main theme the curing of the sick through an intimate knowledge of the nature of the wild animals and plants, while the raris-ta was organized as two opposing war parties, with the southern groups—Wichita, Weco, Kit-

Two Pawnee chiefs photographed by famed Civil War–era photographer Matthew Brady in his Washington, D.C., studio in the 1850s. Many photographs of Native Americans were made in this period to document their traditional costumes and headdress. *Photograph © CORBIS.*

sai, Tawakoni—"attacking" the northern groups or *isati*, the component divisions of the Pawnee.

In both cases a demonstration of power was a successful demonstration of sleight-of-hand, which was referred to as "playing" (*kusisaari*) in the sense of children romping, and of trance-induction, called "fighting" or "shooting" (*patsaku*). The raris-ta, referring to this latter activity as "shooting the image or shadow"—*awai-taaku*. The more aggressive character of this activity in the raris-ta was evident. There is evidence that the Pawnee, like other tribes, used their power of suggestion and trance-induction both on the hunt in relation to the wild animals and toward the enemy in war. It is said that among the tribes of the North Pacific Coast, a war party would

not set out without an able shaman to exercise his powers against the enemy.

After the death of the originator, Kind Warrior, the leadership of the raris-ta was taken over by a Skidi chief, Victory Call, and it became more and more a composite with many typically Pawnee ceremonial features added to the original Wichita nucleus. Among both Pawnee and Wichita, the participants in the ceremony were grouped around a central fireplace into two halves, one part in a northern "arc" and one in the southern. These were again subdivided into two "positions," each in the semicardinal directions: southeast, southwest, northeast, northwest.

In the raris-ta, at each end of these "stations," a number of cult leaders were seated, the positions signifying the ages of a man—southeast, youth; southwest, fully grown men, northwest, men in their prime; and northeast, old men. (The more usual Pawnee symbolism designates the west positions for youth; the cardinal positions for maturity and the east for old age—more particularly the southeast).

The procedure was for **gourds** and ceremonial bows to be brought to the first station at the southeast and for the men to begin to rattle and sing. Then someone would get up and dance, and eventually a feat of sleight-of-hand would be performed. Then further dancing, and for the next round the **rattles** and bows would be taken to the next or southwest station, and they would begin to sing—dancers would get up and another sleight-of-hand performance would be carried out, and so on through the two other stations—northwest and northeast. In the course of these performances the dancers jumped diagonally over the fireplace toward the diagonally opposite semicardinal "station," and a complete performance would include "forming a star," that is, making two diagonal crossings in the opposite direction.

The Pawnee pictograph for a star was an equal-armed cross like our plus sign and the star referred to was Sirius, the star of the southeast—the Wolf Star. The Pawnee referred to this star as *Takirixki-tiuhats,* Wolf–He is deceived, which refers to a legend in the mythology. Performances of trance-induction were also carried out between members of the diagonally opposite semicardinal "stations." Many observers have attested to the great skill of the Pawnee as illusionists. This ceremony was carried out in the fall for ten days after the harvest, nine night sessions, and a tenth all-day episode.

The ceremonies of the Association of Doctor Cults occupied thirty days after the harvest and comprised elaborate animal-mine performances and dances, some of them in the public dance-grounds in the open. An aspect of the animal miming was sleight-of-hand and trance induction between members of the different cults. It was characterized by public parades and was an elaborate Grand Opera with a central theme, an integrated vision story and songs, dances, and performances. In it the Doctors who had charge of the health of the people affirmed their kinship with the living things of nature—the wild animals, the birds, and the plants.

In 1867, the raris-ta was becoming so popular that a bitter rivalry developed between the leaders of the established Doctor Association and the raris-ta leaders. On his death bed, Victory Call attributed his death to sorcery by Big Doctor, of the Doctor Association. There is reason to believe that there were rival cults at an earlier time that finally became integrated into a larger composite cult.

In the Pawnee religious scheme, the Doctors were in charge of the realm of the earth and the water and the official priesthood of the Heavens and the stars and constellations. While all life and creation had its source in the Heavens, the cultivated crops were in a more immediate relationship with Cosmic realm. The palladium of the cosmic theology was an elongated bundle containing ceremonial paraphernalia wrapped in a tanned hide and tied around with a rope of braided buffalo hair, its form and mode of wrapping symbolizing a particular spirit.

Among the Skidi, whose theology was the most highly organized of all the Pawnee

See glossary for definition of boldfaced terms

bands, there were twelve sacred bundles, with a certain variation in the objects they contained, but each having two sacred ears of corn of a special archaic breed grown especially for the bundles and renewed after the harvest each fall. Each of these ears of corn had an individual name, and as the bundles hung over the sacred altar in the earth lodge, offerings were made to it, and the ears of corn were addressed by their names. Every spring the ceremonial cycle began with a ceremony of the five official priests, who went to each bundle in succession, singing of the steps of the creation of the universe, of the star gods, and of the formation of the political federation of villages into the Skidi Band long ago. Many of these songs accompany an elaborate ceremony performed at the time when the ground was first broken for planting the corn. This ceremony is called *Awari,* which signifies activity or motion, and in the course of it, motions of breaking the earth are made with the adze-like hoe, made with a buffalo shoulder blade sharpened along the edge so that it can break the ground.

Like all American Indian groups, raiding parties went into enemy territory, but among the Pawnee, glory was far from the sole motive. Most of all they went to take booty—valuable costumes and decorative objects made of hard-to-get materials and also dried and preserved buffalo meat. There is evidence that this was an old pattern, but horses, as a highly mobile and convenient kind of booty, were certainly a prime objective.

The Pawnee always set out on their raids on foot, particularly with the expectation of getting horses—but they also packed the booty they got on their own backs. Scalps were taken as concrete evidence for the people at home that one had been in the land of the enemy, and honor was given for touching the enemy during battle, provided this could be attested to by an eyewitness or other conclusive evidence, sometimes even an erstwhile enemy during a time of truce.

Among the Plains Indians, the young men formed themselves into military societies under whose auspices raids were undertaken. Among the Pawnee, societies

seemingly comparable in form, were not for this purpose but for national defense against enemy attack of the settlements and for providing official police during the semi-annual tribal buffalo-hunting expeditions.

A primary characteristic of Pawnee life was its dual alternations through the seasons of horticultural activities and tribal migrations south and west across the State of Nebraska to attack the buffalo herds, bringing home the dried and preserved meat for storage. In the spring they lived in settled villages and tended to the planting of the crops; in the summer (the corn being laid by) they migrated for the summer buffalo hunt; in the fall they returned to the villages to harvest, dry, and store the crops; and in the winter again they migrated to the buffalo-hunting grounds to attack the herd.

A storage pit in conjunction with each house held more than a year's supply of dried and preserved buffalo meat, corn, beans, and squash. At the western wall of every house there was a sacred altar on which the buffalo skull rested, and above it hung the sacred bundle with its ears of corn, signifying their dual dependence.

There were songs associated with the veneration of the buffalo, along with songs to accompany the Hoop and Pole Game. It comprised the rolling of a hoop down a long playing field and aiming a spear or pole at it, symbolizing buffalo mating, the hoop representing the female. At the same time the buffalo hunt with a spear was symbolized. This game was a constant and characteristic feature of Pawnee life, the men betting heavily on the sidelines. The gaming grounds were a favorite rendezvous for the men to watch the game, to meet and talk, or just sit around.

Another favorite game of the men was the Hand Game, in which two opposing teams sat on opposite sides of an oblong fire pit, two members of one side hiding a pair of long white tubular beads in their hands and representatives of the opposite side trying to guess the combination of beads and empty hands among the four. This was definitely a game of war symbolism—of attack on the enemy and reprisal—and the betting

was very heavy. The players on opposite sides sometimes tried to strike each other, but the whole group combined to prevent them from actually doing so.

In this brief summary, I have been able only to suggest some of the richness of traditional Pawnee life. The dispossessed Sioux, who, for several centuries, had continued to be pressed westward from their original home around the Great Lakes, carried on a desperate crescendo of attack upon the Pawnee, attempting to take over their lands and their hunting grounds. They early acquired guns from French traders to the east, and as they added to these horses, which came ultimately from Spanish sources in the Southwest, they became a powerful military force, armed and mounted, and more and more displaced peoples who had formerly been settled joined up with them.

It is estimated that in 1780 the Pawnee numbered 12,000, in 1855, 4,000. Epidemic disease was also a major killer. In 1855, the Dakota Sioux alone are said to have had 30,000. In 1865 there were 3,400 Pawnee and on August 5, 1873, while on their summer buffalo hunt, accompanied by an agency-appointed trail agent, the hunters were massacred by a band of 800–1,000 Sioux warriors, who then proceeded to attack the rest of the encampment, including the women, children, and old people who had been rushed to a ravine near Trenton, Nebraska, for shelter. The death toll was very high, and finally, after visiting parties among the Wichita to the south had sounded out the possibility of migrating there, the movement became a landslide in spite of all the chiefs could do to dissuade them from leaving their own territory.

They migrated to Oklahoma in three contingents under different leaders. By 1876 the Pawnee had all left their ancestral home that they had occupied for 600 years. The move was disastrous for many of the people sickened in the new climate and from the hardships of the journey and the need to develop new resources for food, clothing, and shelter. By 1879, three years after the last move, they numbered 1,440, and by the census of 1910, 630—a loss of 94 percent in

See glossary for definition of boldfaced terms

130 years of contact. In 1928, when I first went to Pawnee Oklahoma to record the language, they numbered 750, and today (c. 1965) there are 1,800 on the tribal rolls.

Today remembrance of past traditions is faint, and most of the Pawnee have found their way into professions and trades—numbering among them engineers, accountants and business managers, a journalist and illustrator, a fine artist, a former Major League baseball player, a professional radio entertainer, a psychiatric social worker, nurses, clerical workers, carpenters, and others, with their working homes scattered throughout the country.

But their feeling for the past is not lost, and every year many return to Pawnee, Oklahoma, for a period of homecoming together.

But in 1928 there were a number of old people whose only language was Pawnee, whose youth was spent in Nebraska, living in the traditional villages and going on buffalo hunts. Their memory of their life was vivid, and they hoped to make a final record so people would know "what they had done."

After working on the morphology of the language in order to get materials for its semantic study, I tried to get as detailed an account of old Pawnee life as I could. I enlisted the help of Mark Evarts, who had lived in Nebraska as a boy and migrated to Oklahoma with the last contingent in his early teens. Later he joined a group of his friends and went to Carlisle School in Pennsylvania and, trying to adapt himself in New York, Philadelphia, Newark, and other cities, he returned to Pawnee, lonely and broken in spirit in the early 1890s, when an important religious revival known as the Ghost Dance was in progress.

By religious means, the Indians thought to turn back the clock, "blow away the white people and the devastating new conditions" and bring back their dead and old ways. With all his relatives and friends dead, Mark Evarts embraced this belief wholeheartedly, put away his new ways, returned to speaking only his own language, and, in a series of visions, saw with vivid clarity Pawnee life as he had lived it in his youth. Later, mar-

riage, the birth of a daughter, and a successful farm seemed to bring him satisfaction, but his wife died of tuberculosis and his daughter followed at the age of twelve, and by 1924 his farm was lost through a bank loan in a bad crop year.

When I came to Pawnee in 1928 we first became acquainted through my friend Stacy Matlock and my linguistic interpreter, Henry Chapman, with whom I worked on the South Band Pawnee dialects. I was looking for material on the linguistic differences between the South Band and the Skidi. Henry Chapman continued to act as my interpreter, but finally Mark Evarts became exasperated with the obvious difficulty of direct translation and began to work with me in heavily accented English.

When we came to know each other, I realized that he would be the ideal informant for the detailed account of traditional Pawnee life I was looking for. The plan we devised was to get a complete round of an entire year of Pawnee life in all its detail when Pawnee society was still functioning

and Mark was a small boy, roughly the year 1867. Beginning on a spring morning when he awakened in an earth lodge, he recounted the whole scene: the people, the day's round, etc. From 1929 to 1936 we continued this plan, finally completing the four-seasonal round in its normal course.

This material was collected in my book that was originally published in 1965, titled *The Lost Universe*. In 1936, Evarts came to New York and recorded many of the songs associated with the Pawnee rituals for me. He made a small **water drum** out of a glazed earthenware specimen jar with a piece of tanned hide drawn over the mouth and fastened in the traditional way, filling it partly with water through the skin. The drum that was used by the Pawnee was made of a section of cottonwood log that was partly hollowed out by rotting and then scraping, and then the skin drawn over the mouth and tied as in our substitute. A skin-covered drumstick was also improvised for the occasion and a gourd rattle was used. These recordings were issued on record in 1965 by Folkways.

THE INTERTRIBAL POWWOW IN OKLAHOMA

Gloria A. Young

Gloria A. Young is the education coordinator at the University Museum of the University of Arkansas in Fayetteville. She has authored numerous works dealing with Plains music and dance and the place of the pan-tribal powwow in plains interaction. This essay originally appeared in Remaining Ourselves: Music and Tribal Memory—Traditional Music in Contemporary Communities, *edited by Dayna Bowker Lee, published in 1995 by the State Arts Council of Oklahoma.*

The Oklahoma **powwow** is a dynamic intertribal event that is most notable for its continuing changes over time. It changes because it is made up of a large group of people interacting with each other. The changes are brought about by human initiative. Native Americans are the active players in the history of the Oklahoma powwow, not the passive recipients of styles and activities thrust upon them. Because these players come from so many different backgrounds—tribes, clans, regions, cities, rural areas, schools, and churches—they bring their own ideas, their own songs and dress, and their own history to be a part of the Oklahoma intertribal powwow.

The powwow developed out of historical ceremonial dances that were shared among Indian groups, including the Warrior Society dances, the Ghost Dance, the Gift or Smoke dances, and the Drum or Dream Dance. The styles of all these intertribal dances were greatly influenced by the tribal music, dances, customs, and religion of the

participants. So today's powwows carry a legacy of spirituality from historic ceremonials, both intertribal and tribal. Part of the unique flavor of the powwow, however, comes from the blending of Native American ceremonialism with Oklahoma history's more raucous celebrations, namely, commercial Indian dances. Commercial dances have been held in Oklahoma since territorial times, sponsored by individuals (both Indian and non–Indian), as well as groups such as tribes, commercial clubs, and fair associations.

COMMERCIAL "POW WOWS" OF THE EARLY 1900S

The term "pow wow" [sic] appeared in Oklahoma Territory in 1902 in an *Elk City Record* newspaper article: "Cheyennes from the Hammond Agency held a big pow wow here last week. They were returning from a visit to the Darlington Indians and were about 200 in number." When asked for an

explanation, Cheyenne and Arapaho Agency Superintendent J. Whitewell replied, "They went on request of the merchants and there was no pow wow about it. They simply danced enough times in a circle to satisfy the populace that they had seen an Indian dance." (Whitewell 1902). Perhaps Agent Whitewell understood the term powwow to refer to a meeting such as a tribal council meeting.

"Powwow" was originally an Algonquian word which, according to Roger Williams's seventeenth-century dictionary, referred to curing ceremonies among the New England tribes. (Williams 1827 [1643]). Like the New England words "papoose" and "moccasin," the word "powwow" was quickly adopted into English. By the 1800s it was used widely to mean any gathering at which people were going to be making a decision.

Despite the fact that Agent Whitewell did not consider it a "pow wow," the event described in the newspaper article was something today's powwow-goers would recognize. A large crowd of townspeople paid "their two bits admission." Music was provided by

> ...nine musicians, each having a small stick about two feet long with a rag wound around the end after the fashion of a swab. They sat in a circle around the big drum and sang and pounded that **instrument**. An old timer led the music and began his tune very faintly, gradually increasing in volume, the others joining in and [the women] helping out with the **chorus**. About twenty [men] were gaily dressed with feather and headgear and having strings of sleigh bells around their ankles and about the knees (Whitewell 1902, brackets mine).

This type of public Indian dancing was very popular with the townspeople of the

A modern-day powwow held at Fort Berthold Reservation, North Dakota, in the mid-1980s.
Photograph © Richard A. Cooke/CORBIS.

Twin Territories at the beginning of the twentieth century. For example, a large crowd attended a "pow-wow" sponsored by the Collinsville Commercial Club in 1907. Indian agencies had received a letter that read:

Henry Spybuck, chief of the Shawnees, is anxious to hold one of the greatest Pow-wow [sic] ever pulled off between the full-bloods of the Southwest and requests us to ask you to allow a number of Indians under your charge to be his guests during the 16th to 19th of October (Dickinson 1907, brackets mine).

Some agency superintendents shunned the unabashedly commercial affair. It was probably, however, not an original scheme of the Commercial Club, but rather the continuation of an annual fall dance that had been held by Henry Spybuck at his dance ground, less than ten miles from Collinsville, for years. The Commercial Club may simply

have offered to sponsor it (or Spybuck may have talked them into it).

Held at "what is commonly known as the Collinsville fairgrounds," the powwow was attended by chiefs Geronimo (Apache), Quanah Parker (Comanche), Lone Wolf (Kiowa), O-lo-co-wa-la (Osage), and Rogers (Cherokee). Besides dancing, the event was to include a carnival, greyhound racing, and a beauty contest. The *Collinsville News* of October 24, 1907, reported:

The Indians, though not appearing in thousands in number, did credit to themselves in entertaining the visitors who came a long distance to see them. They danced mornings and evenings, showing the old time customs which they seem to enjoy today. The beauty contest failed to materialize. (*Collinsville News* 1907, pp. 307–310)

Though the Collinsville powwow was well attended by the public, the largest

Map showing the different tribal areas in Oklahoma in the early twentieth century.

KANSAS

MISSOURI

TEXAS

OKLAHOMA

ARKANSAS

TEXAS

commercial dance of the time was a private affair put on by the Miller Brothers 101 Ranch near Ponca City for the National Editorial Association. This first Miller Brothers Round-up, on June 11, 1905, was performed before an audience of over 60,000 spectators, the largest crowd ever assembled in the Twin Territories. The "Indian war dance and powwow" portion of the show featured more than 200 Ponca, Oto, Missouria, Tonkawa, Pawnee, Kaw, and Osage dancers (Hanes 1977, pp. 55–56). The Round-up was the beginning of the traveling "Miller Brothers 101 Ranch Show," with which Native American dancers toured for many years.

DANCING AT EARLY TWENTIETH-CENTURY INDIAN FAIRS

Some commercial dances in the early 1900s were performed at events called Indian Fairs. The 1910 Cheyenne and Arapaho Fair, held at Weatherford, Oklahoma, and cosponsored by the Indian Agencies and the Weatherford Commercial Club, provided for an Indian dance concession charging fifteen cents admission. However, there was also a free "Indian Moon dance in front of the Grandstand the second night with campfire" (Norris 1910). The *Indian School Journal* reported:

> The last two evenings there are picturesque and artistic reproductions of old Indian dances. These exhibits last for an hour and are well understood by the Indians to be merely representations of the old customs which, therefore, are free from the objections usually urged against Indian dances [by the Indian Agency Superintendents]. These reproductions of native games and dances are witnessed by throngs of spectators, both Indian and white, who crowd the large grandstand to overflowing and thus increase the revenues of the [Cheyenne and Arapaho tribal] fair

association. . . . (Freer n.d., p. 308, brackets mine)

In 1921, there was correspondence between the Commissioner of Indian Affairs and the agent at Anadarko over a request from "R.E. Banks and Congressman Gensman" that "a portion of Ft. Sill Military Reservation be turned over to the Interior Department for the Use of the Kiowa and Comanche Indians as a fair ground." The agent was against the idea and noted:

> In the vicinity of the place proposed by Mr. Banks . . . is a resort known as Medicine Park. This resort is right at the foot of Mt. Scott, on a very beautiful stream known as Medicine Creek. Great numbers of persons visit Medicine Park during the spring, summer and fall months, spending their vacations there at the hotel or at small cottages which can be rented from the management. I readily see how an Indian camp and Indian dances would be an added attraction to people visiting this resort, but I do not believe that our Indians should be thus commercialized (Anadarko Agency 1921).

Despite the agent's opposition, a commercial attraction referred to as the Frank Rush Fair was being held near Medicine Park by 1923.

Native American dancers also performed at county fairs. Kiowa Agency superintendent C. V. Stinchecum reported in 1921 that at the Caddo County fair at Anadarko, held during the latter part of September,

> . . . large numbers of Indians came in and camped for several days prior to the opening of the Fair, all during the period thereof, and for sometime thereafter. A group of enterprising Indians built a canvas stockade and held a dance for which they charged admission. This dance was quite liberally patronized by both Indians and whites, as has been the case for a number of years. (Stinchecum 1921)

HOMECOMINGS AND POWWOWS OF THE 1920s AND 1930s

Although not advertised as commercial ventures or performances that charged admission, some of the tribal and all-Indian events of the next decades began to incorporate the more exhibition-like atmosphere of the commercial dances. An event at Haskell Indian School in Lawrence, Kansas, in 1926 may have been the beginning of the modern powwow era. The occasion was the dedication of the new football stadium. Thousands of persons filled the south wing of the new Haskell Stadium for the program that featured Secretary of the Interior Herman Work, Indian Commissioner Charles H. Burke, and Senator Charles Curtis (of the Kaw tribe). A four-year-old Oto "war dancer," Sugar Brown, was the featured dancer at the ceremony, and the climax was the Haskell-Bucknell football game. Some visiting Indians camped at the "Indian Village," which, according to the newspaper *American Indian,* was made spectacular by the Blackfeet tipis (*American Indian* 2, pp. 8–12). The same article also noted that "a caravan of Oklahoma cars from Fords on up took hundreds of Indians to Lawrence." The Quapaws, rich from zinc and lead mine royalties, sponsored some of the events. Many Quapaws remember the caravan of Buicks, Oldsmobiles, Reos, Pierce Arrows, and other large cars that carried them to Lawrence (Young 1981).

Dances were a major part of the Haskell celebration. Daytime was devoted to tribal dances, including an Eagle dance by Potawatomi dancers from Mayetta, Kansas, an Osage Peace Dance, and a Santa Clara Pueblo Eagle Dance. At night there were championship dancing contests. Judges in three world championship contests were Chief Bull Calf (Blackfeet), Chief Bacon Rind (Osage), Pierce St. John (Osage), Victor Griffith (Quapaw), and Chief John Quapaw (Quapaw). According to Frank Turley,

> . . . an intertribal fancy dance contest was held in Lawrence, Kansas. It was then stipulated that the winner's tribe sponsor all future cham-

pionship contests at an annual date. Since a Ponca named August "Gus" McDonald was named winner, the Poncas . . . made the contest a traditional feature of their powwow. (Turley 1961, p. 180)

McDonald has also been credited with the introduction of the fancy dance regalia made of brightly colored feathers. He may have used the bright regalia at first when he was acting in the capacity of a powwow clown (Young 1981).

Two years later the *Daily Oklahoman* newspaper announced that a new dance hall would be dedicated at the 1928 Ponca Powwow. Ponca Agency Superintendent A. R. Snyder explained to the Commissioner of Indian Affairs:

> It was agreed that we should build the hall and then make an effort to pay for it. Accordingly work was done and it was dedicated on July 4th by having a little Indian ceremony. The exercises were just the ordinary Indian dances in costume, and a baseball game between the Ponca team and the Pawnee Indian team. At night, about one and one-half hours was [sic] taken up in a program contesting Indian dancing. Prizes of $5.00 for first, $3.00 for second and $1.00 for third were offered. As I remember it, a Ponca boy was awarded first prize, a [sic] Otoe boy second prize and a Kaw boy third prize. . . . A large crowd was present, and from the proceeds of the stand and admission, about $200.00 was paid on the building. (Snyder 1928)

Two other tribal powwows drew large crowds in 1928. One was the Quapaw Homecoming, a continuation of the Quapaw tribal picnic held at Devil's Promenade, and the other was the Pawnee powwow held at the Pawnee city fairgrounds. The *American Indian* announced both powwows. It reported that

> . . . a rousing powwow given yearly by the Quapaw Indians of Ottawa

See glossary for definition of boldfaced terms

County will start June 28. . . . There will be various kinds of entertainment—baseball games each day, Indian war dances, foot races and contest dancing between different Indian tribes.

Free tables will be set for all visiting Indians—but don't forget your bedding. However, tents will be furnished for those who do not have them. (*American Indian* 1 [9], p. 13)

A Quapaw man described the Quapaw powwow of the 1930s:

In July we have a four day gathering or powwow. We have plenty of beef and good things to eat and have five tables; . . . if you love the Indian you will eat from all the tables. They have games through the day such as ball games, cornstalk shooting, etc., and they dance at night. (Valliere 1937)

The Pawnee powwow of 1928 featured afternoon dances of all kinds plus a terrapin derby and baseball game. At night there were war dances, women's dances, gourd dances, and **stomp dances** by Eastern Indians. As a reporter for the *American Indian* wrote:

Those in charge of the powwow say that over 3,000 Indians were present and over 300 participated in the ceremonies in some manner. Indians from the Pawnee, Kaw, Otoe, Osage, Ponca, Euche, Iowa, Kiowa, Sac and Fox, Pottawattomie, Comanche, Creek, Cheyenne, Arapahoe, and other tribes were present.

The manner in which the Pawnee Indian Junior Council conducted the affair was commendable. The best of order was preserved. The program prepared in advance was carried through each evening. A variety of dances and other forms of entertainment was presented. The committee made preparations to care for the crowd. The visiting Indians went away satisfied and the white spectators were pleased. (*American Indian* 1[9], p. 13).

FAIRS OF THE 1920s AND 1930s

Powwow-type dancing continued at fairs throughout the 1920s and 1930s. Sac and Fox/Iowa tribal fairs were held (Shawnee Agency 1924), and the Cheyenne and Arapaho Fair was revived in 1925. The 1929 Cheyenne and Arapaho Fair at Watonga included an "Indian maiden contest," an event just becoming popular. In 1926, a princess or queen had been selected at the Pendleton, Oregon, Round-up. Esther Lee Montanic (Cayuse) was the first woman chosen for this honor and was lauded as the "prettiest Indian woman in the nation." California Indians had responded immediately, wishing to enter Little Fawn of the Klamath tribe "against all comers." The Tulsa-based periodical *American Indian* carried the story and encouraged nomination from "Oklahoma's forty tribes." (*American Indian* 1, p. 11) In November 1926, the International Petroleum Congress and Exposition in Tulsa had a princess representing the Osage tribe. This may have been the beginning of the selection of Oklahoma tribal and powwow princesses.

The Frank Rush Fair at Medicine Park continued throughout the 1920s. The 1927 fair's Premium Booklet contained information such as "Steve Mopope will have charge of the war dancing. . . . No so-called '49 or social dance . . . will be permitted on the grounds. . . . Frank Rush will give a buffalo to his old Indian friends." Cash prizes were offered for winners of horse races, bow and arrow contests, the wheel game, kickball, and women's shinny. The booklet also stated that "the greatest number of war dancers ever assembled will put on a war dance in front of the grand stand each day," but no mention was made of prizes or dance contests (Rush Fair 1927).

In 1929, however, the Premium Booklet noted, "Special contest war dances and ghost dances will be given each night in front of the grandstand." That year the Oklahoma State Legislature appropriated $1,000 for premiums for the fair (Rush Fair 1929). Perhaps the legislature wanted the Rush Fair to compete favorably with New

Mexico's two new Indian fairs, the Gallup Ceremonial, an unabashedly commercial venture, and the Southwest Indian Fair, an arts and crafts exhibition held in Santa Fe.

In 1931, the Rush Fair and the Cheyenne and Arapaho Fair were both replaced by what was to become the largest all–Indian intertribal fair, the American Indian Exposition. Fair Association President Maurice Bedoka wrote to the Anadarko agency about the

> manner in which our fair association was formed, and how it operated in connection with the Caddo County Free Fair until last year when it held its own fair separately. All tribes under your jurisdiction— Kiowa, Comanche, Apache, Fort Sill Apache, Caddo, Wichita, and Delaware, as well as the Cheyenne and Arapaho of the Concho jurisdiction—constituted the fair association. (Bedoka 1935)

The commercial dances, homecomings, fairs, and powwows of the first half of the twentieth century were the foundation for the Oklahoma-style powwow that swept across the United States and Canada during the 1950s and 1960s. The nature of powwow—interaction between many different people leading to whatever changes were needed to adapt—made the Oklahoma powwow acceptable in any setting. Today, events called powwows continue to change at dizzying speed as people bring new ideas and preferences to the arena. But underneath it all is the solid structure built by Oklahoma Indians interacting in historic intertribal ceremonials and celebrations.

See glossary for definition of boldfaced terms

BIBLIOGRAPHY

American Indian 1, no. 2 (November 1926). Periodical (Tulsa, Oklahoma).

Anadarko Agency. (1921). [Letter to Commissioner of Indian Affairs dated December 20, 1921, re: proposal to set aside land for Indian fair.] (MS. Kiowa: Fairs, Indian Archives Division, Oklahoma Historical Society, Oklahoma City.)

Anadarko Agency. (1930). [Annual Report.] (MS. Anadarko: Law and Order, Record Group 75, Federal Records Center, Fort Worth, Texas.)

Bedoka, Maurice M. (1935). [Letter to W. B. McCowan dated Anadarko, Oklahoma, May 24, 1924, re: American Indian Exposition.] (MS. Kiowa Agency: Central Files 1907–1939, Bureau of Indian Affairs, Record Group 75, Decimal File .047, No. 22512–1935, National Archives, Washington, D.C.)

"The Fair Program." *Collinsville News* 9 (October 10, 1907). Newspaper (Collinsville, Indian Territory).

Freer, William B. n.d. "The Cheyenne and Arapaho Indian Fair." *Indian School Journal,* pp. 307–310.

Hanes, Colonel Bailey C. (1977). *Bill Pickett, Bulldogger.* Norman: University of Oklahoma Press.

Norris, S. W. (1910). [Letter to W. F. Dickens dated Weatherford, Oklahoma, March 23, 1910, re: Indian Fair.] (MS. Cheyenne and Arapaho: Indians with Shows and Exhibitions, Oklahoma Historical Society, Oklahoma City.)

Ponca School. (1928). [Annual Report.]

Rush Fair. (1927–1929). [Premium booklets.] (Anadarko Agency, Central Files 1907–1939, Bureau of Indian Affairs, Record Group 75, Decimal File .047, No. 8105–1927, National Archives, Washington, D.C.)

Shawnee Agency. (1924). [Sac and Fox and Iowa Free Fair Premium Booklet.] (Pawnee Agency, Microfilm PA45, Frame 458, Federal Records Center, Fort Worth, Texas.)

Snyder, A. R. (1928). [Letter to Commissioner of Indian Affairs dated Pawnee, Oklahoma, October 26, 1928, re: Ponca Dance Hall.] (MS. Pawnee Agency: Central Files 1907–1939 Bureau of Indian Affairs, Record Group 75, Decimal File .047, No. 33600–1928, National Archives, Washington, D.C.)

Stinchecum, C. V. (1921). [Letter to Commissioner of Indian Affairs dated Anadarko, Oklahoma, November 2, 1921, re: 49'er dance.] (MS. Kiowa Agency: Central Files 1907–1939, Bureau of Indian Affairs, Record Group 75, Decimal File. 063, No. 58840–1921, National Archives, Washington, D.C.)

Turley, Frank. (1961).

Valliere, Frank. (1937). [Interview.] (MS. Indian and Pioneer History 48:33–34, Indian Archives Division, Oklahoma Historical Society, Oklahoma City.)

Whitewell, J. (1902). [Letter to Cheyenne and Arapho Agency dated Hammond, Oklahoma Territory, September 3, 1902, re: Elk City Dance.] (MS. Cheyenne

and Arapaho: Indian History, Culture and Accultur-ation, Oklahoma Historical Society, Oklahoma City.)

Williams, Roger. (1827). [1643] "A Key into the Language of America or an Helpe to the language of the Na-tives in that Part of America called New England."

Collection of the Rhode Island Historical Society. Vol. 1, pp. 17–163. Providence, RI.

Young, Gloria A. (1981). *Powwow Power: Perspectives on Historic and Contemporary.*

Intertribalism. Ph.D. diss. Indiana University, Bloomington.

CHEROKEE HYMN SINGING IN OKLAHOMA

Charlotte Heth

*Charlotte Heth was formerly a professor at the University of California, Los Angeles, and served as director of the American Indian Studies Center from 1974–94 and as chairperson of the Department of **Ethnomusicology** and Systematic Musicology. She subsequently was affiliated with the Smithsonian Institution as assistant director for public programs at the National Museum of the American Indian. An ethnomusicologist, Heth has published widely on American Indian music. She is an enrolled member of the Cherokee Nation of Oklahoma. The following essay originally appeared in the 1992 Smithsonian Festival of American Folklife program guide.*

The Christianization of a majority of the members of the Cherokee Nation has spawned **hymns** and **gospel** songs—new kinds of Indian music. Cherokees' interaction with whites and blacks on the continually moving frontier also brought **fiddle** and **guitar** music to them. The older Native religious life, and the ceremonial music and dance associated with it, suffered from the changes in this period and has survived to a greater or lesser extent in rural pockets of Oklahoma and North Carolina.

As of the 1990s, approximately 90 percent of the native speakers of the Cherokee language in northeastern Oklahoma were Christian. In Cherokee Christian churches, music plays as important a role as the doctrine preached. While both Cherokees and missionaries adapted some songs directly from Protestant models, others appear unique. All are sung in Cherokee, and the translations often do not match their English counterparts when such counterparts exist.

Sequoyah, a Cherokee man, invented a syllabary for writing his language that was officially adopted by the Cherokee Nation in 1821. Thereafter, official documents, newspapers, letters, gravestones, magical and medicinal formulas, hymnbooks, Bibles, almanacs, minutes of meetings, and public and private records were kept in Cherokee along with (or frequently without) their English versions. America's first Indian newspaper, the bilingual *Cherokee Phoenix,* appeared February 21, 1828. It was edited by Elias Boudinot, a Cherokee, who was assisted by Samuel A. Worcester, a missionary. The majority of extant materials from the nineteenth century printed in Cherokee deal with Christian topics.

The first Cherokee hymnbook was published in 1829 and underwent many subsequent revisions and editions. In all of its editions, the texts are in the Cherokee syllabary without translation into English, and except for a few temperance songs, musical notation is absent. The tunes them-

selves have been handed down now for 160 years or more without ever having been written down. In 1846 the *Cherokee Singing Book,* conceived and compiled by Worcester with the help of Lowell Mason, was published in Boston with four-part **harmonic** settings and Cherokee texts. A close check of these tunes with those used today by the Cherokees in Oklahoma shows no correspondence. Although many of the tunes in the singing book are used by Cherokees (such as "Old Hundred"), the texts associated with them are different from those proposed by Worcester in 1846. There are several Cherokee hymns and gospel songs whose words and music have never appeared in print.

In one of the most recent editions of the *Cherokee Hymn Book* (first published in 1877), there are 132 hymns, 5 doxologies, and 3 temperance songs. In addition to the published hymn texts, there are new songs being composed constantly for Cherokee "sings," or assemblies in which **a cappella** quartets and choirs, particularly family groups, share their music.

One can find original Cherokee hymnals (from 1829–1962) in the Huntington, Newberry, Gilcrease, University of Tulsa, Northeastern Oklahoma State University, and Oklahoma University libraries as well as the Library of Congress. For the most part, succeeding editions in the nineteenth century are duplications or expansions of preceding ones. Two twentieth-century editions located are printed in typefaces different from that of their predecessors and were never widely used. A popular version used today is reprinted from the original plates of the 1877 version. The missionary periodicals *Cherokee Messenger* (1844–1846) and *Cherokee Gospel Tidings* (1898–1901) contain additional hymns.

THE MUSIC

The music itself is similar to Christian singing in Protestant churches, but with several important differences. The vocal quality is for the most part nasal and moderately tense, as are the sounds of the Cherokee language. The hymns usually have some breaks (**glottal stops**) and many sliding attacks and releases, features that also mimic the tonal Cherokee language. (In sliding attacks, the singer begins above or below the principal **pitch** and slurs all the pitches between the attack and the principal one, as on a slide whistle. Releases are endings that slide off the principal pitch.) **Undulating** melodies and **pentatonic scales** are also popular in the hymns, with the **slides** and **glides** exaggerated by a slow **tempo**. The vocal line may be broken up with **chorus** echoes and responses.

Metric hymns find favor among the Cherokees; many tunes can be used for a single text, and conversely, many texts for a single tune. Much of this unaccompanied singing still has rhythmic vocal surges on accented beats.

Repetition, **variation**, and **improvisation** play an important part in each form. The hymns and gospel songs are for the most part **strophic**, as one might expect, but frequently several different tunes and texts are strung together in a song **cycle**. Often the singers choose to end with a quick double-time section.

Two popular hymns, "One Drop of Blood" and "Amazing Grace," were sung on the Trail of Tears, the forced removal in the 1830s of the Cherokees from their eastern homelands to Indian Territory, now the state of Oklahoma. While "Amazing Grace" is familiar to most Christians, "One Drop of Blood" lives primarily in **oral tradition**. It has been copied and recopied for generations. A translation of the text is:

> *What can we do, Jesus, our King?*
> *He's already paid for us.*
> *Our friends, we all must work.*
> *Our King, Your place over which You are*
> *   King.*
> *Our King, Your place over which You are*
> *   King.*

The familiar hymn "Amazing Grace" contains words dealing with Christ's Second Coming:

J. B. Dreadfulwater leads his Cherokee Indian Baptist Choir as it performs a traditional, unaccompanied hymn in the Cherokee language. The photo was taken in the Hall of Musical Instruments at the National Museum of American History in 1988.
Photograph by Laurie Minor Penland, courtesy of the Smithsonian/Folkways Archives.

God's Son, He paid for us.
Then to heaven He went, after He paid for us.
But He spoke when He arose.
"I will come again," He said.

The tradition of Christian hymnody among the Cherokees is among the oldest and best documented examples of change in Indian music brought about by contact with European culture. Other tribes forcibly removed to Indian Territory (Oklahoma) do have similar traditions—the Creek and Choctaw, for example. But the invention of the Cherokee syllabary in 1821 promoted Cherokee literacy and encouraged the spread of hymn singing among them at a time when their Native religion and culture were still viable. Because the first Cherokee hymnals contained only texts, it is safe to assume that some melodies were already alive in Cherokee oral tradition before they were brought west in the 1830s. Cherokee hymns today—performed in church, at home and

in "sings," and printed in newsletters with stories about active family **gospel quartets** and small choirs such as those directed by J. B. Dreadfulwater of Stillwell, Oklahoma—continue to be an active tradition in northeastern Oklahoma.

BIBLIOGRAPHY

Bass, Althea. (1936). *Cherokee Messenger*. Norman: University of Oklahoma Press.

Foreman, Grant. (1938). *Sequoyah*. Norman: University of Oklahoma Press.

———. (1953). *Indian Removal*. Norman: University of Oklahoma Press.

Hudson, Charles. (1976). *The Southeastern Indians*. Nashville: University of Tennessee Press.

McLoughlin, William G. (1984). *Cherokees and Missionaries, 1789–1839*. New Haven: Yale University Press.

Walker, Robert Sparks. (1931). *Torchlights to the Cherokees: The Brainerd Mission*. New York: Macmillan.

Woodward, Grace Steele. (1963). *The Cherokees.* Norman: University of Oklahoma Press.

DISCOGRAPHY

Indian Songs of Today. 1951. Willard Rhodes. AFS L36.

Delaware, Cherokee, Choctaw, Creek. 1951. Willard Rhodes. AFS L37.

Songs of Indian Territory: Native American Music Traditions of Oklahoma. 1989. Willie Smyth. Center of the American Indian, Oklahoma City, Oklahoma.

Creation's Journey: Native American Music. 1994. Smithsonian Folkways CD SF 40410.

A HISTORICAL INTRODUCTION TO BLACKFOOT INDIAN MUSIC

Bruno Nettl

Bruno Nettl is a distinguished ethnomusicologist who has focused much of his work on the music of Native Americans. He a former member of the faculty at the University of Illinois and serves as editor of Ethnomusicology, *the journal of the Society of Ethnomusicology. He is also the author of numerous articles and more than a dozen books, including* The Study of Ethnomusicology *(1983) and* Heartland Excursions *(1995). The following essay is based on the notes he prepared to accompany Folkways 34001, a recording originally issued in 1979 as* An Historical Album of Blackfoot Indian Music. *For an overview of Blackfoot Indian Music that includes more recent scholarship, please consult Nettl's book* Blackfoot Musical Thought: Comparative Perspectives *(Kent State University Press, 1989).*

THE RECORDING OF BLACKFOOT MUSIC

The Blackfoot are among the most thoroughly studied Indian peoples of North America. Since the late nineteenth century, they have been visited by scholars of many disciplines, and, of course, particularly by anthropologists, among them some of the most illustrious figures of the field: George Bird Grinnell, explorer, ethnographer, and folklorist, who was there in the late nineteenth century; Clark Wissler, who went on to provide the most important ethnographies of the Blackfoot; Walter McClintock, explorer and writer; Christian Cornelius Uhlenbeck, the famous linguist, in the first decade of this century; Julian Steward and Oscar Lewis, both of whom were later to be ranked among the world's leading anthropologists in the 1930s; John C. Ewers, the most important scholar of Blackfoot culture and history after Wissler, from the 1950s on; and many others. It is safe to say that there are probably very few older full-blooded Blackfoot Indians in the United States, at least, who have not been interviewed by at least one scholar or graduate student trying to get insight into the history and lifeways of his people.

In the tradition of North American **ethnography**, a great many of these scholars as well as other interested individuals made recordings of Blackfoot music. Realizing the importance of songs and dancing in the lives of the Blackfoot, they made use of whatever recording devices were available as early as the opportunity presented itself. As a result, a large number of collections of Blackfoot music may be found in various archives, but particularly in the Archives of Traditional Music, Indiana University. The first of these were made on wax cylinders, and while their fidelity is modest, they show us how the Blackfoot sang decades ago and permit us to make historical studies of a traditional sort, with concrete sources (rather than merely theoretical reconstructions and the memories of the elderly) that can be compared with the recordings made more recently. Although we cannot be sure that it is indeed the very first attempt at recording Blackfoot music, the earliest collection available seems to be that of George Bird Grinnell, who recorded about forty songs by James White Calf and others in October 1897, in or near the Blackfoot Reservation in Montana. He was quickly followed by Clark Wissler, part of whose intensive studies was a large collection of 146 cylinders made in 1903 and 1904, and by J. K. Dixon, a member of the Wanamaker Expedition No. 2 to the North American Indians, 1908–1909. Dixon recorded several songs sung mainly by Chief Bull, at Crow Agency, Montana, on September 22, 1909.

Public interest in American Indian songs becomes evident soon thereafter, for at least four songs were recorded by the Victor Talking Machine Company on May 23, 1914, in New York City, and two records, Victor 17611 and 17635, were issued. We do not know how these recordings came to be made in New York.

The next large collection was made in 1938 by Jane Richardson Hanks who, with her husband, Lucien Hanks, carried out field work among the Canadian Blackfoot and recorded many songs in Gleichen, Alberta. These were sung by Spumiapi (White-Headed Chief). After World War II, with the invention of the tape recorder, there was a vast increase in the recording of Indian music. Anthropologists, members of the newly established and rapidly growing discipline of ethnomusicology, Indian culture and dance hobbyists, Indian singers themselves, and representatives of record companies serving both general and Indian clienteles must have made countless collections comprising literally thousands of songs.

Complete data on these collections cannot be assembled. Some of them were made systematically, others more or less at random. Among the significant collections made is one by Donald D. Hartle in 1949 on the Blood Reservation, Alberta, consisting of twenty-eight songs recorded on a Webster wire recorder. From the same period comes a collection made by Howard

A famous photograph of a Blackfoot Indian chief recording a song for an early, unidentified folklorist, photographed in Washington, D.C., in 1916. The photo was probably staged, but it has become a symbol of the early interest in recording Native American music. *Photograph © Bettmann/CORBIS.*

Kaufman in Browning, Montana, consisting of some eighteen songs, also recorded on a Webster wire recorder in the summer of 1952. Some of Kaufman's songs were sung by Theodore Last Star and Reuben Black Boy, who were among the great intellectual leaders of the reservation community. Also in the summer of 1952, I recorded over 100 songs sung by Tom Many-Guns, a middle-aged man very knowledgeable in the older traditions, who had come to Indiana University in order to serve as an informant for students of Blackfoot language and culture.

In the summer of 1966, I recorded approximately six hours of music, some 200 songs, mainly in Browning and Heart Butte, Montana. Among the chief singers was Calvin Boy, stepson of the famed Theodore Last Star. Some of these recordings are among the first made of actual, live performances; earlier ones relied on "recording sessions" in which the singers sang especially for the recordist, rather than fulfilling a tribal religious, social, or entertainment function.

In the summer of 1968, Robert Witmer, then a graduate student at the University of Illinois, carried out field work on the Blood Indian Reserve in Alberta under the sponsorship of the Doris Duke Project, the purpose of which was to gather materials needed to help the American Indians study

and understand their own history. A large collection resulted, some of it traditional music and some consisting of European-style music (such as country and western) performed by Indian musicians.

From the 1950s on, professional Indian singing groups began to be established, and recordings by some of them have been released, largely for Indian consumption, through such recording companies as Candelario, Tom-Tom, and, more recently, Taos, Indian House, and others. Among these releases is *Blackfeet Tribal Grass Dance,* issued by American Indian Soundchief (BLKFT–104). The record consists entirely of songs for one very important type of social dance, sung in Canada about 1967 by Edward Morning Owl and Wilbur Morning Owl. Other releases are *From the Land of the Blackfeet,* Canyon Record C–6095, recorded at the annual North American Indian Days celebration in Browning, Montana, in July 1972, and *Blackfeet,* Indian Records and

The Blackfoot Indians live today on reservations in northern Montana and in southern Alberta and Saskatchewan.

Supplies IR220, sung by Pat Kennedy and a number of other leading singers of the Montana reservation. The singers of these records are members of the professional or quasi-professional singing groups which have developed as a result of the pan–Indian movement and the intertribal **powwows** of the 1950s and 1960s.

The history of the recording of Blackfoot music provides us with a broad panorama of late nineteenth- and twentieth-century practices. There are gaps—we have little between 1910 and 1950, the various subdivisions of the Blackfoot people have been treated unevenly, and the musical culture has changed so much and rapidly and is itself so complex that even this large number of collections and songs represents but a small sampling. Still, we have the basis for a better knowledge of Blackfoot Indian music than of most of the world's musical cultures, including even most other North American Indian groups. Despite the large

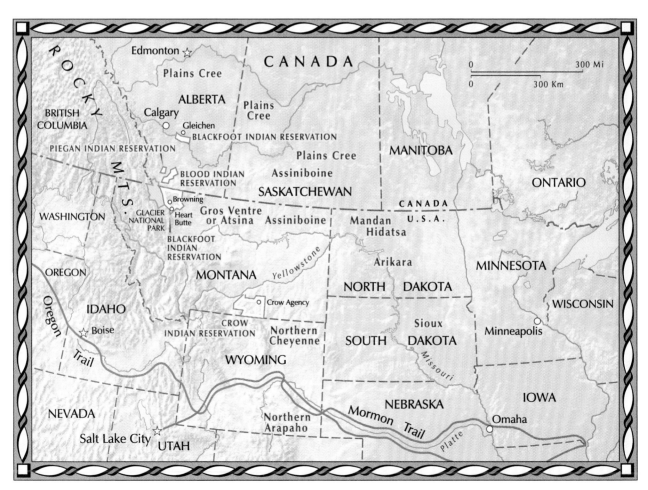

number of collected songs and despite the considerable amount of ethnographic and historical research to which the Blackfoot culture has been subjected, it is curious to find that there have been few studies of the musical culture of this people.[1]

THE BLACKFOOT INDIANS

The Blackfoot have for at least some centuries been divided into three groups that are distinguished by dialect, (relatively minor) variations in custom, and location.[2] The largest of them, the Piegan, are also the southernmost, and after the various treaties that were forced upon them in the second half of the nineteenth century, they came to occupy the Blackfeet Reservation in Montana, immediately East of Glacier National Park. Most of the collections mentioned above were made among the Piegan. The Blood Indians and the Northern Blackfoot, the two smaller branches, lived farther to the North and hence finally took up residence, along with a small group of Northern Piegan, on three reserves in Alberta. There is a great deal of contact among these groups now, and members of other tribes have in small numbers found their way to these reservations as well—particularly Plains Cree and Assiniboine.

The total number of Blackfoot before contact with the whites is estimated to have been about 15,000, which would make them the second-largest tribal group of the Plains, after the Sioux. The number of Blackfoot living today [c. 1979] (counting those of mixed ancestry who choose to enter themselves on the tribal rolls) is somewhere in the vicinity of 20,000. The total number of Blackfoot living in the United States in the 1960s was over 12,000.[3] Of these, some 7,000 live on the Montana Reservation along with several thousand white merchants, employees of the Indian Agency, and caterers to tourists on the way to Glacier National Park. The standard of living of the Canadian Blackfeet appears to be higher than that of the Montana Blackfoot, and, interestingly, the Canadian groups also have held on to their traditional

music, dance, and art more readily than have their southern brothers. But it is the Piegan, in the United States, whose culture is best known to scholars.

Blackfoot culture in earlier times appears to have been rather typical of the North Plains culture area, which also comprises many of the Sioux or Dakota tribes, the Crow, Gros Ventre, Assiniboine, and perhaps the Cheyenne and Arapaho. The Blackfoot language is Algonquian and thus related to that of the Arapaho and Cheyenne, the Cree, and to a very large number of Indian languages spoken in the Midwest and the northeastern United States. When first encountered by whites in the eighteenth century, the Blackfoot were nomadic, dividing into bands during the winter and coming together in the summer. Before the coming of horses they used dogs to pull their belongings while traveling; horses, acquired from tribes to the West, made possible much faster and efficient movement, and therefore the reliance on the buffalo for almost all aspects of livelihood increased in the eighteenth and nineteenth centuries.

Warfare for substantive as well as ceremonial purposes (i.e., for the expansion of hunting grounds as well as to show courage by touching an enemy or stealing his horse) was highly developed. Religion centered on a complex of medicine bundles—groups of objects with supernatural power acquired through instructions given by guardian spirits in visions—and also around the Sun Dance—a large, public ceremony shared with the other peoples of the Plains culture. Being close to the mountains, the Blackfoot also hunted and revered many animals other than the buffalo and other creatures of the Plains. They maintained contacts and traded with other Plains tribes but also with Plateau tribes west of the Great Divide, including the Flathead, Kutenai and Shoshone. In contrast to most of the Plains tribes, they never entered into the peyote cult that was to become so important in the religious life and music of the North American Indians in the late nineteenth and twentieth centuries. [Used by some Native Americans in their religious ceremonies, the peyote plant is a mild hal-

lucinogen that users believe will bring them into closer contact with the spirit world.]

The collections of music which are available for study fall conveniently into two historical periods. Some come from the very beginning of the twentieth century, a time during which the Blackfoot experienced great difficulty because of their rather sudden conversion from an essentially Indian way of life to a culture pattern that was substantially western. They had suffered defeat in wars and had been decimated by diseases brought by the whites (such as measles), and they were confined on what seemed to them tiny spots of undesirable territory. Most of them had been converted to nominal Christianity, and there were great pressures on them to give up their traditions. Nevertheless, the collections of Grinnell, Wissler, and Dixon provide some insight into what Blackfoot music must have been like in the late nineteenth century, before the Indians had come into intensive contact with whites and their music. Many of the songs are sung by older individuals who provide us with a record of music demonstrably a century old.

Most of the other collections come from a period half a century later, a time when the Indians of North America were (and are) seeking a renewal of national identity, when music became the greatest symbol of "Indian-ness," but when tribal distinctions had begun to break down in favor of an intertribal, Indian culture (in which there are nevertheless important tribal and regional differences). The collections by Kaufman, Witmer, and Nettl, and the recently issued commercial records fall into this period.[4]

When these collections were made, after World War II, much of the culture of the nineteenth century and before had been forgotten, or lived only in the vague memories of a few older individuals. Thus, these collections consist mainly of twentieth-century Indian music, not substantially different in style from the older materials, but associated with different functions. The older materials consist chiefly of religious or semireligious music. It seems likely that most Blackfoot songs in the nineteenth century, and certainly those songs that were regarded as most important, were associated with the large and rich complex of religious and semireligious practices—medicine bundles such as the Beaver Bundle or the Medicine Pipe, the Sun Dance, religious music accompanying war activities and the activities of the ceremonial and social men's societies. The recent collections are comprised largely of social dance songs and gambling songs—**genres** surely also present, but less prominent, in earlier times—that are the staple of Indian singing today.

Practically all songs in the collections known to exist are sung by men. Women did and do, of course, know songs and sing. But singing was not considered particularly appropriate for the modest position of women, and men dominated ceremonial life. Moreover, men were more apt to make contact with outsiders such as anthropologists and ethnomusicologists, while women remained in the background. But today, older men often rely on their wives to help them remember songs and even to sing them. Still, even the professional and semiprofessional singing groups that perform at social dances today—and there are some forty or fifty men who are considered "singers" in a new, somewhat western sense on the Montana Reservation today—are comprised of men.

As far as we know, the Blackfoot used only drums and **rattles**, and most of the recordings include drumming. "Flutes," probably **flageolets**, are mentioned by older individuals but seem to have been little used in the last 100 years, if ever. Like most American Indian repertories of the United States and Canada, that of the Blackfoot is essentially vocal.

SONG TYPES

BEAVER MEDICINE SONGS

The Beaver Medicine Bundle was the largest and most prominent of the medicine bundle types used by the Blackfoot. It consisted of literally hundreds of objects—animal and bird skins, sticks for keeping count of days and weeks, pipes, rattles, etc.—with accompanying songs. The objects had supernatural power which was activated when the bundle was opened and appropriate songs, prayers, or other actions were presented. There were few beaver medicine men, and in the twentieth century there have been few who have known much of the ritual. Even around 1910, evidently no one knew the entire ritual, which would have taken several days to perform. Beaver medicine men kept the tribal calendar, helped to bring buffalo, and had a special association with water and the underworld. Most Beaver Medicine Bundle songs were sung solo, and each object in the bundle had its own song, which was sung when the object was taken out of its wrappings. Even the medicine bundle used in the Sun Dance is thought to have been derived from, or in some way associated with, the older and originally more powerful Beaver Medicine Bundle.

MEDICINE PIPE SONGS

The Medicine Pipe Bundle was smaller than the Beaver Bundle and had a less complex ceremony associated with it. It was thought to have been given to man by Thunder, who was, so the Blackfoot myths tell us, temporarily married to a Blackfoot woman. The Medicine Pipe Bundle ceremony was performed each year in the spring, just after the first thunderstorm, and was thought to bring rain and to cure sickness. It consists of a half dozen objects and only a dozen or two songs, some of which accompanied dance. It is known to have been part of Blackfoot religion as early as 1800, and perhaps because it is simpler, its ceremony has been retained better than that of the Beaver Bundle. Indeed, Medicine Pipe songs are still sung frequently, and a Medicine Pipe ceremony is still held occasionally in the summer, but it has been changed from a more or less private, religious event to a public entertainment whose purpose is to keep Blackfoot traditions alive.

SUN DANCE SONGS

The Sun Dance was the most important and largest religious ceremony of the Blackfoot. It was similar to the Sun Dance of other Plains tribes but contained some typical Blackfoot traits such as the use of a Medicine Bundle among its associated activities. The central activity involved dancing around a pole by men who then sought visions of supernatural guardian spirits. During the dancing, the men gazed at the sun and sometimes tortured themselves in various ways. The dancers were accompanied by singers who performed in a group around a drum which they beat in **unison**. Originally, the Sun Dance was preceded by a complex ritual in which the entire tribe participated, consisting of four daily moves of the tribal camp; and during the Sun Dance, various social and athletic events took place, also accompanied by singing. The songs given here are not designated by their collectors as to specific function within the Sun Dance.

In 1887, the Sun Dance, along with many other traditional activities, was suppressed by the Indian Bureau of the United States. It was revived a few years later, and became associated with the July 4 celebrations. Today it is still occasionally held, if appropriate sponsorship can be found; but many of its social functions have been taken over, on the Montana reservations, by the North American Indians Days powwow celebration.

TRADITIONAL WAR MUSIC

Various kinds of songs were associated with war. When a war party prepared itself a dance was held, and songs were sung while the members painted themselves. Warriors sang personal songs when they were wounded or thought they were about to die, or to give themselves courage. When the party returned, a "scalp dance" was held, at which trophies were exhibited and the events of the conflict briefly told in song. The function of these songs disappeared about 100 years ago, and those that are recorded here were doubtless resurrected by older singers from experiences of their youth, or more likely, learned by them outside the context of their original functions. One of the songs is associated with the Scalp Dance, another is simply labeled "Warrior Song." Two others come from the **repertoires** of the men's societies which at one time had a major function in war and social life. These, "Wolf Song" and "Crazy Dog Song," come from such societies, but we do not know specifically whether they were indeed associated with war.

The Piegan had seven men's age-grade societies, each with its own ceremony (which was performed during the Sun Dance complex), its particular function in a tribal war, and other duties. The Wolf Society was one of these—but its function was no longer understood by my informants in 1966. The Crazy Dog Society served frequently as a sort of tribal police force, especially at large gatherings, and this may account for the fact that it is still known, for it provided the white Indian Agent with a ready-made police force. While it no longer performs this duty, having been replaced in Montana by the Blackfoot Tribal Police with its modern police cars, there are still a few older men—among them Uhlenbeck's interpreter of the first decade of this century, the late John Tatsey—who regard themselves as members and who can sing a few of the songs.

See glossary for definition of boldfaced terms

LULLABIES AND LOVE SONGS

Lullabies are known to most American Indian tribes and are still sung to small chil-

dren. Typically, they have no words, and do not differ very much from other songs in their style. Love songs were associated with ceremonies using special secret medicinal formulas—different not in nature but in scope from the medicine bundles—that were taken by lovers whose advances had been repulsed. They are part of a widespread North American Indian repertory whose style differs somewhat from that of the typical songs of most tribes, being short and simple.[5] More dealing humorously with relations between the sexes are referred to as "love songs" by the Blackfoot.

GAMBLING SONGS

Gambling games have long been widespread among the American Indians. Most often they took the form of hiding games in which two teams faced each other, one hiding a small piece of bone, a seed, a bullet, or the like in its hands or in a row of moccasins before it while the other team searched. Men's societies frequently played against each other. The hiding team normally sang special songs. In the nineteenth century these games, like other Indian activities, were frequently suppressed. In the twentieth century they became again important souvenirs of earlier times, and gambling is now a very popular Saturday afternoon pastime. The players sit behind long planks, which they strike rapidly for percussive accompaniment. According to Herzog,[6] gambling songs are different from the main repertory in most Indian musical cultures. This is certainly true among the Blackfoot, whose songs are short and have a breathless quality. The songs on this recording come from recent collections; some of them were especially elicited, but others were recorded during the playing of the game and hence contain the typical extraneous noises of a social event—children calling, babies crying, conversation, cars, and motorcycles.

SOCIAL DANCE SONGS

Social dances were evidently always important in Blackfoot life. In the nineteenth cen-

tury and before, they seem to have been associated with religious events such as the Sun Dance. When these religious practices lost much of their significance, the social dances replaced them as the most important avenue of traditional Indian musical expression. Various social dances were introduced in the late nineteenth and early twentieth centuries from other tribes, laying the foundation for the contemporary intertribal culture pattern that dominates the Plains today, characterized by powwows at which professional singing groups appear, white hobbyists dance, and Indians from various reservations come together for social and cultural exchange. Thus, today, almost all Blackfoot music actually performed consists of social dances, and songs are sung for large audiences by singers who are truly musical specialists. The collections made since the 1950s consist largely of this type of song.

THE MUSICAL STYLE

The musical style of the Blackfoot is essentially that of Northern Plains music at large.[7] **Scales** are typically **pentatonic**, sometimes **tetratonic** or **hexatonic**, with the use of **major** seconds and **minor thirds**, and occasionally perfect fourths, major thirds, and perfect **fifths**. The melodic **contours** descend, often in terrace fashion, and the forms are frequently (but not always) of the "incomplete repetition" variety, in which the second strain omits the (often repeated) initial **phrase**. The older recordings depart most frequently from this form, often exhibiting shorter **stanzas** and ranges smaller than the **octave**, ninth, tenth, or twelfth found in later recordings. The songs are always **monophonic** with the exception of one curious but obviously intentionally **polyphonic** song. This polyphonic example consists of a rather conventional song accompanied at times by a higher voice which concentrates (but also departs from) a single drum tone. Drumming is normally in even beats that slightly precede or follow the beat of the melodic rhythm. The drumming of the Owl Dance songs, however, approximate a dotted rhythm.

Since the older recordings are sung almost exclusively by soloists in especially elicited performances (and this is true of some more recent recordings as well), it is difficult to compare the true performance practice of the period of 1897 to 1910 with that recorded after 1950. The more recent recordings indicate rather standardized practices by singing groups. In Grass Dance songs, for example, the **leader** of a song hits the drum hard once, then sings the first phrase which is repeated by a second singer (and sometimes by the leader as well), after which the rest of the song is sung by the entire group. A song is repeated several times, first softly, with drumming on the rim of the drum, then several times loudly, with full drumming, and then, near the conclusions, with **variation** of the drumming by the use of such techniques as crescendo, skipping of beats, and rests. It is likely that these more complex and standardized performance practices are a recent introduction and have something to do with the development of music as entertainment.

Many of the older recordings have songs with the words, but unfortunately most of the collectors did not take them down or arrange for a translation. About half of the songs in this record have meaningful words. When translations are available for the collector, these are given in the source listing of the songs. The more recent songs rarely have words at all—in part because of the gradual receding of the Blackfoot language, and in part because of the intertribal provenience of the songs. A few have words in English along with meaningless syllables.

A few songs depart rather radically from the general style: the gambling songs, the lullabies, and the love songs. These, as a whole, can be characterized as shorter forms with brief and sometimes repeated phrases. They evidently share a style associated with their functions in other North American Indian repertories.[8]

An examination of recordings of Blackfoot music made over a period of almost a century illustrates many things. Most important among these are the considerable variety of musical style and uses of music, the

great changes occasioned by the modernization and westernization of tribal life, and the extraordinary vitality of Indian musical culture in recent years.

NOTES

1. As of 1973, the major studies specifically treating the music and musical culture of the Blackfoot are Bruno Nettl, "Studies in Blackfoot Indian Musical Culture" (*Ethnomusicology* 11(2):141–60; 11(3):293–309; 12(1):11–48; and 12(2):192–207), a series of four articles which appeared in the May and September, 1967, and January and May, 1968, issues of *Ethnomusicology*. These studies and a number of the recordings included in this album result from work done by Nettl in 1965, 1966, and 1967 with support of the Wenner-Gren Foundation for Anthropological Research and the University of Illinois Research Board. I should like to express my gratitude to these institutions for their assistance, as well as to Dr. Jane R. Hanks, Dr. Howard K. Kaufman, the American Museum of Natural History, the Smithsonian Institution, Mr. F. Gully and the *Calgary Herald* for phonorecordings and photographs used in this album. I am particularly grateful to Frank Gillis for his painstaking work as series editor, which involved a large variety of tasks too numerous to list.

2. The material on Blackfoot ethnography and history given here is largely based on the publications of Clark Wissler and John C. Ewers. A number of separate works are involved, but I should like to mention, as the main sources, only the following: Clark Wissler, "The Social Life of the Blackfoot Indians" (New York: American Museum of Natural History, *Anthropological Papers,* vol. 7, part 1, 1911) and "Societies and Dance Associations of the Blackfoot Indians" (ibid., vol. 11, part 4, 1913); John C. Ewers, "The Horse in Blackfoot Indian Culture" (Washington, D.C.: *Bureau of American Ethnology Bulletin* 159, 1955) and *The Blackfeet: Raiders on the Northwestern Plains* (Norman: University of Oklahoma Press, 1958).

3. "The Montana-Wyoming Indian" (U.S., Dept. of the Interior, Bureau of Indian Affairs, Billings Area Office, 1965), Table I.

4. See William K. Powers, "Contemporary Oglala Music and Dance: Pan-Indianism Versus Pan-Tetonism," *Ethnomusicology* 12(3):357–72 (September 1968), for a discussion of music in modern Plains Indian culture.

5. See George Herzog, "Special Song Types in North American Indian Music," *Zeitschrift fur vergleichende Musikwissenschaft* 3(1/2):27–29 (1935).

6. Ibid., pp. 28–29.

7. Bruno Nettl, *North American Indian Musical Styles* (Philadelphia: American Folklore Society, 1954), pp. 24–30, gives a summary of Plains musical styles.

8. Herzog, op. cit., p. 25, summarizes some of the styles which depart from Indian—particularly Plains—music. His article specifies Ghost Dance, Love, Animal Tale, and Gambling Songs as comprising this group of divergent materials.

BIBLIOGRAPHY

Ewers. John C. (1955). "The Horse in Blackfoot Indian Culture." *Bureau of American Ethnology Bulletin* 159.

———. (1958). *The Blackfeet: Raiders on the Northwestern Plains.* Norman: University of Oklahoma Press.

Herzog, George. (1935). "Special Song Types in North American Indian Music." *Zeitschrift fur vergleichende Musikwissenschaft* 3(1/2) 27–29.

Nettl, Bruno. (1954). *North American Indian Musical Styles.* Philadelphia: American Folklore Society.

———. (1967–1968). "Studies in Blackfoot Indian Musical Culture." Parts 1–4. *Ethnomusicology* 11(2):141–160; 11(3):293–309; 12(1):11–48; 12(2):192–207.

———. (1989). *Blackfoot Musical Thought: Comparative Perspectives.* Kent, OH: Kent State University Press.

Powers, William K. (1968). "Contemporary Oglala Music and Dance: Pan-Indianism Versus Pan-Tetonism." *Ethnomusicology* 12(3):357–372.

Wissler, Clark. (1911). "The Social Life of the Blackfoot Indians." *Anthropological Papers* 7:part 1.

———. (1913). "Societies and Dance Associatons of the Blackfoot Indians." *Anthropological Papers* 11:part 4.

RECORDINGS

Dixon, Joseph K. Collection of five original phonocylinders, deposited in the Archives by the American Museum of Natural History. (Accession No.: Pre '54–094–F).

Grinnell, George Bird. Collection of twenty-one original phonocylinders, deposited in the Archives by the American Museum of Natural History, New York. (Accession No.: Pre '54–095–F).

Hanks, Jane Richardson. Collection of twenty-three original phonocylinders, deposited in the archives by the collector, Columbia University and George Herzog. (Accession No.: Pre '54–019–F).

See glossary for definition of boldfaced terms

Kaufman, Howard K. Collection of first-generation tape copies from three original phonowires, deposited in the Archives by the collector. (Accession No.: 55–003–F).

Nettl, Bruno. Collection of five original phonotapes, deposited in the Archives by the collector. (Accession No.:Pre '54–018–F).

———. Collection of first-generation tape copies from ten original phonotapes, deposited by the collector. (Accession No.: 68–037–F).

Wissler, Clark. Collection of 146 original phonocylinders, deposited in the Archives by the American Museum of Natural History. (Accession No.: Pre '54–096–F).

TURTLE MOUNTAIN CHIPPEWA

Nicholas Curchin Peterson Vrooman

Nicholas Curchin Peterson Vrooman has written widely on Native American music of North Dakota. In 1992, Smithsonian Folkways released a CD entitled Plains Chippewa/Métis Music from Turtle Mountain *(SF 40411), which Vrooman recorded and produced. This essay is derived from the notes he wrote to accompany that CD and subsequently revised for publication in* American Musical Traditions.

The Turtle Mountain Chippewa Reservation in North Dakota is a symbolic—as well as the actual geographic—heart of the North American continent. It is part of the Canadian–United States border region that gave birth to an indigenous American culture evolving from marriages between Indians and Europeans, "marriage *à la façon du pays*—"after the custom of the country." The way of life born of such unions was the foundation of the fur trade and the development of the West from 1670 to 1885; its culmination was the formation of the Canadian province of Manitoba. Manitoba was initially a métis, or mixed-blood, nation—the only native nation that resulted from the reconfiguration of North America. It was led by the schoolteacher–politician–prophet and now legendary culture hero, Louis Riel.

The tribes of the Plains held the last frontier against Manifest Destiny, the belief held by many people in the United States during the nineteenth century that the country was destined to expand westward to the Pacific Ocean. The Chippewa and Cree of the Plains were the westernmost of the Woodland Indians, who followed the fur trade from its beginnings to its height and demise. These tribes experienced generations of trade with the Europeans, golden eras, wars, and near extinction. By the time of the buffalo's decline, they knew their fate and their place in history. Chippewa and Cree people, mixing European blood and culture with their own, became a transitional force in the cataclysmic change inflicted upon this land.

In the late eighteenth and early nineteenth centuries, the fur trade of North America centered around the Northern Plains area. Many French and British fur traders married Indian women of the territory to form trade partnerships as well as for the comforts of family. The children of these unions became a strong and separate society, neither Indian nor European. They held an "in between" position economically, as

the middlemen in commerce. They came to realize that racially and culturally they were also "in between" people; their customs and beliefs were neither Indian nor European, but an amalgam of both. Their new culture gave rise to a new language, called *Metchif,* that was wholly its own, comprised mostly of French nouns and Chippewa/Cree verbs.

On the British side of the mixing it was initially Orkney Islanders of Viking heritage, and later Highland Celts, refugees from the Scottish Clearances following the Battle of Culloden in 1746. For the French, many of the early fur trade workers hailed from France's Celtic provinces of Brittany and Normandy. They became the Creole du Canada of Quebec. These European groups, along with the aboriginal tribes, would pervasively commingle following the mid–eighteenth century, creating and sharing the common customs and language we now call Métis.

The Turtle Mountain Reservation is a contemporary microcosm of the cultures that comprised fur trade society. From their stories we hear of the strength and fortitude of the offspring of those early marriages—we learn that they loved their way of life, and had the best of both worlds. Their children married within their kind, and so their customs were perpetuated. With them came an old-belief Catholicism, large families, French **chansons**, fairy tales, superstitions, celebrations, dance, foodways, and a full gamut of **folklife**, blending native with European. The main elements transferred from the shared English/French **Celtic** heritage was fiddling and **jigging**. All this together was the Metchif way. The strength of these traditions in contemporary Turtle Mountain life is a testament to the love that was born of those first and subsequent marriages between Indian and European peoples.

Today on the Turtle Mountains one can hear ancient **a cappella** (unaccompanied) chansons telling of King Louis, Napoleon, and the common soldiers of the French army. Musicians perform religious songs that are moral tales for the young, songs of married life, songs for holidays, and drinking songs. Many of these are basically unchanged from the time they were brought to

the Northern Plains from France in the mid–eighteenth century. There are also songs and **fiddle** tunes that come from the fur-trade era, composed by fur traders in the traditional French **ballad** and Celtic fiddle styles; songs and tunes about heroes like Louis Riel and Gabriel Dumont; and songs about other events great and small: buffalo hunts and battles, loves and loves lost. All of these together tell of Métis life and the heritage and history of these people.

The cultural region of the Métis reaches from Sault St. Marie, Michigan, to Choteau, Montana, across both sides of the United States–Canada border. The Northern Plains states and Prairie provinces are where the Métis cultural identity coalesced and came to political and national unity. Today the

The Turtle Mountain Chippewa reservation is in northern North Dakota, just south of the Canadian border.

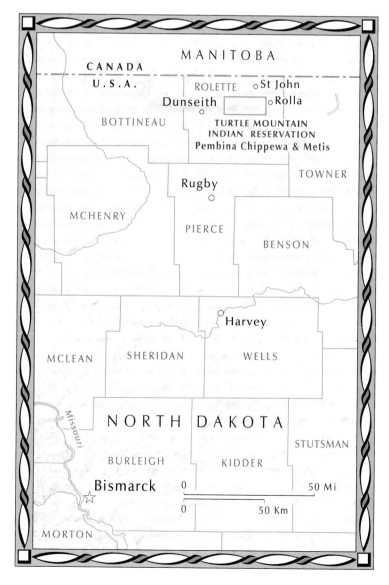

An overview of the beautiful Turtle Mountain region that is situated on the border of North Dakota and Canada.
Photograph © Michael S. Yamashita/CORBIS.

Métis of this area hold more tightly to traditional aspects of their folklife because they are a cohesive population within a vast rural geographic area, where their many isolated communities reinforce the retention of their culture.

Very few people in the United States are aware of the Métis because our government has never recognized them in an official way as a legitimate cultural group. In Canada, the Métis have a little more recognition, coming from the historic fact that the Métis created one of their provinces. But even there they are considered nonstatus Indians with no government-borne responsibilities. For the most part, Métis live on farms and ranches, in communities of their own, or in neighborhoods within larger communities, often called Buckskin and Moccasin Flats, or Breedtowns.

The Turtle Mountains in North Dakota hold the only reservation for Métis in the United States, and that is only because of the goodwill of the Pembina Chippewa (for whom the reservation was created), who allowed them to come when the United States government disowned the Métis. They were accepted on the reservation by their Pembina Chippewa cousins as a way of dealing with a massive political and refugee problem after the Métis' unsuccessful attempt at na-

tional independence between 1870 and 1885. At that time the territories of the Northern Plains were up for grabs, pitting Canada and the United States against each other, and both against the Métis and Indians. To this day the people are called Turtle Mountain Chippewa—a government-invented name.

The Columbian Quincentenary offers us an opportunity to reassess our idea of American cultural identity so that it more fully reflects the contributions of America's aboriginal peoples and more accurately portrays historic processes. The Métis people of the Northern Great Plains offer us a profound example, in blood and culture, of the meaning that those events 500 years ago had for the people of North and South America. That song of change, first sung a half millennium ago on the eastern shores of this hemisphere, still lives. It can perhaps best be heard today at the center of this continent by the descendants of those who lived the epic drama of humanity coming face to face with itself, and merging to become, actually and figuratively, a new people.

The music of the Turtle Mountain Chippewa is a record of being for the Turtle Mountain people and a story for all others to know. From the time these songs and tunes were first created until today, they

have been the primary music heard on the reservation. The music is memorable and jubilant; it shows how the love of music has evolved to take in contemporary forms. This is why it has survived over generations.

There is a wealth of material that gives a sense of the evolution, significance, and vitality of the Turtle Mountain people. Their music is up-close music, made for homes, families, neighbors, and communities. It is performed repeatedly in the cycles of yearly activities. The music represents wonderfully the diversity of this group of people. On the reservation there are special distinctions concerning how it all came together, but, by the ties of history and the structure of reservation life, indeed, it is all together.

By listening to the voices, the presentation and the lyrics, and by envisioning the way performance is integrated into daily life, the listener can begin to feel and understand the intensity, joie de vivre, romance, and history that are all part of the substance of Turtle Mountain existence. When you hear these songs and tunes, remember that the music is being played in kitchens, at weddings, New Year's, reservation bars, and daily celebrations. This is music at home with itself. People need vitality and creativity to survive on the margins of a dominant society. Musical traditions help fulfill the spirit for Turtle Mountain people in spite of the disadvantages of reservation life.

The music is an expression of the vigor, vision, love, and passion of Turtle Mountain life. It blends the ancient with the contemporary, the West with the East, and the red with the white. But more, it's just plain, good music. From the heartbeat sound of the Pembina Chippewa drum to the exploding **bass** of the rock and roll, this music takes its place with the best of America's cultural heritage.

BIBLIOGRAPHY

Blackwell, Lawrence; Dorian, Leah; and Prefontaine, Darren. (2001). *Métis Legacy: A Métis Historiography and Annotated Bibliography.* Winnipeg: Pemmican Publications.

Brown, Jennifer S. H. (1980). *Strangers in Blood: Fur Trade Company Families in Indian Country.* Vancouver: University of British Columbia Press.

Howard, Joseph Kinsey. (1994). *Strange Empire: A Narrative of the Northwest.* New York: William Morrow and Company, 1952. Reprint, with new introduction by Nicholas Vrooman. St. Paul,: MN: Historical Society Press, 1994.

Sealey, D. Bruce, and Lussier, Antoines. (1975). *The Métis: Canada's Forgotten People.* Winnipeg: Pemmican Publications.

Van Kirk, Sylvia. (1980). *Many Tender Ties: Women in Fur-Trade Society, 1670–1870.* Norman: University of Oklahoma Press.

Vrooman, Nicholas Curchin Peterson. (1992). *Medicine Fiddle: How a Tune Was Played and the Metchif Came to Be.* Bismarck: North Dakota Humanities Council.

———. (1991). "Buffalo Voices." *North Dakota Quarterly* 59(4):113–121.

FIRST NATIONS MUSIC OF THE PACIFIC NORTHWEST COAST: KWAKWAKA'WAKW (KWAKIUTL)

Ida Halpern (revised by Paula Conlon)

Ida Halpern was a pioneering ethnomusicologist who documented many of the musical cultures of the Pacific Northwest Coast. This essay is derived from the notes she wrote to accompany recordings she made of the Kwakwaka'wakw (Kwakiutl), released in 1981 on Folkways 4122 as Kwakiutl: Indian Music of the Pacific Northwest. *The material was updated by Paula Conlon, who teaches* **ethnomusicology** *at the University of Oklahoma, where she specializes in Native American music. Her primary research/performing interest is the Native American flute in both traditional and contemporary contexts.*

The First Nations people of the Pacific Northwest Coast are among the most varied and complex to be found north of Mexico. Their tribes include the Kwakwaka'wakw (Kwakiutl), Nuu-chah-nulth (Nootka), Tlingit, Haida, Tsimshian, Nuxalk (Bella Coola), and the Coast Salish. In 1770, on the arrival of the white man, the Pacific Northwest Coast Native population was estimated to be about 70,000 people, while the Kwakwaka'wakw population was between 7,000 and 8,000. In 1882, through infectious diseases, the Kwakwaka'wakw had dwindled to about 3,500. In 1924, there were slightly under 2,000. Since that time, however, the trend has been reversed, and by the late 1970s the Kwakwaka'wakw numbered about 4,000.

The Kwakwaka'wakw occupied territory on the northern corner of Vancouver Island, ranging from Johnstone Strait to Cape Cook. The Kwakwaka'wakw were composed of four phratries (clans): Raven, Eagle, Killer Whale, and Wolf. They were not allowed to marry within the same phratry. The political unit of the Kwakwaka'wakw was the village, which was self-supporting. Only luxuries, including slaves, were traded. The chiefs, who lived in Big Houses, possessed names that, with other rights, titles, and privileges, were handed down from generation to generation. These could include ownership of a song, a crest, a special seat at the potlatch, or the right to membership in one of the secret societies, such as the Hamatsa, or "cannibal society." The Kwakwaka'wakw culture was greatly enriched by totem poles, masks, regalia, and a variety of origin stories and legends. Their masterful artwork included carvings in wood, stone and metal.

Both religion and society placed great emphasis on prestige, rather than power. Much importance was given to wealth, family possessions, and the ownership of slaves, with social climbing and the denigration of rivals acting as strong motivators. Complex rituals and ceremonies were kept according

to strict rules and guided by shamans (priests who used magic to communicate with the supernatural, cure disease, and foretell the future). Goals included the acquisition of supernatural power, spirit quests, the establishment of contact with the spiritual world, and initiation into the secret societies.

HAMATSA

Hamatsa ceremonials were a central part of Kwakwaka'wakw secret societies, with music playing a central role. The Hamatsa secret society was evolved by the Kwakwaka'wakw, and later spread to the surrounding Haida and Nuu-chah-nulth tribes. Initiation as a Hamatsa was a great honor, accorded only to those of high rank, and compulsory for chiefs. Details of the Hamatsa ceremony differ from one tribe to another, as can be seen in the following accounts:

MUNGO MARTIN

An eligible young man was sent alone into the woods where he must stay for four years. [The time varied in different descriptions, sometimes as little as four months.] Then he was sought out and brought back. On his return he jumped at people and bit them. Everybody pretended to be afraid. He then started to dance, getting wilder and wilder.

The ceremony obliged him to dance around the house four times, and to climb the pole four times. At his first appearance he wore nothing but parts of fir trees. At the second dance—the initiation—the Hamatsa wore a mask, like the head of a bird painted in strong colors, and growled instead of speaking because he had lost the power of speech through his long stay in the woods .

There were three Hamatsa costumes: (1) a headdress [mask] with a long beak that opened and shut; (2) no headdress, Hamatsa clad in cedar only, on a naked body; (3) the complete attire [headdress and cedar].

Before the Hamatsa comes out the drums are vibrating quickly. The Hamatsa song "Mosquito" is an initiation song. Mosquitos come from the ashes that are blown out of the chimney before the Hamatsa arrives. Therefore, mosquito bites come from the Hamatsa. When the Hamatsa approaches, the chimney pipes are blowing. The smoke scares them away. The smoke has different colors with different meanings: white smoke, mountain goat; brown smoke, grizzly bear.

After the spirit talks, the Hamatsa is sometimes paralyzed for two years . Whenever he tries to enter, the drums announce him. He tells all about the changes. The women and children in the villages are running about, announcing that the Hamatsa is here. There are feast songs for the Hamatsa. Nobody likes the Hamatsa.

A small Hamatsa accompanies him. Old people believed in small Hamatsas. It was called *Hamasanos* (small people).

When the Hamatsa is dancing everybody is told to be quiet and to watch. One man stands up. There is no more talking. He wants to try to talk. The young man who is a Hamatsa cannot talk. Only an old man who is a Hamatsa can talk. He no longer swears, and he is not angry any more.

The first part of the Hamatsa's initiation was held in secret, with only the members of the Hamatsa society in attendance; the second part was public, with the entire community taking part. Sometimes there were female Hamatsas. The rank was hereditary, and a woman, being the only daughter of a Hamatsa, had to abide by the same rules and

remain in the woods, just as a man would have done. Mrs. Sam Webber, the aunt of Tom Willie, was the only woman Hamatsa in Kingcome. Mungo Martin's wife gave him a Hamatsa song she brought into the marriage, which he planned to give to his sons. His wife inherited the song from her uncle, Johnny Klaotsi of Teina Island, which is fifty miles from Alert Bay.

BILLY ASSU

The Hamatsa must dance around the Big House four times. He climbs up the Hamatsa pole four times to attract the people and make the pole sway. When he first comes out he wears nothing but branches. He must stay four years in the woods. People go there to round him up. He jumps down, fifty feet. He runs away again. This is done to attain a higher standard among the people.

TOM WILLIE

The Hamatsa ceremony lasts from eight to twelve days. The first part of the initiation, there is not yet the Hamatsa. The guests expecting new Hamatsa from the woods are singing eight to twelve songs at the time. Then, after the fourth day, the Hamatsa appears through the roof of the building with hemlock branches. Many boys, about ten, are holding him down to tame him with the smoke of the blanket four times. The big man is asked to bring the Cedar Bark and to change the Hamatsa into the Cedar Bark costume. For four days he is there dancing with the Cedar Bark. After four days, he gets the mask, Long Beak, Crooked Beak, Raven. After the mask is taken off, bearskin comes on [is put on]. The last dance is when the Cedar Bark is washed off. They are singing the whole night and are putting the Cedar Bark away for the next time.

The Kwakwaka'wakw generally use bearskin for the last ceremony, although Chilkat blankets are used when there is a relationship with a northern tribe (Tlingit), as in the case of Stanley Hunt. The Cedar Bark ring on the Hamatsa's head can be worn for four months or even a whole year after the ceremony.

STANLEY HUNT

Hikeles is the first man of the olden days to be a Hamatsa. Hamatsa gives to his own tribe, but he doesn't know the words anymore. Hikeles, old man from Blunden Harbor, he knew how to make that song. It is the first Hamatsa in the world, Pole, when first come out of the woods. Dance. Got pole in the midst of the community. He climbs up on the pole. The old man gave the Hamatsa to all the tribes who wanted it.

Henry Hunt, the son of Johnny Hunt, nephew of Stanley Hunt and Mungo Martin, and grandson of George Hunt (the famous collaborator with Franz Boas and Edward Curtis), gave the following description of the Hamatsa ceremony. His account is based on his recollections of one of the big celebrations his father gave, together with Ed Whonnuck, in Fort Rupert about 1930.

HENRY HUNT

First part, the Hamatsa appears in hemlock branches as a wild man untamed. He dances with hemlock for four days, disappearing and appearing again.

Second part is when he dances with the masks. That means that the masks are put out. There are three dancers in the three-sides mask consisting of a Raven, a Hukuk (Hagok), and the Crooked Beak.

Third part, the people try to put the Cedar on the new Hamatsa, consisting of two rings of cedar on

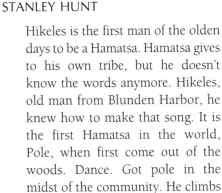

See glossary for definition of boldfaced terms

the neck and head and hands and legs, on the naked body. For four days he dances in this Cedar attire.

Fourth part, the Chilkat blanket is then put on top of the Cedar and the new Hamatsa dances slowly, because he is already tamed, with a woman ahead of him, leading him.

Afterwards, the Hamatsa sits on the floor in the Chilkat blanket when the washing-off ceremony begins. They burn the hemlock, and put the Cedar away for next year. Then they go four times around the house.

[At the Fort Rupert event in 1930] only two special Hamatsas were allowed to fulfill that part of the ceremony: Ed Whonnuck and Alfred Scow [the brother of Billy Scow of Alert Bay].

Nowadays they shorten the ceremony to four days and sometimes even one day, omitting the washing-off ceremony completely. The last time everything was done properly was fifty years ago.

JAMES SEWID

One had to have the right to a name and proper position from his ancestors or his wife's ancestors. The initiation of the Hamatsa took two weeks. In the first ceremony he was clad in evergreen hemlock branches. During the second ceremony he wore Cedar Bark, dyed red, every night. For the third ceremony he was given the mask. The fourth costume was Chilkat blanket and mask. After the final ceremony they took off the Cedar; then comes the bath ceremony, the rubbing down with branches.

CHARACTERISTICS OF HAMATSA SONGS

With regard to **melody** in the Hamatsa song **genre**, three basic melodic types are used:

1. descending melodies,
2. melodies with **angular leaps** but no overall descending or **ascending contour,** and
3. **"pendulum-like" melodies** that undulate approximately similar distances around a central note or notes.

From a study of the Hamatsa song genre, it appears that there are somewhat regular "norms" of each unit assessed: **contour, range, scale,** and certain **intervals**. The nature and use of syllables in the Hamatsa songs is of particular interest. The characteristic syllables in the Hamatsa genre are of clear lexical origin. Song texts often refer to the "cannibalistic" eating of "food." The syllables that are characteristic of Hamatsa songs are HA, MA, MAI, and AM or AN. In their language the word "food" is expressed as "Hama," thus the derivation of the remaining syllables, HA–MA–MAI. Certain syllables or syllable combinations are prefix syllables, others can be used as infixes, and still others appear as suffix syllables. Specific numbers of repetitions and even highly organized patterns of syllables occur in these songs, and definite formal patterns are made by the syllables alone. The syllables, which began as fragments from lexical units in the songs, have become so extended and extensive in the Hamatsa songs that they have an almost independent life, a life that complements the melody and beat, but one which only rarely bonds with these other elements.

POTLATCH

The Potlatch was the celebrated nucleus of the activities of the First Nations people of the Pacific Northwest Coast, the cultural artery of all facets of their traditional life. The word is derived from the Nuu-chah-nulth word *patshetl,* which means "giving" or "a gift." It was customary for the chief of a tribe to host a potlatch and to distribute to his guests nearly all of his possessions, with the exception of his house. The more he could give away, the greater his honor and prestige became. In return, he could expect to receive even more worldly possessions at fu-

A Kwakwaka'wakw totem pole, showing the legendary figure of Tsonoqua and her child Tsiltwalakami, who according to tribal myth founded the Kwakwaka'wakw tribe.
Photograph © Charles and Josette Lenars/ CORBIS.

quisition of a "copper," a large copper plaque indicative of the highest status, sometimes ritually destroyed at potlatches.

A chief might give a "feast" for the men in his household in order to ratify a new decree or ordinance, then the whole community would unite in a potlatch to sanction the new laws for the clan. Within his own house, the chief could celebrate minor occasions, such as the bestowing of minor titles on his children, through the medium of the potlatch. But when he wished such honors for himself, outside chiefs must be called to the potlatch. There was fierce competition for distinguished titles and honors; their acquisition always had to be recognized through the potlatch. In this way, a chief gained the approval of his own house and the respect of others. The greater the title, the greater the potlatch.

It was possible for even commoners to climb the social ladder by giving potlatches, for no sharp line existed between chiefs and commoners. **Oral history** contradicts the assumption that only a chief could give a potlatch. Titles were graded, the highest belonging to the chief who owned more rights than the others. Although the chief held great influence and prestige, he had no legal authority, except over slaves. His influence over the people of his house, as well as their support, was gained through the giving of "feasts." In honoring visitors, he depended on the help of other chiefs in calling a potlatch.

Everything connected with the ceremony had historical precedent, and stringent rules regarding dress and ceremony were followed. At funerals, significant objects were displayed, and people would pay for the opportunity of seeing them. At winter dances, gifts were given with the understanding that they would be returned with added value, according to set rules. Guests of the potlatch were welcomed by the chief and led, each to his appointed place, according to rank and tribe. Each procedure was accompanied by ceremonial singing, appropriate dances were performed by the host chief, and speeches and orations were made glorifying his own position.

ture potlatches given by rival chiefs. The Kwakwaka'wakw tribe carried rivalry and distribution of property to a unique extreme in that they would even destroy possessions in order to indicate superior wealth.

Potlatches were held in the fall, when, after the long season of hunting and fishing, the people were free to participate in winter dances and in the ceremonies of their secret societies. Occasions such as marriage, birth, and death were all marked by the potlatch, but it could also be called in vengeance, to save face, to repay an insult, or to establish rights to certain dances, songs, legends, crests, or regalia. The raising of a totem pole, the building of a house, and the legalization of new titles were considered worthy of the potlatch. It was also held to celebrate the ac-

The order of the potlatch songs, according to Tom Willie, was:

1. Mourning Song (if it was a memorial potlatch),
2. Cedar Bark song,
3. Klasela song, and
4. Feast song.

In traditional times, potlatches took from four to six months. "Everybody got really fat," according to Mungo Martin. In more recent times, the potlatch was compressed to two or three weeks. Mungo Martin remembered when he was a little boy on Teina Island. A chief called a potlatch and he stayed for six months. Then he went away to another potlatch for another six months, being away altogether a whole year. "They had dried salmon, dried berries, dried clams, and sometimes five fires in one house." The only indulgence, in addition to food, was tobacco, smoked in a pipe called a "calumet." Alcohol was unknown until introduced by the white man.

In potlatch ceremonies, custom demanded that everything be repeated four times—each song sung four times, each dance performed four times—because four is a sacred number for the Kwakwaka'wakw, as well as many other First Nations and Native American tribes. At the time of the potlatch, families brought out all their crests to impress the audience. Entertainment played a major role, and many stunts were performed, such as pretending to burn a woman alive or to behead the dancers. Such sleights of hand were pure theater, but, as Chief Billy Assu said, "The white man misunderstood such tricks, and so forbade them, thinking the Indians were cruel."

During the feasting, they told of all the glories of the past and present. The Grease Feast was a very important one during which they gave away olichan (candle fish) oil, one of the most highly valued commodities. On the last night of the potlatch, they took off their headdresses and danced and sang a last song to declare that the potlatch was over. The chief got up and started to sing and then everybody joined in. The potlatch was the social and cultural anchor of their lives. In all of its aspects (as a present-day chief has aptly summed up), "It was a cold war between families because one wants to outdo the other."

In traditional times, animal furs were given away at the potlatch—sea otters, etc. Because animals have the role of intermediary between the supernatural power and man, and are man's guardian spirits, the First Nations people of the Pacific Northwest Coast considered the furs of the animals to be venerable. Therefore, furs at the potlatch were an important trading item. Later on, Hudson Bay blankets obtained through the fur trade were substituted for furs. In more recent potlatches the value of canoes, "grease," etc. were evaluated in terms of these blankets, much like currency. Before Hudson Bay blankets were in vogue, they used dog hair for weaving general-use blankets. One special kind of blanket, the Chilkat blanket, made from mountain goat wool and dyes, was the sole preserve of the chiefs. The potlatch can be considered on one level as a financial system and likewise as a law-abiding and law-confirming institution.

The potlatch also reflected First Nations spiritual belief. To the original inhabitants of the West Coast, there were three distinct levels to the universe: the spiritual world, the animal world, and the world of man. In this cosmology mankind occupied the lowest level. Animals were often cast as the mediators between the purely spiritual forces; they, being closer to nature, were thus nearer to these powers than humans, and were treated with great respect.

REMARKS ON MUSIC

The music of the Kwakwaka'wakw tribe, one of the most complex tribes of the Pacific Northwest Coast, is based on strict sociological rules, which pertain especially to the performance and ownership of songs. Songs are literally "given," for they are "owned" by individuals or families who have paid for them in full. The songs then assume hereditary importance according to established tribal laws.

After the coming of Christianity, First Nations people were reluctant to relinquish, or even to reveal their songs, which were part of their hereditary lineage. So strong was this feeling of ownership that no chief or member of his family would sing a song belonging to another; by doing so, he would be treated as a thief, shamed and scorned by his own people. The chief could inherit a song, acquire it by marriage, or commission it for an important occasion in order to give himself and his clan added prestige.

Songs originated with the songmakers of the tribes and were conceived in a state of spiritual trance, in visions and in dreams. Members of the tribes believed that by learning the song and ritual, they could reproduce the vision. First Nations people derived great strength from their songs, turning to them for supernatural help when they felt the limitations of their own power. Singing was not a trivial matter. Originally the power of the songs was bestowed only upon chosen people. First Nations oral history tells of many great men who were given songs by supernatural powers.

Strict rules were kept in the **oral tradition** of teaching the songs. Great stress was placed on passing songs on to subsequent generations in the proper manner. If a singer were to make a mistake, the consequences would be very serious for him. Mungo Martin said that he "would have to pay very much for one mistake." Certain songs fitted specific occasions, and were meant to convey particular meanings. They would not sing a Winter Dance song in summer, or a Ghost Song except at the time of death. Love songs, crest songs, and some Hamatsa songs are of a hauntingly beautiful quality, while potlatch songs are declamatory. Yet all reveal great dramatic impact and an impeccable sense of timing.

In Kwakwaka'wakw music, there is evidence of a distinct variation principle, not in the Western sense, but in an idiomatic First Nations sense. After the first melody has been sung, the repetitions show slight changes of **pitch** in a persistent upward or downward direction. The voice production

of First Nations people is noticeably different from that of Western singers. Their intonation might appear to Westerners to be out of tune, but this is certainly not so. It is not unvarying intonation but, once begun, follows in strict melodic pattern and **variation**. They vary their melodic material by a slight raising or lowering of pitch, which is a consistent feature of their singing. This raising or lowering of pitch continues several times in a song, often three or four times. This rise or fall may, in our system, amount to only a **half-tone** altogether or as much as one-and-a-half tones. We should never assume, however, that they are out of pitch. Careful analysis and measurement by the collector have proved this. These slight rises or lowerings of pitch represent their variation technique. (When defining **intervals**, the terms "**major, minor,** perfect," etc., are not used in this study because they are measurements of the Western **well-tempered scale** and are accordingly not pure intervals).

An important characteristic of these songs is the use of syllables instead of entire words and texts. These syllables have been referred to as "meaningless" or "nonsensical." In the First Nations music of the Pacific Northwest Coast area, one finds text and syllables interspersed. The generally accepted understanding was that these syllables have no meaning or connection with the song. On the contrary, it was found that the syllables have a specific relationship to the song. They represent part of the meaning and content and are meaningful abbreviations of words referred to in the song. One finds that even the most important part of the song is often given over to the syllables.

The author has already published one study dealing with these so-called meaningless syllables in First Nations music. In the paper "On the Interpretation of the 'Meaningless Syllables' in the Music of the Pacific Northwest Indians" (*Ethnomusicology* 20[2], 1976), the author reported a breakthrough in 1974 dealing with these syllables and their relation to song texts. Research into the enigmatic relationship between these syllables in First Nations song types continues; the syl-

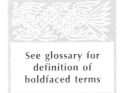

See glossary for definition of boldfaced terms

lables are of paramount importance in the songmaking process, a fact confirmed by discussion with a Native songmaker. The syllables are of critical importance to the songs, and further research on this topic has added numerous further examples, confirmed by many other scholars.

In First Nations music, titles do not exist; instead songs are classified by type or specific genre, such as Hamatsa, Potlatch, etc. By establishing conclusive compositional principles as to genre, one can then establish the basis of their music theory, the rules and regulations for the respective genres. For example, all Potlatch and Hamatsa songs, no matter who composed them or who sang them, have strict rules and compositional techniques in common. In-depth formal analysis shows complexities that are, in turn, found in all of the songs in the same genre. Songs from each genre were analyzed, revealing a different format for each of the genres studied. To be sure of the generic form, many comparable songs sung by different chiefs were examined, revealing complicated formulas for the respective genres. Discovering these principles was especially rewarding after the discovery of a myriad of original expressions within what appears to be a rigid framework.

Similarly, individual songs are characterized by specific properties. One can distinguish the various types of songs by the manner of singing, voice quality, intensity, **vibrato**, **tremolo**, and **glissandi**, along with their individual **rhythmic pulse** or the specific syllables employed.

RHYTHM

Of all the various enigmas encountered in the study of Pacific Northwest Coast First Nations music, none has caused more of a problem that the complex issue of rhythm. Before we may begin to clearly understand the nature of this complicated music, we must come to terms with this fundamental issue. Many musicians attempted, without success, to find a solution to this riddle. The author consulted with professional musicians, conductors, and composers in an effort to find a solution to this problem, but to no avail. None of the methods of notating rhythm in transcriptions was particularly successful. For a demonstration of this problem, one may refer to the film *Potlatch,* which shows Barbeau and Macmillan grappling without success with this problem.

In 1961, the author suggested that melody and the simultaneous percussive beating of sticks, **rattles**, etc. represented two separate musical events which flow independently in parallel courses. If we assess each event separately, we can understand the individual nature of the two events and then develop a composite picture of these two events' subtle interrelationship. It must be stressed that the rhythm of the sung melodic part is in no way subjugated or influenced by the **rhythmic patterns** presented in the beat.

In discussions with First Nations songmaker-chiefs, the author learned many interesting details relating to rhythm, including performance practices. Chief Mungo Martin stressed the independence of the sung melodic material. He emphasized that the rhythmic beat must begin before the singing, or after the singing, but never simultaneously with the start of the singing. To do so was forbidden. This was confirmed by another songmaker, Chief Tom Willie, who talked about the underlying importance of the beat patterns that form, in essence, the skeleton of the song. The beat is the central musical aspect of the songs, and is of greatest importance.

The author came to feel that the most efficient way to treat the beat might be to approach it, not in terms of our present western musical notation, but rather to try rhythmic modal notation, the traditional patterns of poetic scansion, modified as needed to reflect First Nations practices. This worked very well, and more detailed study supported this method as being the most effective way currently at our disposal of reflecting the true nature of the beat. (This theory was arrived at by following the development and evolution of early western

music in the medieval period, from free neumes to modal rhythmic notations.)

Often only a one-beat pattern is used in a given song. However, there are also examples of complexes of two and even three different beat-patterns used within the same song. Further study indicated that within the framework of a specific beat-pattern, there is great musical definition. The specific number of beats is often logically controlled and regular in repetition. For example, if one of two specific sections of a song is completed in the first occurrence within the time span established by seven modified iambs, this time span and that specific number of iambs will remain consistent in subsequent repetitions of the material. Specific numbers of beat patterns form a containing frame for the (parallel) overlaid sung melodic material. Though the beat patterns may be continuous and may be presented without breaks or interruption, it is possible to define melodic sections of songs by stating that they are completed within the time of, for example, five modified iambic beat patterns.

In many songs, the interrelationship of the independent melodic and rhythmic parts is very sophisticated; this is especially true in songs where there is a break or change in the beat pattern. These breaks or changes invariably reflect significant formal changes in the melodic material, the syllables or the text. In this way, there is interplay between beat and melody, though it would be entirely wrong to say that there is direct synchronization. Rather, there are some carefully worked out relationships between these independent entities.

See glossary for definition of boldfaced terms

TEXT AND SYLLABLES

In the First Nations music of the Pacific Northwest Coast, one finds text and syllables interspersed. These syllables have a specific relationship to the song, representing part of the meaning and content of the song. Often they are abbreviations of words referred to in the song or representative of an animal sound. In many songs, these descriptive, quasinaturalistic syllables are used to represent and evoke the animal spirit, the GKA GKA of the Raven, the HO HO of the Wolf, or the NA NA of the Grizzly Bear. In other songs, the abstract evocation of the supernatural power is verbalized in a single sung or spoken expression. The words *Glugwala and Nawala* are used to represent the supernatural power in Hamatsa and Mourning songs, etc. The syllable HAI appears in the Mountain Goat songs to represent the supernatural power. Syllables that are imitative or descriptive of animal sounds can be considered as a religious mediator between man and the supernatural power. M. Schneider explains that "the language of the animal is closer to nature and therefore nearer to the gods" (Fodermayr 1971, p. 94FF). The author believes that this, in essence, is the explanation of First Nations totemism. First Nations people do not consider animals as gods, per se, and did not pray to them. Rather they regarded them as supernatural beings whose guidance they respected and implored. The syllables are of great importance in the songmaking process, as confirmed by discussions with Kwakwaka'wakw chief Tom Willie.

TOM WILLIE INTERVIEW

Ida Halpern: How do they come to make these syllables? They are very interesting syllables; how can you remember if they don't come out of any words of the song?

Tom Willie: When you make songs, . . . Feast Songs or Party Songs, you start with WO JI A—I can make a Party Song—they start out with the WO JI A. We find a tune, we start singing the words.

IH: So you know these syllables and then you start the tune?

TW: We start with that WO JI A first and try to find something. Like a Hamatsa song, we start with HA MA MAI. And when we find good words, we put the words in that, you know. That's what it means, the WO JI A.

IH: Who taught you this?

TW: Well, lots of old people sing together, you know. I've listened ever since I was six years old, I used to listen to those people

singing. [Willie then explained how the song was composed after the syllables were selected.]

IH: You said that first come the syllables, is that right?

TW: Yes. The syllables are always first, first in every song. Then, when the syllables are finished, you repeat those syllables over and over again. And after they finish the syllables, you make the words of the songs. After the words of that song, they start making the songs.

IH: Where do you get the inspiration for the syllables?

TW: Well, the oldest people know how to make songs. Some of these people dream about the songs they want to make. These men know how to sing and make songs. Sometimes they get it from dreaming; they remember their dreaming, and when they wake up the next morning they start singing again, then finish by making the song up. Some of them make songs out of rain blowing. When you hear that blowing, you sing it. When it rains so hard in winter that water drips down from the roof on the corner of the house, it's something like singing. And when you lay down in the boat and you hear the water dripping in the side of the boat, it's like singing.

IH: So after you have your words, then you make the music, the melody to it?

TW: Yes.

IH: Then the melody combines with the rhythm, the beat, or the beat goes independently?

TW: The beat always goes its own way. If we lose the words of the song, then we do a different beat now. Lots of songs have a really difficult beat and difficult words and syllables of the songs.

IH: You put great importance on the beat.

TW: Yes, we can't put any [other] kind of beat besides this beat because [the old] men found this beat for these words. We tried to put different kinds of beats, but we can't sing very well to that.

IH: I see, you have the music, you have your song, then you try to find a beat that will fit, and the beat is the last thing that comes in?

TW: Yes.

[Tom next described how the songs were performed.]

TW: Well, one man starts a song, and all those singers come forward after the first one, on the first **verse** and the second verse.

IH: And after the third verse he tells what the next verse will be as a solo, alone, and then they follow?

TW: Yes.

IH: You see we found that, and we were just wondering if that is only in the Hamatsa or is it always like that, is that the custom with other songs?

TW: All these songs, it doesn't matter what—Kasella songs, Potlatch songs, Women's Dance songs—they're all the same thing.

IH: Who established [the songs], are you taught these rules and regulations, who teaches you that?

TW: My Granduncle Weber in Kingcome. My father [also] used to be good on the songs, used to make songs, used to be a songmaker.

IH: And the **leader** tells them when they have to go higher and lower?

TW: Yes.

IH: How does he say that, or does he start singing it, or what?

TW: Well, he just talks, you know. . . .

IH: He makes a sign, or what?

TW: With a sign sometimes, Indian syllables are "beni."

IH: Is lower?

TW: Lower.

IH: And what was the word for higher?

TW: "Iki" is higher.

IH: So they make the movement with the hand?

TW: Yes, they move the hand.

IH: Higher or lower. That is like our conductors doing it.

TW: Just like that.

IH: We found that it is such a rule, such a straight rule always, so I just wanted to have your documentation on it, if we were right, you see. That is why I asked you for it. It is interesting to find out.

TW: That is a difficult thing to find out. Some people do not find out what it means . . .

IH: That is it, you see. Some people might think, oh well, you just sing like that, but that is what we are doing, to find out the rules and regulations. How long were they teaching you?

TW: Well, I started singing with my old man ever since I was about sixteen. I [would] go sit down and listen to the singing. But he noticed that I am going to know how to do the singing because I never miss the beat, even [though] I didn't watch that beat, the big drum on one side, [I] follow the beat of the people . . .

IH: At the ceremony the singers are separate and the drummers are separate, or are you beating your drum at the same time?

TW: Yes, same time.

IH: You are singing and beating the drum.

TW: Yes.

IH: Just as you are doing here, beating with a stick. Well, now we have it, we have figured it out.

[Finally, he described how the singer chose the pitches for the songs and varied them in the performance:]

TW: In Potlatch songs, sometimes the high . . . keeps on high and did not go down; some songs go way down in the second verse, they come up again and do the same thing as they did before in the first verse, and after that it goes lower. . . .

IH: Still lower?

TW: Still lower, and it comes up again. . . . some people didn't go any lower; some people always go lower [on] some songs.

IH: Some songs always go lower and lower?

TW: Yes.

IH: It is a variety.

TW: Yes.

IH: To make it more interesting, the songs?

TW: Yes, it makes it interesting, that's what it is.

IH: To make it interesting, so they go lower. All the tones always go lower, or some tones always stay the same?

TW: Some tones go higher, some tones lower, then they stop, and get higher and higher, then stop and sing. Some songs go lower and lower.

IH: And if a melody starts going lower, do all the tones go lower or are there some tones which don't move, which stay the same, and others go lower? Are there some fixed tones? You know what I mean?

TW: Yes, you know that Potlatch song and the Feast song, they always go a little bit higher and a little bit lower because [of] the change in the beat. In the Potlatch and Feast songs, they always go higher and they stop, then they come down a little lower. Sometimes they start lower and come higher on the beat.

IH: So, that is also possible, that the whole little melody changes down, or are there some tones which don't go lower, which are always the same?

TW: There are some tones [that] don't go lower, don't move . . . stay the same level.

IH: Some tones don't go lower, that is interesting. Some are fixed. How do you ...which tones do you choose to stay fixed?

TW: I know that, for instance, Ghost songs didn't go lower, didn't go higher sometimes. That is all I know. These melodies stay the same.

IH: The Ghost songs stay at the same level, they don't move.

TW: Don't move.

Every phase of First Nations life is portrayed in songs and dances. The First Nations people have a song for each occasion and endow it with great importance. The author has chosen some specific phases of their lives that can be portrayed or understood as part of a great Potlatch, the mainspring of First Nations existence. The explanations of the songs and their meaning came directly from the informants themselves, focusing

See glossary for definition of boldfaced terms

mainly on the Hamatsa and Potlatch songs of the Kwakwaka'wakw tribe.

The music of the Kwakwaka'wakw tribe is based on strict sociological rules that pertain especially to the performance and ownership of their songs. For this reason, Kwakwaka'wakw music has always presented a problem to the collector. First Nations chiefs are not impressed by the social or professional status of white people who come to hear them sing. They will not give the collector their songs unless he or she can win their complete confidence during years of personal association and by many small tokens of genuine interest and goodwill. It is considered "giving" because they "own" their songs. In permitting the collector to listen and set up a tape recorder, they give him or her a present, a personal privilege. The author gratefully acknowledges that honor.

MUSIC OF THE GWICH'IN INDIANS
OF ALASKA

Craig Mishler

Craig Mishler is a folklorist and cultural anthropologist based in Anchorage, Alaska. From 1989 until 1999 he was a subsistence resource specialist with the Alaska Department of Fish and Game. He is also the author of The Crooked Stovepipe *(University of Illinois Press, 1993), a book on Alaskan fiddle music and square dancing. The following essay is derived from notes Mishler wrote to accompany a 1974 album he recorded and produced entitled* Music of the Kutchin Indians of Alaska *(Smithsonian Folkways 4070). He subsequently revised his essay for publication in* American Musical Traditions.

The Gwich'in Indians are a relatively small Athabaskan tribal group of about 2,500 people occupying a vast area in northeastern interior Alaska and northwestern Canada. Like all northern Athabaskans, they are of the same racial and linguistic stock as their more widely known southern kinsmen, the Navajo and Apache, though with the passage of many centuries, their respective cultures have diverged widely in nearly all respects.

The Alaskan or western Gwich'in are today divided linguistically, socially, and geographically into two main groups. The Gwich'yaa Gwich'in—"People of the Flat Lands"—are comprised of the residents of Chalkyitsik, Circle, Birch Creek, and Fort Yukon; and the Neets'ee Gwich'in—"People of the Mountains"—are those who reside in Venetie and Arctic Village on the Chandalar River. At one time, the people in the flat-lands were isolated into small bands and had more specialized names, but in modern times the outboard motor, airplane, and snow machine have broken down this isolation, and widespread intermarriage has all but erased these former distinctions.

In aboriginal times, the Gwich'in were a nomadic people who followed the game and lived together in large numbers only in the warm summer months when the salmon were running up the Yukon and its tributaries. Indeed, the name "Yukon River" appears to have come from *nyukwanjik,* a Gwich'in word meaning "river where there are moss-covered summer houses." Somewhere along the way, the *-njik* ending, which corresponds to "river," was either dropped entirely or translated directly into English, and *nyukwan* was transformed into "Yukon." The case for this interpretation becomes even more convincing when we discover that the Gwich'in name for Fort Yukon is *Gwich'yaa Zhe*—"Flat-Lands House," and two other early white settlements on the Porcupine River are still referred to as "Rampant House" and "Shuman House."

Fort Yukon, founded in 1847 by Alexander Hunter Murray of the Hudson's

Bay Company, is in many ways the hub of a whole network of rivers whose watersheds define the western territory of the aboriginal Gwich'in. In addition to the Yukon, the Porcupine, the Chandalar, for example, the Black River, and Birch Creek also continue to be occupied by Gwich'in-speaking people, and three other important rivers, the Christian River, Marten Creek, and the Sheenjek ("Dog Salmon River"), were not abandoned until the 1950s and 1960s, although all three are still used occasionally for hunting and trapping. Now a log-cabin community of 583 people with daily scheduled air service from Fairbanks, Fort Yukon has become an important communications, transportation, and supply center for everyone who lives along these river systems.

Though they are in the swirl of rapid acculturation and social change, the Gwich'in are a proud and happy people who still maintain many of their fine traditions. The beadwork sewn by Gwich'in women cannot be matched anywhere in Alaska today—moose hide mitts, slippers, belts, knife and gun sheaths, Bible covers, and mukluks are richly ornamented and colorfully decorated with a dominant four-petaled flower pattern. Twelve of these flowers, symbolizing the twelve disciples, are stitched to the church altar cloths on a background of white bleached moose hide, consummating the art.

Equally impressive are the oral talents of Gwich'in storytellers, who seem to flourish in the more remote outlying villages of Chalkyitsik, Venetie, and Arctic Village, where there is no radio station actively competing for the Indian ear. The Episcopal missionaries, who made many converts well before the turn of the twentieth century, seem to have convinced the people that their animal creation stories were pagan and heathen (probably more for their frank sexuality than for their theological content), so that today the old stories are denigrated by some Indians as being "just like fairy tales."

The stories that are openly encouraged are more on the order of what folklorists like to classify as legends. Popular Gwich'in legends can be roughly divided into tales about famous warriors, tales of survival under extreme conditions, tales about the feats of famous medicine men, and humorous tall tales pregnant with exaggeration.

Still, the most beautiful part of traditional Gwich'in culture is the music. All of the aboriginal ceremonies have now completely disappeared, yet there are still many of the older people around who can sing—and sing well. The style is always solo **a cappella**, and the old-timers say that even before the coming of the whites, no drums or other musical **instruments** were used for accompaniment, except occasionally a couple of sticks of wood that were beat against one another for rhythm. Any public group singing outside of the church is a great rarity now, and individuals perform only upon demand, though elsewhere in Alaska, as

The Kutchin tribe lives in the northeastern interior of Alaska near the northwestern Canadian border.

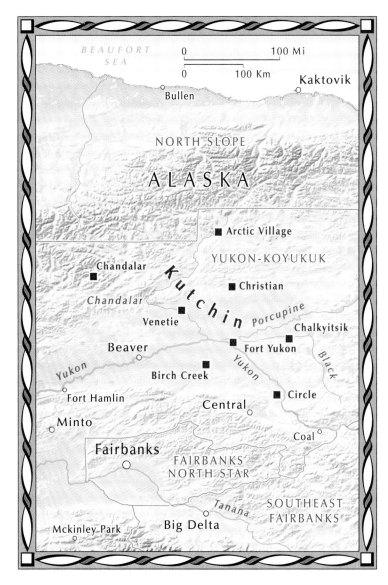

The Nunamta Yupik Eskimo Dancers from Alaska in full tribal uniform. This semiprofessional dance troupe regularly performs in their native Alaska and around the country.
Photograph © 1992 Ilka Hartmann.

with the Koyukon Athabaskans farther downriver, songleaders and public group singing still predominate in a style strikingly similar to the western Apache and Navajo.

Gwich'in songs address a great variety of subjects and tend to fall into the following categories: dance songs, love songs, medicine songs, story songs, songs of tribute and farewell, and New Year's songs. Gwich'in songsters, like Gwich'in storytellers, seem to be remarkably free from taboos or restrictions of any kind. Songs can be performed by women as well as by the men, by day as well as by night, in summer as well as winter.

The **old-time fiddle** dance music that flourishes so well in Gwich'in villages undoubtedly owes its origin to Hudson Bay traders and voyageurs of the mid–nineteenth century. In his journal for the year 1860, Robert Kennicott, an important early explorer and naturalist, describes "a Christmas ball" held at La Pierre's House, on the Up-

per Porcupine River. The principal trader and postmaster at La Pierre's House was one James Flett, an Orkneyman and an old voyageur who had acquired an Indian wife. Also present to celebrate the holidays were a large number of whites and "a dozen or so" Indians. In this earliest account of the Gwich'in dancing to **square dance** tunes, Kennicott writes:

> The dancing was, I may say without vulgarity, decidedly 'stunning.' I should hardly call it remarkably graceful. The figures, if they may be called such, were only Scotch **reels** of four, and **jigs**; and . . . the music consisted of a very bad performance of one vile, unvarying tune, upon a worse old fiddle, accompanied by a brilliant accompaniment upon a large tin pan. (Kennicott 1942)

Thus, the introduction of Scottish and Orcadian folk music and folk dances to the Gwich'in can probably be attributed to

James Flett and his friends. The Flett surname still enjoys a fairly wide popularity among the Gwich'in living in Fort Yukon, and the explorer William Dall, visiting Fort Yukon in the spring of 1867, noted that most of the inhabitants there "are from the Orkney Islands and the north of Scotland, while a few are French Canadians, with a mixture of Indian blood." (Dall 1870)

The late Charlie Peter (1902–1985), recalled that this kind of music was already going strong when he was just a boy, and he remembers such old-time Indian fiddlers as Jacob Luke, Alexander John, and Artie Linklater. So although it was originally a white man's art, this music has been so well incorporated into Gwich'in tradition that many of the tunes are popularly known by their Indian names, and they survive quite independently from the commercial country music played and heard in Alaska's white communities.

As I first saw it performed in the 1970s, the music for Gwich'in dances was provided by a fiddler and a rhythm **guitarist**, and both used small electric amplifiers for their instruments. Today, larger ensembles are common, including electric **bass** and **snare drums**, along with the fiddle and guitar. Usually, when there is an all-night dance, there will be two fiddlers and two guitar players—two teams of partners—who spell each other every two hours or so, for many of the dances take ten or twelve minutes to complete, and at a fast **tempo** in a crowded hall, this can be hot and exhausting work.

In the 1970s male **callers** were often used, but sometimes there was not enough sound equipment on hand, and the amplified music completely drowned out the caller's voice. Nearly everyone knows the basic steps anyway, and the caller only seldomly interjects a variation on the standard patterns. The people are fond of one-steps, **two-steps**, **foxtrots**, **waltzes**, jigs, **schottisches**, **round dances**, line dances, and running sets; and this wide variety generates continuous interest over many hours at a time.

The enormous popularity of this dance music can be measured by the regularity of its public performances. Dances are customarily held on every major holiday of the year: New Year's Day, Easter, Fourth of July, Thanksgiving, and Christmas, as well as for special occasions like weddings, for the ordination of Native priests into the Episcopal clergy, and especially for the annual spring carnivals, when dances are held every night for a week and go full steam until four or five o'clock in the morning.

The geographic extent of Indian square-dance culture in the far north is still relatively unknown. Upriver, it is still possible to observe some of the dances at Eagle, among the Han Athabaskans, and the Han fiddlers claim they hear this music played live on radio CHAK in Inuvik, N.W.T., Canada. There is even good reason to believe that many of the

The Yupik Eskimo remain the dominant cultural presence along this part of the western shore of Alaska.

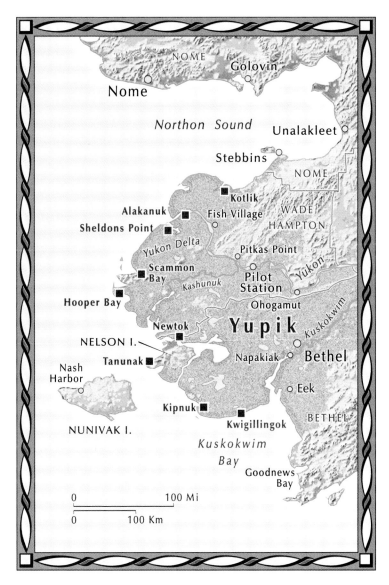

Yupik Dancing

Yupik Dance and Culture Still Thriving

Ann Fienup-Riordan is an independent scholar who has published many books on Yupik Eskimo history and oral tradition, including Eskimo Essays: Yupik Lives and How We See Them *and* Boundaries and Passages. *She has lived with and written about the Yupik people for twenty-five years, and she reports that a revival of their old traditions was under way in 2001. The following originally appeared in the program guide for the 1984 Smithsonian Festival of American Folklife. Fienup-Riordan has also published a book,* The Living Tradition of Yupik Masks *that includes more information about Yupik traditions, including dancing.*

> *Two men came down to the water and entered the open water in their kayaks with only a drum and a spear. They approached the village at night, waiting until the morning to come close. Then they raised their paddles to make their presence visible. They approached slowly, saying, "We fight, some are afraid of death, but still we fight. But spears are meant for killing animals." And they began to beat the drum, and the women came down to the river dancing. Then they said, "We want to come into the qasgiq [communal men's house]." And they did, and took council there. And now they only fight with dancing. And the men who came went home to their old village and said, "No more war."*
>
> —Cyril Chanar, *The Origin of Dancing*

Half a hundred tiny villages, each populated by between 100 and 500 Yupik Eskimos, lie spread along the coast of western Alaska between the mouths of the Yukon and Kuskokwim rivers. First appearances convey isolation and austerity, with man pitted against a cold and inhospitable environment. However, the Yupik area is actually the home of a people committed to harvesting a tremendous natural bounty, including sea and land mammals, birds, and a variety of fish. Thanks to relatively late contact with outsiders and infrequent economic intrusions, it remains one of the most culturally vital areas in Alaska, where English is still the second language of the majority of the residents and Yupik Eskimo the first. As the traditional subsistence activities and language continue to flourish, so do many of the traditional cultural activities, including the lively and rich display we know as Yupik dance.

As in the story above, Yupik dancing is said to have begun where warfare left off. Conversely, one of the more covert battles that western society first waged against Yupik people was the suppression of their dance tradition. During the late 1800s in the delta region, Moravian and Catholic missionaries alike viewed with grave misgiving the *agayuluteng* (masked dances) along with other embodiments of traditional Yupik cosmology. Overwhelmed by the pagan implications of these traditional representations and the ceremonial cycle in which they were a part, the missionaries did their best to discourage their performance. Informal "recreational" dancing survived in the areas missionized by the Catholics, but along the coast south of Nelson Island and along the Kuskokwim River, where Moravian influence prevailed, dance performances were completely suppressed.

In the Catholic communities of the region, dancing as the primary form of religious expression no longer exists. However, the contemporary Yupik have retained several annual formal dance distributions. The winter season, with all its ceremonial activities, is still referred to as *cauyaq* (drum), an essential and central element in the

same tunes heard on this album, like the "Red River Jig," are played all the way down into northern Alberta.

One of the most encouraging things about this dance music is the great number of active practitioners. Among the Neets'ee Gwich'in especially, there are nine or ten young, self-taught fiddlers, and though they do not possess the great **repertoire** of Charlie Peter, they are usually quite skilled and sometimes technically even more proficient. It is also the young people who take the greatest delight in the dancing, and it can be expected that they will still be kicking their heels to the Neets'ee T'yaa for a long, long time yet to come. That's good news.

dance. Along with these major annual events, informal dancing occurs throughout the year. Although more common on stormy winter evenings than during light summer nights when the fish are running, informal dancing is a vital part of village life whenever time permits or an occasion presents itself.

Between one and two dozen participants, including the drummers, are enough to start off the evening, although the group often grows to ten times its original size as the evening progresses. The older men and women of the community are the chief dancers, along with a group of promising youngsters who have been given some of the simpler dances by their grandparents. Early in the evening, as the group begins to assemble in the community hall, several of the middle-aged men take the drums from the closet where they are kept and begin to play softly, waiting.

The drums are made of a rim of bent wood, approximately two feet in diameter, over which a single piece of plastic (formerly walrus stomach or bladder) is tightly stretched. The only instruments to accompany the dancing, they are struck with a thin willow wand. Two to six drums are used, the drummers rotating during the evening as their voices become weary and their arms grow tired.

Each dance has its own *yuayun* (song), which the drummers, accompanied by up to a dozen singers, perform to the beat of the music. Each song consists of three parts: two or more *apullat* (**verses**) sung to an *agenra* (**chorus**) repeated between verses, and a *cauyarialnguq*, an irregular drum sequence accompanied by motions but without words. Both chorus and verse elicit highly stylized dance gestures that tend to be more abstract and are danced according to a formal pattern, while those of the drum sequence are often realistic imitations of animal and human behavior, and follow no set pattern. Each verse is danced through twice between choruses. The sequence is repeated again and again, becoming faster, louder and more exaggerated with each repetition, until by the end of the dance the precise **syncopation** between the drum beats and the movements of the dancers makes it seem as though the dancers themselves were making the sound.

A dance begins as one old man or woman softly sings the verse, which contains both **vocables** (lexically meaningless syllables) and words descriptive of the action or events the dance will depict. As the singer finishes, the audience begins to generate the dancers, pushing and calling them forth. The heads of older matrons turn around, searching for the appropriate dancers—those who in years past have been given particular dances as their prerogative by the older men and women who have written the songs. A man and his wife or two cousins come from different parts of the seated mass and join together in public, as the drummers tighten their drum heads and prepare to begin. From two to a dozen individuals perform in each dance. The women dancers stand in a line towards the back facing the audience and the drummers, while the male dancers kneel in front of them, also facing the drummers.

Both men and women hold fans while they dance; if no fans are available, they wear gloves, some say out of respect for what they perform. The men use circular wooden fans decorated with five or six large feathers (mallard or snowy owl) extending around the rim. In the Nelson Island area, women's fans are made of grass coils along the edges of which they sew the long and graceful neck hairs of reindeer. On the Yukon delta, women hold small wooden finger masks by means of two holes carved at their bases. The small masks are bordered with a combination of short full feathers and long thin ones, topped with tufts of down. Both the flowing hairs and the stiff feathers serve to accentuate the arm and hand movements of the

(Continued on next page)

Afterword: In November 1983, Athabaskan fiddling received a major boost in recognition when funding from the National Endowment for the Arts made possible the first Athabaskan Old-Time Fiddling Festival at Eagles Hall in Fairbanks, Alaska. Now the social event of the year for interior Indians from Alaska and Canada, this festival has been held annually ever since. It features musicians from two distinct traditions—the fast "upriver style" featuring the Gwich'in and the slower-paced "downriver style" featuring the Lower Tanana and Koyukon. The "upriver style" features the older jigs and **contras** introduced by Hudson's Bay Company traders, while the "downriver style" is

(Continued from previous page)
dancers, rendering the women's movements more fluid and the men's more staccato.

On special occasions, women may also wear broad strings of beads around their necks, as well as beaded crowns topped with wolverine and caribou hair. The beaded fringe of these headdresses often covers the eyes of the performers, studiously cast down as another stylized mark of respect. Both the encircling crowns and the rounded, perforated dance fans, fringed with both fur and feathers, are reminiscent of the mask worn traditionally by the central dancer. The open-work design of the fans held by the men is explicitly compared to the pierced hand found as an appendage to many traditional dance masks. The hole in the hand's center, like the opening in the dance fan, is a symbolic passage through which the spirits of fish and game came to view their treatment by humans; if they found it acceptable, it was believed they would repopulate the world. Although the traditional masked dances have been abandoned, the dancers, with fans and arms extended in the motions of the dance like gigantic transformation masks, call forth many of the traditional meanings, including the continued interrelation between the human and nonhuman worlds.

When the singer has completed the verse once and the dancers have assembled, the drummers and chorus begin to play and sing. They are led by an older man or woman, the official dance director, who encourages and teases the dancers during each verse by calling out directions during the chorus pantomime, such as "Raise the gun!" and "Shoot!" The director's motions may be accompanied by the steady back-and-forth movement of a dance wand, a three-foot-long piece of decorated driftwood. From a quiet beginning, the scene grows more and more raucous, with the audience shouting back and forth, pulling people off and on to the dance floor, and calling for the dancers to begin again, as the performers play up to an audience that continues to egg them on.

During the dances, women stand, feet flat, body swaying with an up-and-down motion, and knees bending to the beat, while the men kneel directly in front of them. The dance songs themselves are about everything from winning at cards or war to escaping from a ghost. Since all songs deal with daily experiences, a catalogue of the changes that have come to the area since the mid-1960s can be read from Yupik dance songs: songs about basketball, **guitar** playing, having fun on the swings at the school playground, or going to Anchorage.

Yupik dancing is as vital today as ever on the Yukon/Kuskokwim delta. Men and women continue to dance to the steady rhythm of the hooped drum traditionally said to represent the beating heart of the spirits as well as the lively movements of the spirits of humans and animals over the thin surface of the earth. Although many traditions have changed or vanished, the drum continues a steady and meaningful beat.

BIBLIOGRAPHY

Fienup-Riordan, Ann. (1983). *The Nelson Island Eskimo: Social Structure and Ritual Distribution.* Anchorage: Alaska Pacific University Press.

———. (1983). *Nick Charles: Worker in Wood.* Fairbanks: Rasmuson Library.

———. (1996). *The Living Tradition of Yupik Masks.* Seattle: University of Washington Press.

Ann Fienup-Riordan

a later development shaped by music of the gold rush era and popular country music of the early 1950s.

BIBLIOGRAPHY

Dall, William Healy. (1870). *Alaska and Its Resources.* Boston: Lee & Shepard.

Gibbons, Roy W. (1980). "'La Grande Gigue Simple' and 'The Red River Jig': A Comparative Study of Two Regional Styles of a Traditional Fiddle Tune." *Canadian Folk Music Journal* 8:40–48.

Kennicott, Robert. (1942). "Journal." In *The First Scientific Expedition of Russian America and the Purchase of Alaska,* ed. James A. James. Evanston: Northwestern University Press.

Lederman, Anne. (1986). "Old Native and Métis Fiddling in Manitoba: Origins, Structure, and Question of Syncretism." *Canadian Journal of Native Studies* 8(2):205–230.

Mishler, Craig. (1987). "Athabaskan Indian Fiddling: A Musical History." *Alaska Magazine* 53(11):47–51.

———. (1993). *The Crooked Stovepipe: Athapaskan Fiddle Music and Square Dancing in Northeast Alaska and Northwest Canada.* Urbana and Chicago: University of Illinois Press.

———. (1999). "Athabascan Fiddlers and Dancers: An Alternative Musical Standard." *Fiddler* 6(2):4–7.

THE CHANGING SOUNDSCAPE IN INDIAN COUNTRY

Thomas Vennum, Jr.

MUSIC AND CHANGE

Please see the introduction to this volume for biographical information on Thomas Vennum, Jr.

By its very nature, music is never to-tally static; over time, even the most conservative of musical traditions have been susceptible to change, however slight. In "never to be altered" traditions, such as European classical music, which depends upon scores precisely notated by their composers, each performer applies personal nuances of technique and interpretation. Thus no two performances, say, of a Beethoven piano sonata will ever be exactly identical, even by the same player.

Change in music—like that in other kinds of cultural performance—is a response to changes that may occur in many areas of society, ranging from the migration of peoples, to the acceptance of a particular religion, to shifts in critical notions of "authenticity," to the stylistic innovations of some creative genius. Music might change from within its tradition if the musicians have deliberately altered their performance practices, invented new musical instruments, or purposely affected the style of their music in

some other way. Change might come from outside the tradition through contact with another culture, such as when foreign musical **genres** are imposed on a people (Christian **hymns**, for instance) or when certain traits of the foreign idiom (vocal styles) or whole genres (**fiddle** dance music) are adopted willingly. The folk and tribal musics of the world—in practice more conservative than popular musics—seem mostly affected by external change. Classical traditions, on the other hand, tend to exhibit internal changes. Sometimes the change may represent a return to earlier practices to recover the original intention of the music. In the pursuit of more "authentic" performances, for example, the musical instruments of Europe's past have been reconstructed according to our historical knowledge of their former properties—their exact shapes, sizes, and materials of manufacture. Museum specimens of Baroque harpsichords are carefully measured and copied so that performers can replicate the sounds of that period rather

106

than relying on nineteenth-century pianos to produce them, as was customary.

When change occurs in tribal music, the combination of new and old musical traits results in hybrid styles of music. When Indian peoples were (sometimes forcibly) taught to sing Christian hymns, missionaries translated the texts into the Native language and allowed the hymns to be sung in **unison** (that is, without **harmonies**) to facilitate learning. In so doing they created a hybrid form—albeit one that was linguistically unchallenging and musically acceptable to Native ears accustomed to unison singing of Indian melodies. Of primary importance to the missionaries were the musical and religious meanings expressed in tunes and texts—European in origin and foreign to Indian cultures.

These new, Native hymns became a powerful tool in attempts to convert Indians to Christianity. They were particularly well received by southeastern tribes forcibly removed to Indian Territory in the 1830s. In a state of extreme culture shock, many of them abandoned traditional ways of life and belief systems, taking up the new religion and its music to address a spiritual crisis. Once in Indian **repertoires**, however, some translated European texts were set to traditional Native melodies. Indian composers even created new tunes for them using Indian tonal systems. In performing these hymns, Indian people continued to use their own vocal style. Their characteristically flat, nasal delivery with its **glissandi** and, to European ears, "imperfect" intonation contrasted markedly with the European bel canto (operatic) ideal of singing, with its vocal **vibrato** and clear attack of musical **pitches**. This hybrid tradition of Christian hymn singing in Indian languages continues, especially among the Choctaw, Cherokee, Comanche, and Kiowa, some performed without instrumental accompaniment in unison or in two-, three-, or four-part **harmonies**.

THE POST-COLUMBIAN PERIOD

European exploration and colonization of the Western Hemisphere set into motion changes that affected every aspect of Indian culture, including music. Indian exposure to European music, especially that of the church, occurred early. In the wake of Cortés's conquest of Mexico in 1519, the Spanish made immediate efforts to Christianize the Native peoples, building countless small churches and cathedrals, importing musical instruments from Spain to accompany the Mass, and training Indians to sing. As early as 1530 a small organ from Seville was installed in the Cathedral of Mexico City to accompany Indian choirs.

Efforts to train Indians to play a variety of European instruments for church services apparently became so excessive that in 1561 Phillip II complained in a *cedula* (royal decree) about the mounting costs of supporting the musicians. He cited the large number of players of trumpets, clarions, *chimirias* (oboe-like reed instruments), flutes, sackbuts (trombones of the Medieval and Renaissance eras), and other instruments and requested a reduction in the number of Indians being paid for such services. As the Spanish moved northward into present-day New Mexico, similar practices are recorded. During the 1630s at Hawikuh (Zuni), the pueblo used as Coronado's first headquarters, a Franciscan was giving intensive instruction to Indians in organ, bassoon, cornet, Gregorian chant, and counterpoint.

Indians quickly became proficient in making a wide range of instruments. At first they began making flutes but went on to construct *vihuelas* (**guitars**), lutes, and even pipe organs under Spanish supervision. It soon became unnecessary to import instruments from Spain. In summing up the sixteenth-century musical activities of Indians in New Spain, Frey Juan de Torquemada wrote in his *Monarquia Indiana* (Seville 1615), "The other instruments which serve for solace or delight on **secular** occasions are all made here by the Indians, who also play them: rebecs, guitars, trebles, viols, harps, **monochords**."

The English and French were equally active in their New World colonies in exposing Indian peoples to their musical traditions. Thomas Heriot in *A briefe and true*

report of the new found land (London 1588) wrote of the local Indian chief on Roanoke Island that he "would be glad many times to be with vs at praiers, and many times call vpon vs both in his owne towne, as also in others whither he sometimes accompanied vs, to pray and sing in Psalmes." By 1648 John Eliot was translating metrical psalms into the language of "the praying Indians" at Natick in Massachusetts.

Hymnals in the Native tongues continued to be published throughout the nineteenth century, particularly by the American and the Presbyterian Boards of Foreign Missions. An Iroquoian hymnal, *Gaa Nah shoh* (1860), was created for use by the Seneca at Cattaraugus Reservation, while a Siouan hymnal, *Dakota Odowan* (1879), went through several printings. Asher Wright and his wife, who collated the Iroquoian hymns, induced the Indians to sing them to the accompaniment of a melodeon (a small reed organ) that had been donated by a Sunday school in Massachusetts. At the Indians' insistence (according to the Wrights), they set the melodeon up in the middle of the longhouse—the traditional Iroquoian religious structure—"where by the grateful young people, who loved it as a human being, it was gorgeously decorated with hemlock boughs and a profusion of red berries."

Some Christianized Indians went on to become hymnal collators themselves. Thomas Commuck, a Narragansett, published a Methodist hymnal in 1845 containing tunes claimed to be Native in origin and variously attributed to famous chiefs (Pontiac, Tecumseh) or such tribes as the Flathead, Osage, Algonquin, and others. In the publication the melodies were set to harmonic accompaniment by Thomas Hastings.

As would be expected, European secular music was also brought to the new colonies, and Indians had ample opportunity to hear it. Marin Mersenne in his *Harmonie universelle . . .* (Paris 1636) could state that Indians were already singing the songs of French fur traders living among them. In 1655 Claude Dablon (born 1619) traveled from Quebec to Iroquois country and brought with him several musical instru-

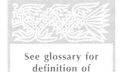

See glossary for definition of boldfaced terms

ments he had mastered as a youth. Although it is not recorded which instrument he played for them, the Indians are reported to have crowded the missionaries' bark hut to hear Dablon "make the wood talk." The trader John Adair, living forty years among the southeastern tribes in the late eighteenth century, was accustomed to singing Irish tunes such as "Sheela na guria" to his Indian friends. Song schools sprung up throughout New England for itinerant singing masters to teach not only colonists but also Indians to read music and sing in harmony. In the 1760s, Eleazar Wheelock at his Indian Charity School in what is now Connecticut taught his Delaware pupils to perform in three-part harmony. These schools quickly made fluent sight-singers of the Indians, having introduced them to the totally foreign concepts of musical notation and **polyphony**, which contrasted with the **oral tradition** of unison singing to which they were accustomed.

Not all exposure to European music took place in the New World, however. Indians were brought back to France to perform in Parisian court entertainments such as *Ballet de la Reine* (1609), which included pastoral American scenes. Apparently a sensation was caused when a naked Tupinambá Indian was introduced on stage in the score of *Ballet de l'Amour de ce Temps* (1620), and the famous composer Lully incorporated Indian actors into several ballets performed before Louis XIV.

ADAPTATION AND ADOPTION

Through long and constant exposure to European culture, Indian people not only absorbed foreign vocal repertoires but sometimes altered their musical instruments as well. One of the hallmarks of Native music in the Western Hemisphere is the almost universal accompaniment of unison singing to percussion provided by the singers or dancers. Of all percussion, **rattles** and drums have always been the most commonly used. Contact with European cultures affected both types of percussion, but in different ways, as Indian people adapted material items from

the foreign culture. In the case of rattles, the greatest change was in the nature of the vessel and the loose material inside that struck the container to produce the sound. An example of this kind of change occurred sometime early in the twentieth century in the western Great Lakes area. Formerly, the rattle used in religious ceremonies of the Ojibwa (Chippewa) medicine lodge was made of bark or hide formed into a cylindrical vessel, filled with pebbles and sewn shut with spruce roots before a wooden handle was inserted. Once Euro-American canned goods became available to Indians, however, it eventually became commonplace to substitute metal containers, usually a baking powder can, for natural materials. Instead of pebbles, buckshot might be used to produce the sound. The shape of the rattle remained the same, but the materials used in its manufacture and the resultant sound changed—apparently not enough to be rejected aesthetically. (The Winnebago, Ojibway neighbors to the south, continue to use traditional **gourd rattles** in their medicine lodge and jokingly assert that the Ojibway have abandoned tradition and are now using beer cans for rattles!)

Rattles accompany the **Stomp Dance**, common among southeastern tribes. Traditional Stomp Dance music is cast in a **call-and-response** pattern: the leader of a line of dancers sings a brief melodic **phrase**, and the dancers repeat it exactly or answer it with a similar phrase. Although the leader carries a rattle in his hand, most of the percussion in the Stomp Dance is produced by vessel rattles made of turtle shells tied in bunches around the calves of the dancers. Their stomp-like dance steps produce the rattling sound from pebbles inside the turtle carapaces. In this century, however, many Stomp dancers have begun to substitute milk cans for the turtle shells; they are easier to come by and simpler to make rattles from, and many feel that the sound is even enhanced in volume and quality.

Precontact drums were usually made from logs hollowed by charring and scraping, with animal skins stretched over their openings for drumheads. To be sure, this type of drum continues to be made—the large, **two-headed cottonwood drums** of Pueblo peoples, for instance. But when the Grass Dance, with its ritually prescribed large drum, spread to northern Plains Indians in the late 1800s, they found it expedient simply to substitute the commercially available marching band drum, long familiar to them from military bands on frontier outposts. To perform Indian music using this drum, they merely turned it on its side so that the singers could surround it. Today such drums with their plastic heads are commonplace, and Indian singing groups usually decorate them by painting Indian designs or motifs of the name of the group on the exposed head. But, in yet another change, a rejection of the marching band drum and a return to building drums the traditional way appears to be part of a general musical revitalization in Indian Country.

ADOPTION AND JUXTAPOSITION

One European folk instrumental tradition adopted by Indian people throughout North America was fiddle music. The Indians learned fiddle-playing and step-dancing from French fur traders throughout the Great Lakes region beginning in the 1600s. Later, settlers from Ireland and Scotland, who did trapping in the 1700s and lumberjacking in the 1800s, brought their fiddle repertoires as far west as the Athabaskan interior of Alaska, where Indian people maintain them today. Intermarriage between Europeans and Indians accelerated the acceptance of European instrumental and dance traditions.

The Saturday night **square dance** began to challenge Indian as well as Christian religious ideals. Traditional Ojibway medicine lodge ceremonies, customarily lasting several days, found their attendance dwindling as people took time off to attend local square dances. A Catholic missionary to the Menominee was reported to have chopped to pieces a fiddle belonging to one of his parishioners, telling him that he would never play "the devil's instrument" another Saturday night.

Many Indians developed their fiddle talents while working in lumberjack camps. Others were self-taught, spending spare moments in the woods practicing. In all–Indian logging camps, square-dance **callers** would perform in the Native tongue, and the repertoire of fiddle tunes often included Indian compositions whose titles were derived from names of Indian settlements or activities. Fiddlers at the west end of Lake Huron, for example, played "Manitoulin Island **Waltz**," named after an island reservation in that lake; Algonquian speakers on the St. Mary's River had a tune "Whitefish on the Rapids," referring to the great fishery between Lake Superior and Lake Huron, which for centuries provided an important subsistence staple for Indians living nearby.

Most Indian fiddles were of European manufacture, but some were homemade from cigar boxes and fish line, and others were modified in some way to make them "Indian." In his film "Medicine Fiddle" (1991) Michael Loukinen interviewed a number of western Great Lakes performers who provided some of the rich lore surrounding their fiddle traditions. One man told of his deceased father who converted a store-bought fifteen-dollar fiddle to Indian use; to make it louder he put porcupine quills inside the fiddle's body and attached a deer bone to its neck. Having applied his "Indian medicine" to the instrument, he allowed no one to touch it. Some Indians interviewed on film told stories about chance encounters with horned people playing fiddles in the woods or abandoned cabins. Because drawings of horns on human heads in Great Lakes pictography traditionally signified spiritual power, the horned performers may be understood as spirits, although in this instance there may also be the concept of the fiddle as the "devil's instrument."

A number of distinct Indian fiddle traditions began with this culture contact. Thus we find Indian fiddling contests today among the Cherokee of Oklahoma and among interior Athabaskans of Alaska, a métis ("mixed") French–Ojibway–Cree style on the Turtle Mountain Reservation in North Dakota, and a slightly different Red River

style further north in Manitoba among the Saulteaux, where fiddlers **jig** with their feet while playing. There are also fiddlers among the Houma of Louisiana and the Apache of Arizona, which is the only tribe also to have an indigenous one-string fiddle of its own, totally unrelated to the European variety and used for playing traditional Apache music.

Another tradition of Euro-American culture that was adopted by Indian people was the symphonic (mostly brass) band. This was a late nineteenth-century emulation of Anglo culture; as small towns had athletic teams and marching bands to perform on July 4 in parades or under pavilions, so did many reservations. Just as baseball supplanted lacrosse in many Indian communities, so the marching band grew in importance at the expense of Native musical events. Many learned to play trumpets, trombones, and clarinets by attending primarily Anglo schools. Others, in all-Indian boarding schools, had band performance imposed upon them as part of their programmed acculturation to deprive them of their Indian musical heritage, just as they were forbidden to speak their Native tongue or dress in tribal attire. Further erosion of traditional Indian music on some reservations was aided by the governments free band instruction as part of the WPA program in the 1930s.

In Mexico and Central America the various *banda* (band) traditions were adopted by Indian communities from the dominant culture. Their repertoire continues to include *marchas, pasadobles*, and other compositions arranged and scored by late nineteenth-century composers—the Spanish equivalents of John Phillip Sousa. Many of the performers were musically illiterate and had to learn the music by ear. Most of them lacked music teachers, so their techniques of playing and the tones they achieve from self-developed performance styles on clarinets, trumpets, and trombones do not produce the polished, in-tune, dynamically controlled sounds to which we are accustomed. These features of Anglo performance style are absent, and certain Indian aesthetic qualities of banda music might offend us, but they please their audiences.

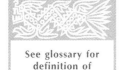

See glossary for definition of boldfaced terms

Banda schools have in fact become cultural institutions in Indian communities, such as in Oaxaca, where rural Zapotec Indian children sometimes live in banda communities away from their families. The town banda has become part of Indian cultural identity for these people—one that distinguishes one Indian community from another. Furthermore, the Zapotec banda has social prestige within the community and functions much like an artisans' guild. In the *tequio* system of social organization, members of the banda are exempt from such communal responsibilities as road building, to which all others in the town owe their services. The banda members' performance at all secular **fiestas** and religious feasts and processions is considered their paramount duty to society.

While band traditions have been transmitted mostly through oral tradition in Indian communities, the mass information media of the dominant society have played a key role in introducing Indians to the latest in Euro-American musical forms. Rapid changes in twentieth-century technology have had a dramatic effect on music in Indian Country. Through exposure, first to radio, then the phonograph and television, Indian people have been bombarded with the musical culture of the dominant society for decades. Rather than being passive consumers of American popular music, they have adopted many of the styles and musical instruments commonly found in Euro-American society. In some instances they have adapted them to their own musical traditions; in others, they have accepted them along with the associated musical genres. Thus throughout Indian Country today one finds older traditions of non–Indian origin functioning as contemporary popular music as well as the latest forms of Anglo popular music used by Indian people for a variety of purposes.

Take, for instance, a prevalent style of dance music called **waila**, performed in southern Arizona by its creators, the Tohono O'odham (formerly known as Papago). Waila

A typical late-nineteenth century Native American brass band. This one is the Metlakahtla Cornet Band, whose members lived in Alaska. Native American bands like this one played western instruments and performed the typical brass band repertoire of the day.
Photograph © Michael Masian Historic Photographs/CORBIS.

is also called "**Chicken Scratch**" by some who compare the way dancers kick back their feet on the hard, dry, dusty ground to the way a chicken searches for food. The music is clearly derived from Mexican and Anglo neighbors of the O'odham; parts of the tradition had already formed a syncretized style by the mid–nineteenth century. German and Czech settlers along the Texan Rio Grande brought European button **accordions** with them in the nineteenth century to play the **polka** traditions of the Old World. The accordions as well as the polka repertoires and styles were in turn taken up by Mexican performers, and a new music called **norteño** emerged. Scholars believe this music reached the O'odham by about 1850, when it began to be performed by an ensemble of fiddles and guitars (introduced by missionaries) with a rhythmic accompaniment of **snare** and bass drums, each played by a different individual. Eventually this ensemble changed its character and sound; the contemporary **button accordion** was adopted, and saxophones, whose playing techniques were learned in high school bands, replaced the fiddles in the 1950s and 1960s.

Today's waila rhythm section includes an **electric guitar**, **bass**, and **traps** (a set of drums and **cymbals** played by one person). Commenting on the irony of this phenomenon, folklorist James S. Griffith observes, "Thus the two great institutional attempts at changing Tohono O'odham culture—the Spanish mission system and the Indian schools—are reflected in, of all things, the organization of O'odham popular dance bands!"[1]

"Chicken Scratch" bands typically perform a set of tunes in succession, moving from a waila (a fast tempo polka), to a two-step *chotiz*, to a *cumbia*, a Caribbean borrowing. Occasionally they include a waltz or a **mazurka**. Like most Indian music the tradition is an oral one, not learned or read from score. Some of the tunes are quite old, while others have been taken from commercial recordings of Mexican norteño groups. Some popular American melodies such as "Rudolph the Red-Nosed Reindeer" have been incorporated into the repertoire.

Waila music has by no means replaced older O'odham music. Like musics of many American Indians, the traditional O'odham repertoire consists principally of unison songs accompanied by percussion, either rattles or a notched **rasp** using an inverted basket drum as **resonator**. Such traditional instruments are used in the semi-sacred *chelkona*, or "skipping and scraping" dance, performed to induce rainfall in their desert homeland by lines of male and female dancers with special costumes and body paint in cloud and lightning designs. Also traditional is the *keihina*, a **round dance** which, though somewhat social in nature, is still thought to bring rain, as the dancers stamp vigorously on the ground to encourage rain clouds to appear. While this religious repertoire remains intact, waila bands perform Saturday night social music, thus functioning as a popular music tradition for most O'odham.

While the O'odham and most other Native peoples of North America carefully separate their traditional sacred music from evolved, European-influenced secular forms such as waila, there are isolated examples where the two have been juxtaposed. This has occurred in the Pascola/Deer Dance complex, a traditional religious practice of Yaqui Indians living in Sonora, Mexico, and of those in southern Arizona, who fled persecution by the Mexican government in the late nineteenth century.

The history of the Yaqui helps explain the evolution of the Pascola/Deer Dance celebration. During the Spanish conquest of Mexico in the early seventeenth century, an expedition against the Yaqui in 1610 was defeated by the tenacious Indians. Possibly as a strategy against further military action by the Spaniards, the Yaqui requested that missionaries be sent to live among them. Two Jesuits settled in their territory in 1617, and gradually a type of ceremonialism developed that syncretized Indian and Christian elements, such as is evident in the Pascola/Deer Dance complex.

The ritual is performed at fiestas to honor God and certain saints. It consists of successive performances by two musical ensembles—the first reflecting European mu-

See glossary for definition of boldfaced terms

sical traditions, the other exclusively Native ones. The transition between them, however, is not marked, as one flows into the other. The performance begins to the accompaniment of a folk harp and folk fiddle, both modeled after classical European counterparts and offering clear evidence that the Indians began to copy Spanish Renaissance string instruments shortly after the Cortés invasion. The players are seated on chairs, and the style of their music is decidedly European, although Indian interpretation of European tonalities and counterpoint are evident, and performance techniques are more folk than classical. Dancers for both the Pascola and Deer Dances wear cocoon rattles strung around their calves—clearly an indigenous musical instrument. Pascola dancers wear masks positioned to one side of the head rather than over the face.

Once the Pascola part of the ritual has concluded, the completely Native musical ensemble begins. A tampelo begins to beat a small hand drum with a stick while simulta-neously playing a three-hole **flageolet** (flute). The other musicians are three males seated on the ground—an Indian tradition—playing a **water drum** and using rasps with **scrapers** and resonators. They perform songs with poetic texts in an archaic form of the Yaqui language unintelligible to most Yaqui today. Meanwhile, the dancer removes a sistrum rattle (Native) that had been tucked in his belt during the Pascola section of performance and relocates the mask to cover his face. A Deer dancer, wearing a deer's head atop his own, begins his dance and completes the flow from music of Spanish origin to a probably older Native tradition.

THE CHANGING SOUNDSCAPE

Waila, brass bands, Pascola music, and the music of other Indian string ensembles are examples of external traditions syncretized in the past by Indian peoples with their own styles of performance. But today on Indian reservations and in urban Indian communi-

Robby Romero and Benito Concha, the leaders of the contemporary Native American group Red Thunder.

Photograph courtesy of the Agency for the Performing Arts, Inc.

Red Thunder

Please see the sidebar accompanying Chapter 3 for biographical information on Nick Spitzer. This essay originally appeared in the program guide for the 1995 Folk Masters concert series, held March 10–April 15 at the Barns of Wolf Trap in Vienna, Virginia.

Driving from Taos to Santa Fe at night the radio crackles with remote reception, but the station from one of the pueblos has the first Red Thunder CD coming in loud and clear. Red Thunder is arguably the most popular Native rock group making the circuit from the "Res" to the earnestly chic Hard Rock Café—their synthesis of roots and rock is reminiscent of Los Lobos' beginnings, though the connection of Indian traditional forms to Western pop and rock involves a greater musical leap in some ways for performers and audiences alike. In local live performances, band founders Benito Concha and Robby Romero are joined by various older traditional players from Taos Pueblo, most notably Benito's father, José Miguel "Mike" Concha, the governor of the pueblo and a worker at the Millicent Rogers Museum devoted to Indian arts and culture.

Red Thunder's musical mix is a fascinating blend of pan-Indian big drum, Puebloan drumming and song, Native flute in traditional and rock styles, and socially conscious folk-rock lyrics. The trap set of rock drumming is there, but the hard *electric guitar* is absent. The effect is one of purposeful traditionality and pop contemporaneity in the same moment. Revolving around the songwriting, *guitar* and singing of Robby Romero and the traditional drumming of Benito Concha, Red Thunder is the product of their pride in Native American heritage and a self-proclaimed commitment to give their lives a "present tense in mainstream culture." While they tend to eschew both the synthesizer keyboards and declarative *rap* style found in so many new age and pop Indian bands, they are committed to using technology for broad reach—Red Thunder's video "Heartbeat" was seen on VH–1.

Romero and Concha divide their time between life on the road and life in Indian Country. Of Apache descent, Romero practices the traditional religion of his Lakota extended family in Wanbil, South Dakota. Concha, who is part of the emerging leadership of his Red Willow People, is active in the religious and cultural life of the Taos Pueblo.

Flute player Robby Romero has long participated in both worlds. He left Taos, where he had been living as a teenager, encouraged after meeting Dennis Hopper to move to Hollywood. There he grew to be friends with a circle of musicians that included Rick Danko of The Band, Gene

ties one also encounters groups playing country and western music, rhythm and **blues,** and even forms of **jazz** fusion.

During the period of American social unrest in the late 1960s, the figure of the "protest singer" with an acoustic guitar emerged, not only in Anglo society but in Indian Country as well. Paralleling Anglo counterparts, Indian protest singers created songs depicting a wide range of social injustices visited upon Indian peoples. Performers such as the Dakota singer Floyd Westerman and the Cree singer Buffy Sainte-Marie began to compose, give public concerts, and eventually record an Indian repertoire not unlike that of Pete Seeger or Peter, Paul, and Mary. But the issues they articulated resonated principally with Indian audiences, since it was they who were injured by the dominant society's despoilment of the environment, government interference in Indian affairs, poverty on the reservation and its attendant social ills such as alcoholism and suicide, and past injustices inflicted on Indian people.

In the early 1970s, Westerman's album *Custer Died for Your Sins*—its title a double-barbed missionary and military irony—became a best-seller among Indians overnight. The sarcasm characteristic of in-group Indian humor is also reflected in the names contemporary Indian ensembles choose for themselves. Expropriating Anglo stereotypes, an Onondaga blues band from upstate New York calls itself "White Boy and the Wagon Burners" (the keyboardist is non–Indian), and a rock group from Phoenix with members of several tribes—Navajo, Ojibway, Menominee, Hopi, and Blackfoot—is named "Wild Band of Indians."

Clark of the Byrds, guitarist Ed Jesse Davis (himself a Kiowa Indian), Paul Butterfield, and Bob Dylan. Johnny Rivers produced some of his music and urged Romero to write about his own culture.

After a decade plus of the ups and downs in the music scene, Robby returned to Indian Country in the early '80s to seek the help of the elders and to be restored. In his words he was "beaten, but not broken." In this period Romero reunited with a childhood mentor, activist Dennis Banks, who founded the American Indian Movement, and he traveled the country with the charismatic leader, meeting others who ultimately shaped both his politics and music. In 1988, Robby and Suzan Harjo, then executive director of the National Congress of American Indians, formed Native Children's Survival to promote environmental and human rights issues. The organization's policy circle includes Onondaga Faithkeeper Oren Lyons, Winnebago leader Reuben A. Snake, and Onondaga Clanmother Audrey Shenandoah.

A continuing focus on environmental issues from a spiritual perspective led to Romero and Concha's involvement in Earth Day 1990, when they performed on the Capitol steps in Washington, D.C., along with a variety of rock and popular musicians. This event cemented their will to form Red Thunder. In an act of pan–Indian musical evolution that moved a step past the powwow

synthesis, Robby and Benito brought friends, elders, and other musicians from the North and South American Indian world into their fold, periodically including flute player Mazatl Galindo.

"It's a traditional groove," asserts Romero. "The drums can't be bought; they have to be made. Materials such as deer and elk skin tied to cottonwood, aspen, and cedar as well as hooves and **gourds** are used to warm the sound." Benito Concha, whose drums provide a backdrop for many of Romero's songs, adds, "The drum is the heartbeat of Mother Earth." Concha also performs a number of traditional pieces from his Taos Pueblo background, saying, "This traditional set changes for practically every show." For his part, Romero continues to adapt folk, rock, country—even **reggae**—to his needs. "It's like glass beads and horses," he says. "They were not native to Indians either, they were something that was traded with us and we became expert in."

Suggested Listening

Red Thunder's music, including the CD *Red Thunder,* is available through Eagle Thunder Records. For information, contact Canyon Records and Indian Arts, 4143 N. 16th Street, Phoenix AZ 85016; 602/266–4823/4659.

Nick Spitzer

The tradition of protest song continues in Indian Country and is reflected in the repertoires of many contemporary performers. While the message is much the same as in the 1960s, its vehicle has changed; the lyrics of satirical songs performed on electric instruments in blues ensembles comment on political power ("Everyone is white at the White House") on constant harassment of Indians from law enforcement officials ("Please Mr. Officer, let me explain, I got to get to a **powwow** tonight"), or on the arbitrary mapping of Indian lands by government planners that results in social upheaval ("Someone drew a line"). The Bureau of Indian Affairs is an especially favorite target of Indian protest singers, who perceive its Native bureaucrats as entrenched, self-serving, and worthy of the appellation "the true Washington Redskins."

Many Native American performers come from very conservative backgrounds; some are even religious practitioners, maintaining and providing the music required for ancient ceremonies. But some chose to go beyond the traditional music they were brought up with, to adopt other styles, to take up non–Indian musical instruments, to create songs with English texts in a contemporary idiom, and to perform before non–Indian as well as Indian audiences. This musical direction probably began with the protest singers of the 1960s.

Some performers have chosen their musical direction as a means of "getting the Indian message across." This incentive is well expressed by the Oneida singer Joanne Shenandoah in a statement entitled "1991: The Year of the Native American," as she describes how she became a protest singer and active composer:

ever hopeful their work will finally be taken seriously; that they will be given the chance to show the world we are more than images from times past. . . . Their music is creative, lively, and rooted in their ancient traditions. It isn't all drums around a fire. Give us a listen and watch as we peel away your misconceptions. (Promotional flyer 1991)

Others present the music with which they were familiar since childhood. Although European origins may be discernible in what they do or play, it is Indian music, played by and for Indian people. Thus waila functions as a popular idiom for the O'odham on a Saturday night in Arizona, as does country and western or blues in bars or nightclubs on or near reservations in other parts of North America, or **marimba** or brass bands in small town festivals throughout Mexico and Central America. Because music is never static, traditions continue to evolve, and we can certainly expect further changes in the soundscape of Indian Country.

SUGGESTED LISTENING

Because of the many recordings available, readers should consult catalogues from Canyon Records and Indian House Records, where evolved forms of Indian music are usually listed as "contemporary." For information, contact Canyon Records, 4143 N. 16th St., Suite 1, Phoenix, AZ 85016; and Indian House Records, P.O. Box 472, Taos, NM 87571.

NOTE

1. From James S. Griffith's *Southern Arizona Folk Arts* (Tucson: University of Arizona Press, 1988), p. 72.

BIBLIOGRAPHY

Griffith, James S. (1988). *Southern Arizona Folk Arts*. Tucson: University of Arizona Press.

Medicine Fiddle. 1991. Michael Loukinen. 81 mins. Marquette, MI: Up North Films. Video.

Native Americans protesting in January 1974 in Kashena, Wisconsin. Protest rallies of various kinds have become common among Native Americans, and often they are accompanied by singers who write songs about the grievances that started the protest.
Photograph © Bettmann/ CORBIS.

As a Native person brought up surrounded by non–Indians I ached to find a way to communicate my history to my American friends; perhaps . . . a popular film, or a top 40 song about Indians which would give us the basis for discussing a different reality than the one they had come to believe was paramount in the world. . . . For a society extraordinarily dependent upon the media for its perceptions and beliefs . . . it is necessary to remove the stereotypes which have for so long kept [Indian people] down. Presently, there are many Indian performers on the road and in the studio. They are filming, dancing and recording,

REGGAE RHYTHMS SPEAK TO AN INSULAR TRIBE

Bruce Weber

Bruce Weber is a regional writer on music who specializes in the music of the Southwest. This essay originally appeared in the New York Times *on September 19, 1999.*

From the top of Second Mesa, one of three flat-topped mountains here that are the foundation of the remote Hopi reservation, the view of vast high desert, empty to the horizon, is the sort to inspire ruminations on man's existential solitude. And when the cloudburst came late on Friday afternoon, with prongs of lightning blanching the enormous sky, thunderclaps to wake the dead and hailstones dropping like bullets of the gods, it almost seemed as though the natural spirits that are worshiped by the Hopi were reminding the mortal of their mortality.

But maybe it was merely Mother Nature's sense of moment. The storm passed, a full rainbow appeared across the western face of the mesa, and at sunset the red rock glowed like an ember, warm and welcoming. And just about then, the visiting **reggae** bands on the Teva Spirit of Unity Festival tour took the stage at the Hopi Veterans Center, just below the lip of the mountain ledge, and some 2,000 reggae fans went crazy. For

six hours, the gymnasium-like auditorium throbbed with life, in spectacular isolation under a thrillingly bright half-moon.

The concert—featuring top-flight bands like Steel Pulse, Third World and Culture, and singers like Maxi Priest and Monifah—was, in the words of one Hopi, "the biggest nonreligious event of the year on the res." But beyond that, it was the high point of a cross-cultural tradition that has been building here for more than two decades.

Reggae—the Jamaican–born, Rastafarian music characterized by a lilting, insistent **syncopation** and a defiant live-and-let-live message—has long provided anthems of anti-oppression for third world peoples around the globe, and it is popular on Indian reservations throughout the western United States. (At the Friday concert, there were Apache, Navajo, Havasupai, Ute, and other tribe members, along with a fair number of Pahana—white people—who came from three surrounding states and up to 150 miles away.)

But it has found a special welcome—and an unlikely one—among the insular and secretive Hopi, a farming tribe with a complex and closely held set of spiritual beliefs whose history in this area goes back to the beginning of the millennium and who are known for guarding their ancient culture from outside influences. Children are initiated into the tribal religion as teen-agers; those who are never initiated are never fully in the know. And everyone is discouraged from being too forthright with outsiders.

"My uncles say that those who do not know anything will tell you everything, and those who know something will not tell you anything," said Lance Polingyouma, who grew up in Hopiland and now works as a "cultural interpreter" at the Hyatt Regency in Scottsdale, explaining the Hopi to tourists on their way to the reservation. "It's a pretty good axiom for Hopi life."

The reservation—eleven villages on three mesas in the midst of a vast desert highland the size of Rhode Island—holds between 8,000 and 10,000 people. Entirely surrounded by the much larger Navajo nation, with which the Hopi have a continuing land dispute, "the res" provides a life that Hopi describe as fiercely clannish, with all the pride and resentment that entails, and with many of the conflicts that go with wanting to get along in the world at large and still maintain a private way of life. The people are poor, but reject the lionization of money. Alcohol is forbidden on the reservation, but alcoholism is a problem. Homicide is rare; suicide is not.

Especially for a younger generation of Hopi, reggae is the music that speaks for them and the preciousness of their heritage. It isn't as though dreadlocks are rampant on the reservation—Hopi longhairs favor ponytails and the occasional braid—and it isn't hero worship. There are more Michael Jordan jerseys being worn here than Bob Marley T-shirts. But ask Hopi under fifty what draws tribe members to reggae (some older Hopi do view a devotion to the music, particularly because of its association with marijuana, as a diminution of traditional values),

and they use words like "relevance" and "identification."

"It's mostly the lyrics," said Jennifer Joseph, a painter and graphic artist who grew up in a traditional Hopi family on the reservation. "They sing about the same things we feel. They sing about oppression, and we feel that here. And they sing about peace and unity in the world, which is what our religion teaches us. But it's the beat, too. It has the same feel as our tribal drumming."

The relevance and identification go both ways.

At Friday's show, Joseph Hill, the lead singer for Culture, a Jamaican band that has been here half a dozen times in the last decade, paused between songs to declare: "Christopher Columbus discovered America—that's a damn lie." Resplendent in a white suit, his dreads flying, he was speaking indigenous North American to indigenous North American, exploited people to exploited people. The cheers were wild.

Indeed, one reason the Hopi accept reggae so easily, said Mr. Polingyouma, is that "they're not trying to take anything from us."

"They just come to bring us music," he said.

In an interview after he came offstage, Mr. Hill said of the Hopi: "This culture is quite specific and lonely in its own right. But they are not the only ones. The Rastafarians make two. The black man suffered the same as the Hopi, but until this day we have never brushed against each other. The only thing that has kept us apart is the journey between homes."

Mr. Hill, asked what made a Hopiland gig special, replied, "Boy, everything." And he spoke of the percussion in Hopi music "that could well blend in with reggae," and of the local landscape.

"If you are artistic, you can see tons of pictures in these rocks," he said. "That brings me home."

In keeping with both cultures, as the language on both sides indicates, the bond between them seems spiritual, and genuinely felt.

See glossary for definition of boldfaced terms

"There's something you just feel with this audience that you can't put into words," said Richard Daley, who plays with the band Third World, and was making his second trip to Hopiland. "They look at you with this glow, as if to say, 'Hey, we've been waiting for you.'"

In a way they have. People here generally credit Bob Marley, the Jamaican singer who died in 1981, and his band, the Wailers, with instilling a love of reggae among the Hopi in the early 1970s. Those were the days of reggae's peak popularity around the country, if not the globe. They were radio days on the reservation, where there was little live music but for the occasional country dance, and where television was not yet ubiquitous.

"I remember I first heard it through my cousins, and I just got the groove," said Burt Poley, thirty-six, who is now a woodcarver whose specialty is the kachina dolls that represent Hopi spirits. In the early 1980s, he was one of a group of particularly intense devotees that ended up being the first importers of reggae to the res. For years they had been so hungry for reggae that they took to traveling to Phoenix for concerts by local bands, a four-hour drive each way.

"We'd drive down late in the afternoon, go to the show, get back at 4:00 A.M. and go to work that morning," said Gerry Gordon, a white man who lived and taught elementary school on the reservation for two decades until he began working in a Phoenix school this year. It was partly, if not entirely, out of sheer exhaustion, he said, that they conceived the idea that would bloom into a tradition.

"Finally we just thought, 'You know? Maybe it would be easier to bring the reggae to us.'" He and his friends, a group of half a dozen, all of whom were Hopi, arranged for a Phoenix band to play in an elementary school gym on the reservation in the fall of 1983. Two hundred people showed up, "and for most of them it was the first time they'd ever heard live reggae," Mr. Gordon said.

It was a couple of months later that he got a call from a record company in Washington that had somehow got wind of the Hopi interest in reggae, and which offered to send some of its artists out for a show. In 1984, the first Jamaicans to play the reservation, Freddie McGregor, and a band called Michigan & Smiley, arrived. Since then, there have been some thirty-five shows there, presented under a general billing in mock–Jamaican patois: "Reggae Inna Hopiland." Most of the shows have been produced by Mr. Gordon and Mr. Poley's group, Culture Connection. Along with a promoter in Phoenix, Artist Resources, they arranged for the Spirit of Unity tour to stop in Hopiland between dates in Santa Fe and Phoenix.

The bands were eager. To make the stop in Hopiland, they agreed to play for about a fourth of their usual rate and did without a lot of the perks—dressing rooms and specially ordered food. "They're basically doing the Hopiland show for free," said Terri Larsen, the president of Artist Resources, who also produced the show in Phoenix tonight. "Basically they're just charging us for sound and light and transportation. It's costing us $12,500." A third of the profits will go toward building a playground in the Hopi village of Polacca.

The Hopi have yet to produce much reggae music of their own, though one young singer and songwriter, Casper Lomayesva, has produced a first CD and has been performing in Arizona and in neighboring Western states. Mr. Lomayesva, thirty, grew up largely on the reservation, listening to reggae on the radio and helping his grandfather tend the cornfields.

The CD is on his own label, Third Mesa Records, which is based in Phoenix, where he now lives; it is called "Original Landlord," a reference to the Hopi claim on its land. (The Hopi have lost land over the centuries, but unlike many Native American tribes, they have never been relocated by the federal government.) The title song, a kind of melodic rap, sad and angry, with local subject matter but some locutions

borrowed from the Caribbean, goes this way, in part:

> *Our Hopi reservation no stretch far and wide*
>
> *It gives us sense of purpose, me say sense of pride*
>
> *Religion and our culture help keep us strong*
>
> *I'm proud of these people, that's why me sing this song*
>
> *Just check the history books, it is not what I say*
>
> *The government, the policies they take my land away*

Standing in the family field, fingering the cornstalks, impossibly healthy in the sandy soil, he pointed to a distant tree.

"I've written songs right in this field," he said. "I wrote 'Original Landlord' sitting under that tree." So are Hopi who love reggae made. Reggae musicians who love Hopiland are made with a visit.

"It's an ancient place, a very spiritual place, that's how it looks to me," said David Kirton, a singer from Barbados, shortly after he arrived in Hopiland for the first time. "I'm one for picking up vibes. And the vibes are very good, too."

RECENT BIBLIOGRAPHY/ DISCOGRAPHY/VIDEOGRAPHY

Compiled by Jennifer C. Post

Amiotte, Arthur. (1987). "The Lakota Sun Dance: Historical and Contemporary Perspectives." In *Sioux Indian Religion: Tradition and Innovation,* ed. R. J. DeMallie and D. R. Parks. Norman: University of Oklahoma Press.

Bahr, Donald. (1987). "Pima Heaven Songs." In *Recovering the Word: Essays on Native American Literature,* ed. Brian Swann and Arnold Krupat. Berkeley: University of California Press.

Bahr, Donald; Paul, Lloyd; and Joseph, Vincent. (1997). *Ants and Orioles: Showing the Art of Pima Poetry.* Salt Lake City: University of Utah Press.

Barker, James H. (1990). "'There's my ancestors singing to me.'" *Journal of Alaska Native Arts.*

Brisbin, James S. (1986). "The Poetry of Indians" [1878]. In *Native American Folklore in Nineteenth-Century Periodicals,* ed. W. M. Clements. Athens, OH: Swallow Press; Ohio University Press.

Burch, Sharon, et al. (1994). "New Directions in Native American Music." *NARAS Journal* 5 (1):81–93.

Burton, Bryan. (1993). *Moving Within the Circle: Contemporary Native American Music and Dance.* Danbury, CT: World Music Press.

Callahan, Alice Anne. (1990). *The Osage Ceremonial Dance i'n-lon-schka.* Vol. 201 of "The Civilization of the American Indian" series. Norman: University of Oklahoma Press.

Clements, William M. (1996). *Native American Verbal Art: Texts and Contexts.* Tucson: University of Arizona Press.

Contreras, Don. (1996). *We Dance Because We Can: People of the Powwow.* Marietta, GA: Longstreet Press.

Cronk, Michael Sam. (1988). "Writing While They're Singing: A Conversation about Longhouse Social Dance Songs." *New York Folklore* 14(3–4):49–60.

———, comp. (1990). *Sound of the Drum.* Brantford: Woodland Cultural Centre.

Crowell, Aron. (1992). "Postcontact Koniag Ceremonialism on Kodiak Island and the Alaska Peninsula: Evidence from the Fisher Collection." *Arctic Anthropology* 29(1):18–37.

Dailey, Truman W., and Hopkins, Jill D. (1993). "Native American Church Songs of the Otoe-Missouria and Ioway." *Proceedings of the 1992 Mid-Atlantic Linguistics Conference and Conference on Siouan/Caddoan Languages,* ed. E. Smith and F. Zephir. Columbia: University of Missouri.

Daniels, Edwin. (1998). *Ghost Dancing: Sacred Medicine and the Art of J. D. Challenger.* New York: Stewart, Tabori & Chang.

De Cesare, Ruth, ed. (1988). *Myth, Music and Dance of the American Indian.* Van Nuys, CA: Alfred Publishing.

Densmore, Frances. (1990). *Teton Sioux Music and Culture.* Lincoln: University of Nebraska Press. Originally published as *Teton Sioux Music.*

Deyhle, Donna. (1998). "From Break Dancing to Heavy Metal: Navajo Youth, Resistance, and Identity." *Youth and Society* 30(1):3–31.

Diamond, Beverley M.; Cronk, Sam; and von Rosen, Franziska. (1994). *Visions of Sound: Musical Instruments of First Nations Communities in Northeastern America.* Chicago Studies in Ethnomusicology. Chicago: University of Chicago Press.

Ellis, Clyde. (1990). "'Truly Dancing Their Own Way': The Modern Revival and Diffusion of the Gourd Dance." *American Indian Quarterly* 14(1): 19–33.

Enrico, John James, and Stuart, Wendy Bross. (1996). *Northern Haida Songs.* Lincoln: University of Nebraska Press.

Evers, Larry, and Molina, Felipe S. (1989). *Wo'i bwikam: Coyote Songs from the Yaqui Bow Leaders' Society.* Tucson, AZ: Chax Press.

———. (1987). *Yaqui Deer Songs, maso bwikam: A Native American Poetry.* Tucson: University of Arizona Press.

Faris, James C. (1990). *The Nightway: A History and a History of Documentation of a Navajo Ceremonial.* Albuquerque: University of New Mexico Press.

Farnell, Brenda. (1991). "Nak'ota mak'oc'e: An American Indian Storytelling Experience." *Yearbook for Traditional Music* 23:79–99.

Fletcher, Alice C. (1970). *Indian Games and Dances with Native Songs: Arranged from American Indian Ceremonials and Sports.* New York: AMS.

———. (1996). *The Hako: Song, Pipe, and Unity in a Pawnee Calumet Ceremony.* Reprint. Lincoln: University of Nebraska Press.

Frisbee, Charlotte J. (1987). *Navajo Medicine Bundles or Jish: Acquisition, Transmission and Disposition in the Past and Present.* Albuquerque: University of New Mexico Press.

Gelo, Daniel J. (1999). "Powwow Patter: Indian Emcee Discourse on Power and Identity." *Journal of American Folklore* 112 (443):40–57.

Gidley, Mick. (1987). "R. B. Townshend's 1903 Snake Dance Photographs in Focus." *European Review of Native American Studies* 1(2):9–14.

———. (1987). "'The Vanishing Race' in Sight and Sound: Edward S. Curtis's Musicale of North American Indian Life." *Prospects* 12:58–87.

Giglio, Virginia. (1994). *Southern Cheyenne Women's Songs.* Norman: University of Oklahoma Press.

Gombert, Greg, ed. (1997). *Native American Music Directory,* 2nd ed. Summertown, TN: Book Pub. Co. Revised ed. of *A Guide to Native American Music Recordings,* 1994.

Gooding, Erik D. (1998). "Songs of the People: Plains Indian Music and Recordings, 1968–1996." *Notes* 55 (1):37–67.

Griffith, James S. (1997). "*Waila*: The Social Dance Music of the Tohono O'odham." In *Musics of Multicultural America: A Study of Twelve Musical Communities,* ed. K. Lornell and A. K. Rasmussen. New York: Schirmer Books.

Havnen-Finley, Jan. (1994). *The Hoop of Peace.* Happy Camp, CA: Naturegraph Publishers.

Heth, Charlotte, ed. (1992). *Native American Dance: Ceremonies and Social Traditions.* Washington, D.C.: National Museum of the American Indian, Smithsonian Institution.

Hilliker, Rebecca. (1987). "Alaska's Lost Heritage: The Unprecedented Flowering of Drama, Dance and Song in the Nineteenth-Century Potlach of the Northwest Coast Indians." *Journal of Popular Culture* 21(4):63–76.

Hittman, Michael. (1992). "The 1890 Ghost Dance in Nevada." *American Indian Culture and Research Journal* 16(4):123–66.

———. (1998). *Wovoka and the Ghost Dance.* Expanded ed. Lincoln: University of Nebraska Press.

Hofmann, Johanna. (1997). "Le tambour du pow-wow nord américain, battement du coeur d'un peuple et rythme de sa spiritualité." *Cahiers de musiques traditionnelles* 10:249–72.

Johnston, Thomas F. (1987). "Athabascan Music and Dance in Alaska: A Survey." *Inter-Nord* 18:77–85.

———. (1988). "Community History and Environment as Wellspring of Inupiat Eskimo Song Texts." *Anthropos* 83(1–3):161–71.

———. (1988). "Drum Rhythms of the Alaskan Eskimo." *Anthropologie* 26(1):75–2.

———. (1988). "Tlingit Dance, Music, and Society." *Acta ethnographica* 34(1–4):283–324.

———. (1989). *Koliganek Dance Songs.* Anchorage: University of Alaska.

——. (1989). "Song Categories and Musical Style of the Yupik Eskimo." *Anthropos* 84(4–6):423–31.

——. (1990). "The Northwest Coast Tlingit Indian Musical Potlatch." *South African Journal of Musicology* 10:77–99.

——. (1992). ""The Socio-Mythic Contexts of Music in Tlingit Shamanism and Potlatch Ceremonials." *The World of Music* 34(2):43–71.

Jonaitis, Aldona, ed. (1991). *Chiefly Feasts: The Enduring Kwakiutl Potlatch.* Seattle: University of Washington Press; New York: American Museum of Natural History.

Jones, Judy, and Olsen, Loran. (1996). "Women and Music in the Plateau." In *A Song to the Creator: Traditional Arts of Native American Women of the Plateau,* ed. L. A. Ackerman. Norman: University of Oklahoma Press.

Kan, Sergei. (1990). "The Sacred and the Secular: Tlingit Potlatch Songs Outside the Potlatch." *American Indian Quarterly* 14(4): 55–66.

Keeling, Richard, ed. (1989). *Women in North American Indian Music: Six Essays.* Special Series, No. 6. Bloomington, IN: Society for Ethnomusicology.

——. (1997). *North American Indian Music: A Guide to Published Sources and Selected Recordings.* Vol. 5 of Garland Library of Music Ethnology; Vol. 1440 of Garland Reference Library of the Humanities. New York: Garland.

Kozak, David L., and Lopez, David I. (1999). *Devil Sickness and Devil Songs: Tohono O'odham Poetics.* Smithsonian Series in Ethnographic Inquiry. Washington, D.C.: Smithsonian Institution.

Kurath, Gertrude P. (1998). "Menomini Indian Dance Songs in a Changing Culture" [1959]. In *Wisconsin Folklore,* ed. J. P. Leary. Madison: University of Wisconsin.

Lassiter, Luke E. (1997). "Charlie Brown: Not Just Another Essay on the Gourd Dance." *American Indian Culture and Research Journal* 25(4):75–103.

——. (1998). *The Power of Kiowa Song: A Collaborative Ethnography.* Tucson: University of Arizona Press.

——. (1999). ""Southwestern Oklahoma, the Gourd Dance, and Charlie Brown." In *Contemporary Native American Cultural Issues,* ed. D. Champagne. Walnut Creek, CA: AltaMira Press.

Lassiter, Luke E., and Ellis, Clyde. (1998). "Applying Communitas to Kiowa Powwows." *American Indian Quarterly* 22(4):485–91.

Lee, Dayna Bowker. (1995). *Remaining Ourselves: Music and Tribal Memory—Traditional Music in Contemporary Communities.* Oklahoma City: State Arts Council of Oklahoma.

Lee, Dorothy Sara. (1979). *Native North American Music and Oral Data: A Catalogue of Sound Recordings, 1893–1976.* Holdings of the Archives of Traditional Music. Bloomington: Indiana University.

——. (1992). "Historic Recordings and Contemporary Native American Culture: Returning Materials to Native American Communities." In *Music and Dance of Aboriginal Australia and the South Pacific,* ed. A. M. Moyle. Sydney: University of Sydney.

Leighton, Alexander H., and Leighton, Dorothea C., comps. (1992). *Lucky, the Navajo Singer.* Albuquerque: University of New Mexico Press.

Levine, Victoria Lindsay. (1997). ""Music, Myth, and Medicine in the Choctaw Indian Ballgame." In *Enchanting Powers: Music in the World's Religions,* ed. L. E. Sullivan. Cambridge, MA: Harvard University Center for the Study of World Religions.

——. (1997). "Text and Context in Choctaw Social Dance Songs." *Florida Anthropologist* 50 (4):183–87.

Levine, Victoria Lindsay, and Chace, Amanda. (1999). *Music in the Ruben Cobos Collection of Spanish New Mexican Folklore: A Descriptive Catalogue.* Colorado Springs: Hulbert Center Press of the Colorado College.

Lewis, Thomas H. (1990). *The Medicine Men: Oglala Sioux Ceremony and Healing.* Studies in the Anthropology of North American Indians. Lincoln: University of Nebraska.

Lincoln, Bruce. (1994). "A Lakota Sun Dance and the Problematics of Sociocosmic Reunion." *History of Religions* 34 (1):1–14.

List, George. (1993). *Stability and Variation in the Hopi Song.* Vol. 204 of Memoirs of the American Philosophical Society. Philadelphia: American Philosophical Society.

——. (1997). "Hopi Kachina Dance Songs: Concepts and Context." *Ethnomusicology* 41 (3):413–32.

Little Coyote, Bertha. (1997). *Leaving Everything Behind: The Songs and Memories of a Cheyenne Woman.* Norman: University of Oklahoma.

Mails, Thomas E. (1998). *Sundancing: The Great Sioux Piercing Ritual.* Tulsa: Council Oak Books. Originally published as *Sundancing at Rosebud and Pine Ridge,* 1978.

Masco, Joseph. (1995). "'It Is a Strict Law That Bids Us Dance': Cosmologies, Colonialism, Death, and Ritual Authority in the Kwakwaka'wakw Potlach." *Comparative Studies in Society and History* 37 (1):41–75.

Matthews, Washington. (1995). *The Night Chant: A Navaho Ceremony.* Reprint. Salt Lake City: University of Utah Press. Originally published in 1902.

———. (1997). *The Mountain Chant: A Navajo Ceremony.* Reprint. Salt Lake City: University of Utah. Originally published in 1887.

McAllester, David. (1995). "Two Navajo Airplane Songs." In *The Essence of Singing and the Substance of Song,* ed. L. Barwick, et al. Sydney: University of Sydney.

Merriam, Alan. (1989?). *Music of the Flathead Indians.* N.p.

Mishler, Craig. (1993). *The Crooked Stovepipe: Athapaskan Fiddle Music and Square Dancing in Northeast Alaska and Northwest Canada.* Music in American Life. Urbana: University of Illinois Press.

Morrison, Ann. (1996). "Christians, Kyries, and *kci niwesq:* Passamaquoddy Catholic Songs in Historical Perspective." *European Review of Native American Studies* 10(2):15–21.

Mount, Guy, ed. (1993). *Serrano Songs and Stories.* Cottonwood, CA: Sweetlight.

Nettl, Bruno. (1989). *Blackfoot Musical Thought: Comparative Perspectives.* Kent, OH: Kent State University Press.

———. "Music of European Origin in Blackfoot Indian Musical Culture." In *Tradition and Its Future in Music,* ed. Tokumaru Yosihiko.Tokyo: Mita Press.

Olson, Ted. (1995). "Walker Calhoun: Cherokee Song and Dance Man." *Appalachian Journal* 23 (1):70–77.

Osterreich, Shelley Anne, comp. (1991). *The American Indian Ghost Dance, 1870 and 1890: An Annotated Bibliography.* Bibliographies and Indexes in American History, No. 19. New York: Greenwood Press.

Payne, Richard W. (1989). "Indian Flutes of the Southwest." *Journal of the American Musical Instrument Society* 15:5–31.

Powers, William K. (1986). *Sacred Language: The Nature of Supernatural Discourse in Lakota.* Norman and London: University of Oklahoma Press.

———. (1987). *Beyond the Vision: Essays on American Indian Culture.* Norman and London: University of Oklahoma Press.

———. (1990). *War Dance: Plains Indian Musical Performance.* Tucson: University of Arizona Press.

Rahkonen, Carl. (1998). "Special Bibliography: Natalie Curtis (1875–1921)." *Ethnomusicology* 42 (3):511–22.

Rosman, Abraham, and Rubel, Paula G. (1990). "Structural Patterning in Kwakiutl Art and Ritual." *Man* 25 (4):620–40.

Schlottner, Michael. (1997). "'World Music' and Native Americans: How Ethnic Are Indians?" *European Review of Native American Studies* 11 (2):43–46.

Smyth, William, ed. (1989). *Songs of Indian Territory: Native American Music Traditions of Oklahoma.* Oklahoma City: Center of the American Indian.

Smyth, Willie, and Ryan, Esmé. (1999). *Spirit of the First People: Native American Music Traditions of Washington State.* Seattle: University of Washington Press. Includes one sound disc.

Speck, Frank, et al. (1993). *Cherokee Dance and Drama.* Norman: University of Oklahoma Press.

Stevenson, Robert M. (1994). "American Tribal Musics at Contact." *Inter-American Music Review* 14 (1):1–56.

Swann, Brian, ed. (1992). *On the Translation of Native American Literatures.* Washington, D.C.: Smithsonian Institution.

———. (1993). *Song of the Sky: Versions of Native American Song-Poems.* Amherst: University of Massachusetts Press.

Toelken, Barry. (1991). "Ethnic Selection and Intensification in the Native American Powwow." In *Creative Ethnicity: Symbols and Strategies of Contemporary Ethnic Life,* ed. S. Stern and J. A. Cicala. Logan: Utah State University Press.

———. (1996). "From Entertainment to Realization in Navajo Fieldwork." In *The World Observed,* 1–17, ed. B. Jackson and E. D. Ives. N.p.

Turner, Edith. (1990). "The Yaqui Deer Dance at Pascua Pueblo, Arizona." In *By Means of Performance: Intercultural Studies of Theatre and Ritual,* ed. R. Schechner and W. Appel. Cambridge: Cambridge University Press.

Underhill, Ruth Murray. (1993). *Singing for Power: The Song Magic of the Papago Indians of Southern Arizona.* Reprint. Tucson: University of Arizona Press.

Valencia, Anselmo; Valencia, Heather; and Spicer, Rosamond B. (1990). "A Yaqui Point of View: On Yaqui Ceremonies and Anthropologists." In *By Means of Performance: Intercultural Studies of Theatre and Ritual,* ed. R. Schechner and W. Appel. Cambridge: Cambridge University Press.

Vander, Judith. (1988). *Songprints: The Musical Experience of Five Shoshone Women.* Music in American Life. Urbana: University of Illinois Press.

———. (1997). *Shoshone Ghost Dance Religion: Poetry Songs and Great Basin Context.* Music in American Life. Urbana: University of Illinois Press.

Vennum, Thomas. (1982). *The Ojibwa Dance Drum: Its History and Construction.* Vol. 2 of Smithsonian Contributions to Anthropology. Washington, D.C.: Smithsonian Institution.

———. (1989). "Ojibway Drum Decor: Sources and Variations of Ritual Design." In *Circles of Tradition: Folk Arts in Minnesota.* St. Paul: Minnesota Historical Society.

———. (1994). "The Songs of the Great Lakes 'Big Drum' Societies: A Study in Repertoire Diffusion Among American Indian Tribes." In *Themes and Variations: Writings on Music in Honor of Rulan Chao Pian,* ed. B. Yung and J. S. C. Lam. Cambridge: Department of Music, Harvard University.

Wild, Regne. (1995). "The Ethnomusicologist as Cultural Broker: Natalie Curtis and Indian Songs." *European Review of Native American Studies* 9 (1):1–4.

———. (1996). *Lieder der nordamerikanischen Indianer als kompositorische Vorlagen: in der Zeit von 1890 bis zum Ersten Weltkrieg.* Bd. 1 of Berliner Musik Studien. Cologne: Studio.

Williams, Maria P. (1995). "The Wolf and Man/Bear: Public and Personal Symbols in a Tlingit Drum." *Pacific Review of Ethnomusicology* 7:79–92.

Witmer, Robert. (n.d.) "Stability in Blackfoot Songs, 1909–1968." In *Ethnomusicology and Modern Music History,* ed. S. Blum, P. V. Bohlman, and D. M. Neuman. Urbana: University of Chicago Press.

Woodside, Jane Harris. (1995). "'Everybody Needs Identity': Reviving Cherokee Dance." In *Communities in Motion,* ed. S. E. Spalding and J. H. Woodside. Westport, CT: Greenwood Press.

———. (1995). "'I Want to Show These Young People What We Used to Do': A Cherokee Revivalist Remembers—An Interview with Walker Calhoun." In *Communities in Motion,* ed. S. E. Spalding and J. H. Woodside. Westport, CT: Greenwood Press.

RECORDINGS

American Pow-Wow. 1993. Sound of America Records SOAR–142. Performed by the Cathedral Lakes Singers.

American Warriors: Songs for Indian Veterans. 1997. Ryko RCD 10370.

Amérique du nord: Takini. 1994. Le chant du monde CDM CMT 2741000. Lakota Sioux.

Arawak Mountain Singers: Feel the Thunder. Sound of America Records SOAR 167–CD. New York State.

Canyon Records 45th Anniversary Vintage Collection. 1998. Canyon CR–6000. Vol. 1: *Natay: Navajo Singer* (CR–6160); Vol. 2: *Navajo: Traditional Navajo Songs* (CR–6064); Vol. 3: *Hopi Butterfly* (CR–6072); Vol. 4: *Pueblo Songs from San Juan* (CR–6065); Vol. 5: *Apache: Traditional Apache Songs* (CR–6053); Vol. 6: *Papago: Traditional Papago Songs* (CR–6084); Vol. 7: *Old Time O'odham Fiddle Music* (CR–8082); Vol. 8: *Yaqui Ritual and Festive Music* (CR–6140); Vol. 9: *Native Music of Northwest Mexico* (CR–8001); Vol. 10: *Utes: Traditional Ute Songs* (CR–6113); Vol. 11: *Traditional Music from Warm Springs* (CR–6123); Vol. 12: *Old Peyote Songs* (CR–6054); Vol. 13: *Pow-Wow!: Southern Style Pow-Wow Songs* (CR–6088); Vol. 14: *Kiowa: Traditional Kiowa Songs* (CR–6145); Vol. 15: *William Horncloud: Traditional Lakota songs* (CR–6150); Vol. 16: *Porcupine Singers: Traditional Lakota Songs* (CR–8007); Vol. 17: *Young Grey Horse Society: Songs of the Blackfeet* (CR–6164); Vol. 18: *The Drums of Poundmaker: Cree Pow–Wow Songs* (CR–6157); Vol. 19: *Drum Dance Music of the Dogrib* (CR–6260); Vol. 20: *Traditional Voices: Anthology of Music from Twenty Tribes* (CR–7053).

Creation's Journey: Native American Music. 1994. Smithsonian Folkways CD SF 40410.

Dancing Buffalo: Cornel Pewewardy and the Alliance West Singers. 1994. Music of the World CDT MOW 130. Kiowa and Comanche.

Heartbeat: Voices of First Nations Women. 1995. Smithsonian Folkways SF CD 40415.

Heartbeat 2: More Voices of First Nations Women. 1998. Smithsonian Folkways SF CD 40455.

Honor the Earth Powwow: Songs of the Great Lakes Indians. 1990. Ryko RCD 10199.

Music of New Mexico: Native American Traditions. 1992. Smithsonian Folkways CD SF 40408s.

Navajo Songs. 1992. Smithsonian Folkways CD SF 40403.

Navajo Songs from Canyon de Chelly. 1990. New World Records 80406–2. Arizona.

Oku shareh: Turtle Dance Songs of San Juan Pueblo. 1993. New World Records 80301–2.

Plains Chippewa/Métis Music from Turtle Mountain. 1992. Smithsonian Folkways CD SF 40411.

Songs and Dances of the Eastern Indians from Medicine Spring and Allegany. 1985. New World Records 80337–2.

Songs of My People. 1995. Peter Garcia. Music of the World CDT–133. Pueblo.

Songs of the Navajo: Kee Kinlechene and Yátzá. 1994. JVC VICG–5334.

When the Earth Was Like New: Western Apache Songs and Stories. 1994. World Music Press WMP 015 CD.

Wood That Sings: Indian Fiddle Music of the Americas. 1997. Smithsonian Folkways SF 40472.

VIDEOS

The American Indian Dance Theatre: Finding the Circle. 1989. 60 min. New York: WNET.

The American Indian Dance Theatre, Volume 2: Dances for the New Generations. 1996. 60 min. New York: WNET; distributed by Canyon Records and Indian Arts.

Ceremonial Music of San Juan Pueblo: Butterfly and Turtle Dances. 1978. Charlotte Heth. 57 min.

Ceremonial Music of San Juan Pueblo: Eagle, Buffalo, Evening, Cloud, and Deer Dance. 1978. Charlotte Heth. 57 min.

Dancing to Give Thanks. 1988. 30 min. Lincoln, NE: Native American Public Telecommunications. Omaha Indian annual powwow.

Dream Dances of the Kashia Pomo: The Bole-Maru Religion Women's Dances. 198?. W. R. Heick. 30 min. Berkeley, CA : University of California Extension Media Center.

The Drummaker. 1990. Mike Herter and Thomas Vennum, Jr. 27 min. Smithsonian Folklife Studies, no. 2A. University Park, PA: Media Sales, Pennsylvania State University. Northern Wisconsin.

Indian Dances of the Zuni Pueblo. 1996. Fernando Cellicion and Millard Clark. 30 min. Moore, OK: Indian Sounds.

Into the Circle: An Introduction to Native American Powwows. 1992. Scott Swearingen. 58 min. Tulsa, OK: Full Circle Communications.

JVC Smithsonian Folkways Video Anthology of Music and Dance of the Americas I: North American Indians. 1988. 55 min. Tokyo: JVC, Victor Company of Japan.

Kashia Men's Dances: Southwestern Pomo Indians. 1990. W. R. Heick. 39 min. Berkeley: University of California Extension Media Center.

Medicine Fiddle. 1991. Michael Loukinen, producer/director. 81 min. Marquette, MI: Up North Films. Métis fiddling and dancing of northern Michigan and Canada.

Music in the World of the Yurok and Tolowa Indians. 1978. Charlotte Heth. 56 min. Los Angeles: Office of Instructional Development, University of California; Advanced Video.

Music of the Creek and Cherokee Indians in Religion and Government. 1978. Charlotte Heth. 60 min. Hollywood, CA: Ampac Video.

Music of the Sacred Fire: The Stomp Dance of the Oklahoma Cherokee. 1978. Charlotte Heth. 56 min. Hollywood, CA: Ampac Video.

Naamikaaged: Dancer for the People. 1994. Thomas Vennum. 25 min. Washington, D.C.: Smithsonian Folkways Recordings.

Navajo Traditional Music: Squaw Dance and Ribbon Dance. 1978. Sam Yazzie and Charlotte Heth. 60 min. Hollywood, CA: Ampac Video.

Pepper's Powwow. 1995. Sandra Osawa. 57 min. Seattle: Upstream Productions. Jim Pepper, a contemporary Native American **jazz** musician.

Rockin' Warriors: A Film. 1998. Andy Bausch. 56 min. Luxembourg: Lynx Productions. Native American musicians in Arizona, New Mexico, Germany, and Luxembourg.

Sam Yazzie: Navaho Singer. 1989. Charlotte Heth. 61 min. Burbank, CA: Office of Instructional Development, University of California.

Singing Our Stories. 1998. Annie Frasiér Henry. 49 min. Montreal, Quebec: National Film Board of Canada. Women in Native American music.

Song Journey. 1994. Jeanine Moret and Arlene Bowman. 57 min. New York: Women Make Movies. Women in the powwow circuit in the United States and Canada in 1993.

The Sunrise Dance. 1994. Gianfranco Norelli. 55 min. New York: Filmmakers Library. Documentary about the Apache puberty rite of a young girl.

Teaching the Music of the American Indian. 1990. Michael Blakeslee. 37 min. Reston, Va.: Music Educators National Conference.

Traditional Music of Native Northwest California: Brush Dance, Feather Dance and Gambling Songs. 1978. Charlotte Heth.. 61 min. Hollywood, CA: Ampac Video.

Winnebago Women: Songs and Stories. 1992. Jocelyn Riley. Madison, WI: Her Own Words Productions.

Wisconsin Powwow. 1996. Thomas Vennum. 42 min. Washington, D.C.: Smithsonian Folkways Recordings.

GLOSSARY

A

a cappella Unaccompanied vocal music; singing without instrumental accompaniment.

Accordion A free-reed, bellows-driven instrument developed in the early nineteenth century. There are various forms of accordions; most common are the button accordion (with a keyboard made up of one or more rows of buttons) and the piano accordion (with a piano-style keyboard). *See also* Diatonic accordion.

Alabado A free-form lament of Arab-Spanish origin that is heard in Texas-Mexican communities of the southwestern United States.

Angular leap An abrupt jump between two intervals in a melody.

Antiphony See Call-and-response.

Ascending contour or **melody** A melody that generally rises in pitch over its duration.

Autoharp A musical instrument invented by C. F. Zimmerman in the late nineteenth century. It is tuned chromatically, covering about three and a half octaves. The strings are stopped by the player pressing down on "chord bars;" these bars automatically block all the notes except those found in a specific chord. Sold through mail-order catalogs and by traveling salesmen/teachers in the early twentieth century, the

autoharp became a popular instrument for accompanying songs and ballads.

B

Bagpipe A common musical instrument found throughout Europe. There are many varieties made in different sizes with different features. The basic bagpipe consists of a large bag (sometimes made of the body of a goat or another animal) that is pumped to provide the air supply for one or more pipes. In the top of each pipe is a single reed that produces the sounds. The chanter is a long pipe with holes in it that produces melody notes; the drone pipes are shorter and play only a single, continuous note. *See also* Uillean (bag)pipes.

Bajo sexto A large-bodied, guitar-like instrument popularized in Mexico. It has a much deeper body than a standard guitar.

Ballad A song that tells a story. Ballads are usually long, and their main subjects are love and death.

Banjo (five-string) An African American–derived instrument featuring a skin or plastic head stretched across a wooden or metal hoop, with four long strings and one short "drone" string. The banjo was originally used in African American dance music and in minstrel music and is now commonly played in old-time and bluegrass music. *See also* Tenor banjo.

Barbershop harmony Traditional four-part harmonies developed by so-called barbershop quartets during the late nineteenth and early twentieth centuries. Barbershop quartets often featured an independent, and active, bass part. This style of singing was carried forward by gospel quartets and other popular harmony groups.

Barrel drum A drum with a long body that is slightly flared at its center, like the shape of a barrel. These drums can have either one or two heads and may vary in size from small to very large. The Japanese *taiko* and Puerto Rican *barile* are examples of barrel drums.

Bass An acoustic or electric four-string instrument used to play the bass harmony accompaniment to a melody.

Bass drum A large cylindrical drum of indefinite pitch with heads on both sides.

Batá drums Sacred drums (imported from Africa) that are played as part of Afro-Caribbean religious ceremonies. They have an hourglass shape with a head stretched across each end of the body. The drums are held vertically across the player's body, and each end is struck with one hand. Batá rhythms have been carried over into secular/popular musical styles from this region.

Bebop A style of jazz involving new harmonic concepts, rapid tempos, and small ensembles. It was developed in the 1940s and is especially associated with saxophone player Charlie Parker.

Big band The primary ensemble of the swing era of American jazz and popular music of the 1930s and 1940s. Big band music is scored for multiple trumpets, trombones, clarinets, and saxophones (melody group), while small groups usually employ, at most, one of each instrument. Usually the sections of the band perform alternately, in call-and-response style. In both big and small bands, the rhythm section is piano and/or guitar, drum kit, and double bass.

Big circle dance An Appalachian dance performed in a large circle. Couples pair off in sets of two to perform figures similar to those in square dances, then fall back into a big circle to perform larger group figures.

Blue note A note that is slightly flattened to give it a "bluesy" effect; often the third or seventh degree of the scale.

Bluegrass A style of music invented by mandolinist Bill Monroe based on old-time string band music, blues, and Western swing. Monroe put together a band that included the rhythms of popular music, the bluesy inflected vocals of African American music, and the tight harmonies of gospel and old-time church singing. The typical bluegrass band is modeled on Monroe's original group that featured mandolin, guitar, banjo, fiddle, and bass.

Blues A traditional African American musical genre. It is in 4/4 time, with a melody characterized by lowered third and seventh (blue notes), and has developed into a stereotyped, twelve-measure harmonic pattern. The term has also been used to describe any song that expresses "blue" or sad feelings.

Bodhrán *See* Frame drum.

Bolero Medium-tempoed dance in triple time, with intricate steps, popular in Spain, Latin America, and the Caribbean.

Bongo drums/Bongos Two small, shallow, single-headed drums that are played with the palms and fingers of the hands. Popular in Latin-Caribbean musical cultures.

Bottleneck A style of playing the guitar in which the guitarist places a glass bottleneck around a finger on the noting hand and slides it over the strings of the instrument, creating a sliding or whining sound. This is a common technique among blues guitarists, who use either a glass bottleneck or a metal bar (called a slide).

Brass band A band made up entirely of brass and wind instruments, popularized by bandleader/composer John Philip Sousa at the turn of the twentieth century.

Break dancing/Breaking A solo, urban dance style featuring elaborate athletic moves, including spinning, moonwalking, flipping, and popping (isolating certain parts of the body to mimic robot-like movement).

Broadsheet/Broadside ballad A single sheet of paper on which the text (and sometimes music) of a song was printed. Beginning in the seventeenth century, broadsides were popular as a means of spreading new and traditional songs.

Buck dancing *See* Clogging.

Button accordion *See* Accordion.

C

Cajun music A style of music that originated among natives of southeastern Louisiana of French descent. It often consists of dance music or lyrical songs sung in the local dialect (which is itself a mixture of English and French dialects). Typical Cajun bands feature fiddle, accordion, triangle, and guitar.

Call-and-response A vocal or instrumental style in which a short melodic line (the "call") is sung (often by a song leader) and then a second, "responding" phrase follows it (often sung by a group). In European and American classical music, the style is called "antiphony."

Caller A dance leader who "prompts" the dancers by calling out the figures before they are to be performed. Common today among square, contra, and big circle dances.

Calypso A Caribbean song form popularized in the United States during the 1930s featuring improvised songs of topical or humorous content with a syncopated beat.

Camp-meeting song A religious song associated with large nineteenth-century camp meetings, the purpose of which was to convert people to Christianity. Hundreds of congregants converged on a single spot to spend several days praying, sermonizing, witnessing, and exchanging and learning simple songs that were easy to sing by ear.

Canción A traditional love song of the Latino communities of the southwestern United States, Mexico, and Latin America.

Ceili Gaelic for "dance." Thus, any gathering where Irish dancing is performed.

Ceili or **Ceilidh band** An Irish dance band that combines traditional Irish melody instruments—fiddle, flute, bagpipe, and accordion—with a regular, heavy rhythmic accompaniment provided by piano, bass, and military-style drumming.

Celtic music Music of the Celts, the original inhabitants of Ireland and Wales; often used to describe Irish traditional music in general.

Chanson A short lyric song in the French language.

Chanter (1) A song leader. In the Native American tradition, the chanter (usually male) may also serve as the drummer who accompanies dancers. (2) The melody pipe of the bagpipe.

Chantey *See* Shanty.

Chanteymen Sailors who sing traditional shantys; also used to describe any sailors who work on a boat.

Chicago blues A style of urban blues that emerged on the South Side of Chicago after World War II, centering around performers such as Muddy Waters and Howlin' Wolf. Generally, Chicago blues is performed by a combo featuring electric guitar, piano, harmonica, and drums.

Chicken scratch music A common name (regarded by some as disparaging) for a type of dance music played by Native American and Tex-Mex bands that is derived from European styles such as quadrilles, waltzes, and polkas.

Chinese opera An elaborately staged and costumed musical theater tradition of China. Different Chinese regions have their own operatic styles, which are referred to as Peking opera, Cantonese opera, and so on.

Chorus (1) *See* Refrain. (2) A large vocal group made up of voices of different vocal ranges.

Chromatic scale All twelve divisions of the octave (not just the eight of the do-re-mi scale.) On a piano, for instance, the chromatic scale includes all of the white and black keys within the span of an octave.

Cittern A Renaissance-era string instrument similar to a guitar.

Clave rhythm The defining rhythm of much Latin-Caribbean music. It is a repeated two-bar pattern around which all other rhythmic patterns are organized. It goes "123-123-12 34-12-12-34," keeping an even pulse and stressing "1."

Claves Two sticks that are beat rhythmically together in Latin-Caribbean musical styles. *See also* Rhythm sticks.

Clog (1) *See* Clogging. (2) A dance tune to accompany clogging or step dancing, usually in 2/4 or 4/4 time.

Clogging Complicated step dances often performed by a solo dancer, with movement restricted to the lower legs and feet, while the remainder of the body is held straight. Similar to Irish step dancing and perhaps derived from it. Styles that involve keeping the feet close to the ground are known as "flat-foot clogging" or "flatfooting." Also called "buck dancing."

Coda An ending passage of a musical composition.

Combo A small instrumental ensemble.

Concertina A name loosely given to a wide variety of free-reed, bellows-driven instruments. The concertina played by German, Polish, and other immigrants in the American Midwest is really a form of button accordion. The Irish concertina is much smaller and plays a different note on the push and pull.

Conga drums *See* Tumbadoras.

Conjunto (1) A small ensemble, usually led by an accordion, popular in the southwestern United States and Mexico. (2) The type of music played by such an ensemble. *See also Norteño music/La música norteña.*

Contour Literally, "shape." The shape of a melody—whether it moves up or down gradually or in leaps—is called its contour.

Contra dance A New England form of couple dance, danced in two facing lines. The figures are performed by two couples and are similar to those found in square dancing. Chorus figures are performed by the entire line. Couples progress up or down the line as they become "active" (initiators of a figure) or "inactive."

Contradanza *See* Contra dance.

Contredanse *See* Contra dance.

Corrido A narrative folk song or ballad (often tragic and with elements of social protest) found among both Native American and Tex-Mex traditions in the southwestern United States and Mexico, its country of origin.

Cotillion A French ballroom dance of the late eighteenth and early nineteenth centuries that was popular in the American colonies as well as in England. It involved couples in square formations performing repeated figures and was a predecessor of the quadrille and square dance.

Cotillo *See* Cotillion.

Countermelody A contrasting second melody played simultaneously with the principal melody.

Counterrhythm A second rhythmic line played in contrast with the principal rhythmic line.

Couplet Two lines of a song's lyric that form a complete thought.

Cowbell A small, hollow metal bell—similar to those placed around the necks of cows—that is struck with a metal stick.

Csárdás A stylized Hungarian folk dance in 2/4 time that became popular in the first half of the nineteenth century. The melodies are noted for their minor keys and dramatic changes in tempo.

Cuatro A Puerto Rican guitar-like instrument, but with a smaller body and five pairs of strings.

Cubop A blend of Cuban rhythms and drums with bebop-style music. Pioneered by Dizzy Gillespie's bands of the 1950s.

Cycle (1) A group of songs or instrumental compositions that are usually performed together. (2) In square dancing, a group of four couples who form a single square. Also called set.

Cymbals Paired percussion instruments consisting of two brass discs that are struck together. They can be very small (for example, finger cymbals) or quite large.

D

Deejay *See* Disc jockey.

Descending contour or **melody** A melody that generally falls in pitch over its duration.

Diatonic accordion An accordion with buttons that play different notes when the bellows are opened (pulled) or closed (pushed). Sometimes called "push-pull accordions" for this reason.

Diatonic scale The eight-tone scale from octave to octave; the do-re-mi scale without chromatic tones.

Diddley bow Traditional African American one-stringed instrument. The string is made of hay baling wire stretched over two cans or jars and fastened horizontally to a wall or a board at each end.

It is plucked with the fingers of one hand. Different tones are produced by stopping the string with a small bottle or other slide.

Disc jockey An announcer who selects, introduces, and plays records, either "live" or on the radio. Commonly called a "deejay" or "DJ."

Disco Dance music of the 1970s noted for its loud, regular beat.

Dissonance In Western classical music, any harmony part that is based on seconds, sevenths, augmented, or diminished intervals. More generally, a harmony part that sounds unpleasant to the ear. "Consonance" is the term used to describe simultaneously played tones that are pleasant to the ear.

DJ *See* Disc jockey.

Dominant The fifth degree in the Western major or minor scale. Also, the chord built on this note.

Dorian mode A sequence of tones from one octave to the next, neither major nor minor, which can be sounded by the eight white keys of the piano starting and ending on "D."

Drone A continuous, unchanging tone that sounds throughout a musical composition or a portion of it.

Drop-thumb/double-thumbing (banjo) *See* Frailing.

Drum-rattle A skin-headed drum that features small rattles, either mounted on the outside of the instrument or along the rim of the drumhead itself, so that it can create both percussive and rattling sounds.

Dulcimer (Appalachian dulcimer or **lap dulcimer)** A three- or four-stringed instrument held on the lap. The strings run the length of the instrument over a fretted fingerboard, and the player frets the notes either with a small stick or the fingers while strumming the strings with a feather quill or pick. Not related to the hammer/hammered dulcimer.

Duple time/beat A rhythm that is divisible by two or with two primary accents.

E

Electric guitar An amplified guitar; the guitar's sound is enhanced through pickups that translate the sound into electrical energy that is amplified and broadcast over speakers. Amplification further allows changing the guitar's timbre.

Ethnography The systematic description of human culture.

Ethnology The scientific comparison of human cultures.

Ethnomusicology The study of people making music, all over the globe.

F

Fa-sol-la singers *See* Shape-note.

Falsetto An artificially high voice; often a male singer singing well above his normal range.

Feis An Irish competition/festival in which musicians and dancers compete for prizes.

Fiddle A bowed lute with four strings, ordinarily tuned GDAE like the European violin. Although fiddles and violins are now structurally more or less identical, fiddle players use different techniques and sometimes modify their instruments (flattening the arc of the bridge, for example) and play in nonstandard tunings.

Field holler An a cappella, African American work song.

Fiesta A religious celebration popular in Latino communities and among some Native Americans.

Fife A short, open-holed, transverse flute with six to eight holes.

Fifth The fifth scale degree; the related interval between the tonic and the fifth scale degree.

Fill An embellishing musical phrase, often improvised by an ensemble musician not responsible for carrying the main melody.

Finger cymbals Tiny paired cymbals that are attached to the fingers with small leather straps.

Finger pick To play a banjo or guitar with the tips of the finger or finger picks (metal or plastic extensions attached to the thumb or fingers to enable the player to produce a louder sound) rather than strumming across the strings with a flat pick held between the thumb and first finger.

Fipple flute A flute with a mouthpiece that has a plug with a notch at one end, such as that found on the recorder.

Flageolet A simple flute, often made from a reed or bone, that is blown from one end. It features four fingering holes and two thumb holes to vary the tones produced.

Flatfooting *See* Clogging.

Floating stanza or **verse** A common set of lyrics that moves from one song to another.

Folklife Study of the day-to-day lives of ordinary people in close-knit communities, with special attention to traditional ways of thinking and doing.

Folklore The oral and customary traditions of a group of people, including their stories, songs, recipes, clothing, holidays, architecture and use of space, and so on.

Foodways The traditional eating habits and cooking practices of a specific cultural group.

Form Musical structure; the way the musical design coheres as a whole.

Fox-trot Popular dance form of the 1920s and 1930s in duple time that has survived as one of the standard couple dances.

Frailing (banjo) The old-time style of playing the banjo that involves brushing

the back of the nail of the second or third finger across the strings while "catching" the thumb on the short drone string in a rhythmic pattern. Also called clawhammer, rapping, banging, thumping, or drop-thumb (a more melodic variation of frailing, where the thumb is used to pick notes as well as to hit the drone string). *See also* three-finger style (banjo) and two-finger (up-picking) style (banjo).

Frame drum A round drum with a shallow body. The rim of the drum is often made from a single bent piece of wood. Examples of frame drums are the bodhrán, which is used in Irish traditional music, and the tambourine.

Free reed A small, single reed—made of metal, bamboo, or some other material—that is held firmly at one end, usually in a frame. A Jew's harp is a simple free-reed instrument. Accordions, concertinas, the Japanese shō, and harmonicas are also free-reed instruments.

Freedom song Song performed during the civil rights movement of the 1950s and 1960s expressing the message of the movement.

Frolic An older term for a dance, often held at a private home, that might last all night long.

Funk (1) An African American popular music that developed in the 1960s from African polyrhythms and call-and-response textures. Funk music often uses a single chord or a few alternating, sometimes complex harmonies, through which clipped, syncopated lines emerge in the electric guitar and bass parts, drums and percussion, keyboards, winds (saxophones, trumpets), and vocal parts. Interjections by different instruments and voices, often repeated, is another typical element. Funk has been able to blend into successive styles, exerting influence on reggae, disco, hip-hop, and rap. (2) A roots movement in jazz during the

1950s that drew on blues, rhythm and blues, and gospel music in a reaction against increasingly abstract bebop and cool jazz styles.

G

Gaelic The family of traditional languages of Ireland and Scotland.

Genre A named type of musical composition and performance, such as jazz, blues, bluegrass, zydeco, and so on.

***Gesangverein* ("Singing society")** A private, German American social club dedicated to choral singing, often of patriotic and sentimental songs, traditionally sung in German.

Gigue Originally a popular Baroque dance in a rapid tempo that was performed by men. In the Franco-American tradition, the gigue has evolved into a virtuosic solo step dance performed by both men and women. *See also* Jig.

Glide A smooth, rapid movement from one note to another, slurring over the intermediate pitches. In classical music, called "portamento" or "glissando."

Glissando *See* Glide.

Glottal stop An abrupt interruption of the breath by rapidly closing the glottis (the elongated open space between the vocal cords).

Gong A large, round, metal plate that is often suspended in a frame. It plays a single note when it is struck with a metal stick or mallet.

Gospel music Modern Protestant religious music that is more personal and informal than the traditional Christian hymn.

Gospel quartet A small ensemble of four or more singers who sing religious-themed songs in four-part harmony.

Gourd rattle A dried gourd that has been hollowed out and filled with seeds or small pebbles. When shaken, it makes a rattling sound.

Grace note An ornamenting or embellishing note, usually performed before the primary tone.

Griot An African storyteller; specifically applied to the master harpists of the Gambia who accompany themselves on a harp known as the kora while relating their political and cultural history.

Guitar A six-stringed instrument of seventeenth-century Spanish origin, successor to the lute. It was popularized among folk and amateur musicians in the United States in the late nineteenth century as an accompaniment for songs.

H

Habanera A traditional Latin-Caribbean dance form with a 3+3+2 rhythmic structure.

Half-tone or **half-step** The smallest interval in the Western scale; also called a semitone. For example, the interval C-C# is a half-step.

Hammer/hammered dulcimer A traditional instrument found in many regions of the world. It consists of a square or trapezoidal-shaped body with strings running across the length of the box. The strings are usually paired (i.e., each note is produced by two strings). The player strikes the strings with two small "hammers" made of wood (sometimes covered with felt). Unrelated to the Appalachian lap dulcimer, despite the shared name.

Hammond organ An electronic organ developed in the late 1940s that was far less expensive and much smaller and lighter than a conventional pipe organ and therefore appealed to smaller churches and home organists. Besides organ sounds, this instrument was also capable of producing some "special effects" electronically.

Harmonica A small, free-reed instrument. A series of reeds are mounted in small air chambers that are open at one end. The player either sucks or blows into these openings to make the reeds sound. By cupping their hands over the harmonica and opening or closing them while playing and by playing in keys other than what the harmonica is meant for, blues musicians have created many different timbres and effects. Also called a "mouth harp," "harp," or "mouth organ."

Harmonium A small reed organ. The reeds are set in motion by air from a bellows pumped by the player's feet.

Harmony Musical tones sounded at the same time. *See also* Melody.

Heterophony Two or more slightly different vocal or instrumental parts played simultaneously. Slight intentional variations in ornamentation and attack may account for some of the differences.

Hexatonic A six-note scale.

Highland fling The Irish name for traditional Scottish tunes played briskly in 4/4 time.

Hillbilly music The recording industry's pejorative, in-house name for early country music (c. 1923–1930).

Hip-hop African American popular dance music of the last two decades of the twentieth century that became the underlying musical basis for rap. While inheriting the strong beat of disco, hip-hop re-emphasized the backbeat of 1960s popular music and also drew upon house music of the late 1970s. It developed as sampling technology evolved, allowing musicians and producers to "sample" or record small excerpts from earlier popular songs. These small pieces were then electronically treated, looped (or repeated), and put one on top of another to form a dense musical texture.

Hoedown A community dancing party, originally in the rural American South and West, featuring square dances with calling and old-time music.

Honky-tonk A small bar or club featuring country music. Marked by the sound of electric guitars and pedal steel guitars, honky-tonk music emerged as a popular style in the late 1940s and early 1950s.

Hornpipe Since the sixteenth century, a dance and tune in 4/4 or 2/4 time. Originally played slowly to accompany step dancing, hornpipes are now often played as quickly as reels.

Hula Originally a form of religious dance from Hawaii; subsequently popularized as a show dance style.

Hurdy-gurdy A stringed instrument most commonly found in Eastern Europe and France (Brittany). The fret board is covered with an elaborate mechanism that allows the player to fret the strings by pushing down on a key (like the keyboard of a piano). The notes are sounded by turning a crank that activates a rosin-covered wheel that rubs up against the strings from underneath.

Hymn A religious song praising God.

I

Idiophones Musical instruments whose sounds are produced by striking or shaking a metallic, wooden, or other surface directly. Thus, idiophones produce their sound by the substance of the instrument itself. Cymbals, rattles, rhythm sticks, and triangles are examples of idiophones.

Improvisation The creation of new melody, lyrics, or harmony parts in the midst of performance.

Instrument A device that produces musical sounds.

Interval The distance in pitch between two notes. Intervals are usually measured from the lower tone to the higher. In the C major scale, the interval C-E is a major third.

J

Jam/jamming A dance competition held on the street; "jamming" is to compete with other dancers. *See also* Street dancing; break dancing/breaking.

Jam session An informal gathering of musicians to play tunes.

Jazz A number of popular musical styles invented by African Americans beginning around the turn of the twentieth century based on improvised melodies and syncopated rhythms.

Jew's harp A small musical instrument consisting of a metal tongue (or reed) mounted in a frame. The player holds it up against his or her open teeth, and, while vigorously plucking the instrument's tongue, breathes in and out to create a whirring sound. Also called "jaw harp."

Jig An Irish dance tune in triple time; also the rapid movement of the feet in a "jig" step.

Jubilee An African American religious song that has had different meanings over time and that may refer to (1) songs sung during the emancipation celebrations of 1862 and that refer to a liberation, (2) songs that are uptempo and rhythmic (such as "When the Saints Go Marching In"), and (3) the Fisk Jubilee Singers and their strong influence on a new singing style and songs written during Reconstruction. The Fisk singers and these new songs were important in the development of gospel quartets. Written in the context of freedom, not slavery, this music exhibited a different attitude and style.

Jug band An informal jazz group, often featuring homemade or inexpensive musical instruments, including the kazoo, washboard, washtub bass, and a large, empty jug. The jug player either blows or sings into its opening in a rhythmic fashion to create a bass harmony part.

Junkanoo music A style of vibrant, Bahamian percussion music performed

by costumed marchers (Junkanooers) at special parades and festivals that were originally held during the Christmas season but now occur at other times of the year as well.

K

Kazoo A small wind instrument featuring a thin membrane that is set into vibration when the player hums or speaks into one end of the instrument. A simple version can be made by placing a piece of tissue paper over a comb and humming through it.

Kitchen racket or **kitchen junket** An informal dance held in the home; the term was most commonly used in New York and New England for informal contra dances.

Klezmer A Yiddish term literally meaning "vessel of melody," it was the name given to Jewish American dance bands of the 1920s and 1930s who played a mixture of traditional and jazz-influenced music. Klezmer music has enjoyed a strong revival since the mid-1970s.

Konpas Haitian small-band music that incorporates elements of rock, jazz, disco, soul, and funk.

L

Ländler A couple dance in 3/4 time that originated in alpine central Europe in the early nineteenth century.

Leader *See* Song leader.

Lining out A term used to describe a style of hymn singing in which a group leader first sings a line of music and the leader and congregation then repeat the words to a different but related melody. The hymn continues in this way line by line.

Long bow style A fiddle technique in which several notes are played on a single bowstroke; smoother than playing "short bow" style, in which the direc-

tion of the bow is changed with the majority of notes.

Longways Dances performed in two long lines. *See also* Contra dance.

Lulus *See* Vocables.

Lute A generic name for a variety of plucked string instruments, most popular from the sixteenth through the eighteenth centuries. The body of the lute is shaped like half of a pear, with its neck turned back at a right angle. It usually has five sets of double strings, plus a single string for the highest sound, and they are plucked with the fingers. The mandolin is of the lute family, as are the Chinese pipa and the Japanese biwa. *See also* Guitar.

Lyric song A song that primarily expresses an emotion (e.g., love, loneliness, or anger). Lyric songs are shorter than narrative ballads. Usually in a verse-refrain format, a common structure in which one melodic part (a verse whose lyrics often change) is alternated with a repeated chorus or refrain.

M

Major The primary Western classical scale since the eighteenth century. A major chord consists of a first, major third, and fifth intervals.

Mambo A ballroom dance derived from the rumba. It appeared in Cuba during the 1940s and by the 1950s had spread to non–Hispanic audiences in the United States. The mambo uses forward and backward steps (beginning on the upbeat) to percussive polyrhythmic accompaniment.

Mandolin An eight-string, guitar-like instrument. The mandolin's strings are paired in four and tuned like those of a violin. Mandolin orchestras were popular in the early twentieth century. Today they have largely disappeared, but the instrument is featured in bluegrass music.

Maracas Popular Latin-Caribbean gourd rattles.

Mariachi A modern musical ensemble—often heard along the border between Texas and Mexico—consisting of vocalists accompanied by various stringed instruments, including guitars and violins and usually brass (trumpets) as well.

Marimba A wooden-keyed instrument with small resonators placed below the bars. It is played with a stick or a pair of sticks. A type of xylophone.

Matachina and *Matachines* *Matachina* are dances of conquest, originally Spanish in origin but later adapted by the Pueblo Indians; *matachines* are the male dancers who perform them. The matachines dance in two lines facing each other, often wearing elaborate crowns featuring long ribbons and carrying rattles. They may also perform circular dances around a maypole.

Mazurka A Polish dance style in triple time brought to the United States by immigrants beginning in the mid–nineteenth century.

Mele Chanted poetic texts that express the relationship of Hawaiians to everything around them (the land, the ocean, their gods, and all living things) and also serve as orally transmitted records of the legends and lore of the Hawaiian people, including family histories, plant names, place names, and medical practices.

Melisma Characterized by singing three or more tones per syllable of text.

Melody A succession of musical tones. *See also* Harmony.

Membranophones Musical instruments that produce a sound through a vibrating membrane, or skin head. Drums are the most common membranophones.

Merengue or **meringue** Characteristic Afro-Cubanesque song dance of Venezuela, Haiti, and the Dominican Republic. It uses four-line stanzas and refrain verse forms. Responsorial singing, polyrhythms, and 5/8 effects are layered over the basic 2/4 beat.

Metallophone Similar to a xylophone, but with metal keys instead of wooden ones.

Microtone Any interval smaller than the half-tone; often used to describe tiny divisions of a tone (such as 1/4 of a tone).

Minor The second most common Western classical scale, also known as the Aeolian mode.

Minstrel show A nineteenth-century American amusement in which actors and musicians mimicked African American dialect, music, and dance.

Mixolydian One of the Greek modes, rarely heard today in classical music, although still common in some folk traditions. Neither major nor minor, it is a sequence of tones that can be achieved by playing the eight white keys of the piano starting and ending on G.

Monochord A single-stringed instrument, such as the diddley bow.

Montuno The call-and-response section of Cuban son. It features a short, simple harmonic ostinato that forms the basis for call-and-response passages and solo instrumental improvisation.

Motown A type of African American popular music (created specifically to appeal to teenagers of all races) that was produced by the Detroit-based record label of the same name during the 1960s.

Music notation Any system of symbols for writing down music.

N

Narrative song A song that tells a story or relates history; a ballad.

Norteño **music/***La música norteña* Contemporary accordion-based folk music of Tex-Mex origin characterized by stylistic simplicity and working-class themes. The style is known inside Texas as conjunto.

Note value The length of time or duration that a specific note is sounded. Also called "time value."

O

Octave The eighth or final scale step; the interval whose distance is eight diatonic tones, as from middle C to C above middle C on the piano.

Off-beat A beat that is normally not stressed or accented.

Old-time (1) The traditional songs and fiddle tunes of the southeastern United States. (2) Songs and tunes that were popular in the past but now are remembered by only a small group of musicians. (3) A term used by many European American cultures of the Midwest to describe the ethnic-based styles of social dancing and social dance music centered around waltzes, polkas, and often the schottische. Ballroom dances (such as the fox-trot) that have developed in more recent years are considered part of the "new-time" tradition.

Oral history (1) History that is passed from generation to generation by the telling of stories rather than through written texts. (2) A method of collecting history by means of interviews.

Oral tradition Songs, stories, and other customs that are passed down from generation to generation by imitation and by word-of-mouth rather than by being written down.

Ornament Formulaic decoration or embellishment of a musical tone.

Ostinato A melodic phrase that is persistently repeated (usually in the same voice part and at the same pitch) throughout a composition.

P

Panpipes A collection of reeds of different lengths that are tied together. The player blows across the top of the reeds to play different notes. Panpipes are found in many Pacific and Latin American musical traditions.

Parallel thirds A type of harmonic accompaniment in which the melody line is doubled by another part, two scale tones above it, in parallel movement.

"Pendulum-like" melody A melody that predominantly alternates between two notes.

Pennywhistle *See* Tin whistle.

Pentatonic scale A five-note scale, common in folk and traditional styles. On the piano, it can be obtained by playing the black keys only.

Phrase A short musical or lyrical thought; a portion of a melody.

Piano accordion *See* Accordion.

Pipa A short-necked, Chinese wooden lute.

Pitch The acoustical highness or lowness of a musical tone resulting from its frequency of vibration.

Play-party song A short, often nonsensical song sung primarily by children at informal parties to accompany a dance or a game involving physical activity (musical chairs, for instance).

Plena A Puerto Rican ballad similar to the calypso songs of Trinidad.

Polka A vigorous Eastern European couple dance in 2/4 time, introduced by immigrants to the United States in the mid–nineteenth century.

Polyphony More than one vocal or instrumental melodies sung or played at the same time.

Polyrhythm Two or more conflicting rhythmic parts played simultaneously.

Powwow A modern, intertribal gathering of Native Americans to perform traditional dance and song forms.

Pulsation A slight interruption in breath; a continuous revoicing of a note in rapid succession.

Q

Qeej A bamboo-reed mouth organ of the Hmong people of Cambodia. Similar to the Japanese shō.

Quadrille A precursor of the square dance, the quadrille originated in the ballrooms of France and attained its greatest popularity in the early nineteenth century throughout Europe, Russia, and the United States. It is performed by either four or eight couples and features five main figures (patterns of movement).

Quills See Panpipes.

R

R&B *See* Rhythm and blues.

Race records A term used by record companies to describe the special line of recordings marketed primarily from the 1920s through the 1940s to the African American audience.

Ragtime Originally a piano style with a regular, repeated bass line and a syncopated melody; later, any syncopated composition. Ragtime was developed by African Americans in the late nineteenth century.

Range In describing a melody, the overall intervallic distance covered between lowest and highest notes.

Rap A style of urban African American popular music characterized by (often) improvised, sung-spoken rhymes performed to a rhythmic accompaniment. Rap is frequently performed a cappella, with sexual, socially relevant, or political lyrics. The music itself became known as hip-hop.

Rasp/Rasping sticks A rasp is a small, notched piece of wood that is rubbed with a stick or scraper to make a grating sound. Rasping sticks are also notched in such a way that when they are rubbed together, they produce a similar effect.

Rattle A gourd, shell, or can filled with pebbles that makes a rattling sound when it is vigorously shaken.

Reel A fast Anglo-American dance tune, often played on the fiddle, in 4/4 or cut (2/2) time.

Refrain The repeated chorus of a song that alternates with the verse. Unlike the verse, the words to the refrain usually do not change. Sometimes a refrain is shorter than a chorus.

Reggae A popular Jamaican musical style that melds Western rock instrumentation with a loping, syncopated beat and often topical lyrics.

Repertoire The songs, dance tunes, or other musical pieces that are characteristically performed by an individual or a group of people.

Resonator An empty vessel—often a gourd—placed under a musical instrument to increase the sound produced.

Rhythm and blues (R&B) A generic term used to describe African American popular song styles in the late 1940s and early 1950s. Imitation soon led to rock and roll, the white equivalent of rhythm and blues.

Rhythm sticks Two sticks that are rubbed together to create a percussive rhythm.

Rhythmic pattern The patterns of beats that occur throughout a piece of music.

Rhythmic pulse The underlying beat.

Riff A short, memorable melodic phrase that is repeated throughout sections of an instrumental composition or accompaniment. *See also* Ostinato.

Ring shout Historically, a circular African American dance song expressing religious feeling. The song is half-sung, half-shouted as the dancers move slowly in a ring formation. Also called simply a "shout."

Rock and roll A popular white American style of the 1950s that was copied from

black rhythm and blues and featured a percussively heavy reinforcement of the meter (beat) played by combos consisting, minimally, of piano, bass, drums, and guitars, often with a single saxophonist or small wind section. Blues harmonic structures were common, but without the corresponding mood. By the mid-1960s, rock and roll had run out of steam, only to be revitalized and transformed into rock by the so-called "British Invasion" of musical groups that emphasized electric guitars and nonblues harmonic patterns. *See also* Rhythm and blues.

Rockabilly A musical style of the late 1950s and early 1960s that blended country music with rock and roll's sensibility, instrumentation, and heavily accented beat. The term was coined from a combination of "rock" and "hillbilly."

Round dance Any traditional dance that is performed in a circular figure. *See also* Big circle dance.

Rumba A syncopated Latin American dance form, originally from Cuba, that was popularized in the United States in the 1930s.

S

Sacred Harp, The The name of a religious songbook first published in the early nineteenth century; now applied to any song from this book or others in the shape-note tradition.

Salsa A vigorous Latin American dance form combining Latin rhythms with big band instrumentation. Based on the traditional Cuban son style.

Samba A Brazilian American dance style featuring a medium tempo and pronounced rhythms.

Scale A sequence of tones, arranged in ascending or descending order, and used in a characteristic way in a musical performance or composition.

Schottische An Eastern European dance that is a variant of the polka. It is performed by couples in a circle, in 2/2 time, at a slower pace than the polka.

Scraper A small stick used to rub against another object to make a sound.

Scratching A technique used by disc jockeys in which records are spun back and forth while being played so that a percussive, scratching sound is created.

Sean-nós singing A traditional Irish singing style. Highly ornamented, it is particularly suited to singing songs in Gaelic but is also used for English-language songs.

Secular music Music without religious content; music performed for entertainment, not to express religious feelings.

Seísun Literally, "session." An informal gathering of Irish musicians.

Set A generic term for any square dance. The group of four couples who perform the dance are often described as a "set." Also called cycle.

Shanty A short lyric song sung by sailors to aid in their work or pass the time.

Shape-note A system of musical notation in which different scale notes are represented by notes of different shapes, including diamonds, circles, squares, and triangles. Singers can therefore learn their parts without "reading" conventional music by associating the shape with its scale tone (sung as "fa-sol-la," etc.). This method was used to promote music literacy and teach hymn singing to people both in the northern and southeastern United States. *See also* Sacred Harp, The.

Shellshaker In the Native American tradition, a turtle shell filled with small pebbles that is usually attached to the leggings or boots of a female dancer. The name "shellshaker" may be applied to the turtle shell or to the dancer herself.

Shō A Japanese musical instrument consisting of a group of thin bamboo pipes (each containing at its base a small reed) clustered around a small wind

chamber. The player blows into the chamber to sound the reeds. Small fingering holes at the base of each pipe are used to regulate which reed sounds. Variants of this instrument are found throughout Southeast Asia.

Shout *See* Ring shout.

Shuffle (step) (1) A walking step in which the feet are dragged slightly. (2) A syncopated beat.

Slide (1) Moving from one tone to another without a break; similar to a glide but usually covering a smaller range. (2) In reference to the guitar, the use of a bottleneck or metal bar to stop the strings; this technique is known as slide guitar. (3) In Irish music, a jig in 12/8 time, often in three or more parts.

Snare drum A small, two-headed drum of wood or metal, across the lower head of which are stretched several gut strings or strands of metal wire (snares), whose rattling against the head reinforces and alters the tone. The upper head is struck alternately or simultaneously with two drumsticks.

Soca Caribbean music that combines traditional calypso with disco rhythms and soul vocal styles.

Son (1) Generic name of indigenous songs of Cuba and neighboring islands, reflecting the influence of African rhythms and set usually in a strongly accented 2/4 time. *Son* was the principal form of Cuban popular music in the twentieth century and remains an important form of expression in New York's Cuban and Puerto Rican community. It is characterized by a two-part structure in which two or three verses (usually sung by a lead soloist but sometimes by a chorus) are followed by a call-and-response section known as the montuno. *See also* Salsa. (2) A traditional dance piece performed by Mexican mariachi musicians. It varies in style from region to region in Mexico, but is often fast-tempoed with raucous and sometimes

improvised lyrics containing social commentary.

Song leader (1) In call-and-response form, the person who sings the melody first, unaccompanied ("the call"), to whom the chorus then answers or "responds." (2) Anyone who leads a large group in song, whether in a religious or secular setting (as, for example, during the rallies of the civil rights movement).

Soul music A term used to describe the gospel-flavored performances of popular African American singers such as Ray Charles and Aretha Franklin.

Spiritual A genre of popular religious songs, chiefly from the nineteenth century. Spirituals composed by African Americans during the slavery period are the best-known examples.

Square dance A traditional American dance form, usually performed by four couples in a square formation. Specific "figures" (dance patterns) are performed by the couples in succession, as prompted by a caller.

Squeezebox or **squeeze-box** A common name for any bellows-driven instrument, such as an accordion or a concertina.

Stanza *See* Verse.

Steel band A large ensemble of steel drum players.

Steel drum/steel pan A Caribbean musical instrument made out of the shell of an oil drum. Small indentations are made in the face of the drum. By striking in different areas with a metal or wooden stick, the player can sound different scale notes.

Steel guitar An electric guitar that is held, face up, on the player's lap (and is therefore sometimes called a "lap steel"). The instrument is tuned to an open chord and played with a metal bar that is moved across the fret board. Also called a "fry pan," because early models were small and thin; the small

body attached to a long neck resembled the common piece of cookware.

Step dancing A dance style of European origin that features rapid movement of the lower legs and feet while the remainder of the body is held rigidly. Similar to clogging.

Stomp dance In the Native American tradition, the term used for a variety of both secular and sacred dances in which the movement of the dancers' feet provides the rhythmic accompaniment. The percussive sound is often provided by rattles tied in bunches around the calves of the dancers.

Strathspey A Scottish dance tune named for the valley of the River Spey. It is characterized by its "Scotch snap" rhythm: a sixteenth note followed briskly by a dotted eighth note. In traditional Scottish fiddling, the sixteenth note is played with a slight upbow, followed by a sharp downwards stroke for the dotted eighth, giving the characteristic "snapping" sound. Played in 4/4 time, but slower than a reel.

Strawbeater In some traditions of the southeastern United States, a strawbeater would hold two small pieces of reed or straw and beat them rhythmically on the strings of the fiddle while the fiddler was playing. This would add a rhythmic texture to the fiddle's sound.

Street dancing A highly virtuosic, exhibition dance style, often performed on urban street corners. *See also* Break dancing/Breaking.

String band A group of musicians who accompany dances, usually consisting of stringed instruments such as banjos, fiddles, guitars, and mandolins. Non-stringed instruments—such as harmonicas—can also be heard in a string band.

Strophic Made up of stanzas or strophes; songs based on a repeated melody line that is used to accompany a series of stanzas.

Swing A style of big band jazz that was a major type of social dance music from the 1920s through the mid-1940s. Small swing groups featured improvisation, while the larger groups presented lavish arrangements of songs with interpretations that accented smoothness.

Symmetrical rhythm A balanced, or repeating, rhythmic pattern used consistently throughout a musical composition.

Sympathetic strings Strings that run under the neck (or in the body) of a musical instrument and thus are inaccessible to the player for either fretting or strumming. Instead, these strings vibrate "in sympathy" when the instrument is played; that is, they may vibrate when either the body of the instrument or the other strings vibrate. The Scandinavian hardanger fiddle is an instrument that features sympathetic strings.

Syncopation Accenting the off-beat; placing an accent on a beat that is usually unaccented.

T

Taiko A Japanese double-headed barrel drum, usually of great size.

Tambourine A small, shallow hand drum featuring a single head with small metal "jingles" placed in the frame.

Tamburitza An Eastern European folk lute.

Tango An Argentine dance form first popularized in the 1920s and 1930s that is marked by dramatic, strongly syncopated melodies.

Tap dancing A popular dance form of the 1920s and 1930s that has been revived over the past few decades. It is an elaborate form of step dancing in which the performer wears metal taps on the bottom of his or her shoes in order to emphasize the percussive sounds. Most of the movement occurs as the dancer alternates between tapping the front of the shoe and the heel; arm movements and other gestures are added for emphasis.

Tarantella A popular and energetic folk dance of Italian origin.

Tempo The rate of speed of a musical performance.

Tenor banjo A four-string instrument based on the original banjo but developed at the turn of the twentieth century specifically for playing accompaniment work in ragtime and early jazz. Tenor banjos were adopted by Irish musicians for playing melody as well.

Tex-Mex music *See Norteño* music/*La música norteña.*

Texture The interrelationship of the musical lines in a composition or performance.

Third The third scale degree; the related interval between the tonic and the third scale step.

Three-finger style (banjo) A more modern method of playing the banjo in which patterns are picked by the thumb and two fingers. This is also called bluegrass style because it was popularized by Earl Scruggs and other bluegrass banjo players.

Timbales Paired tom-tom drums mounted on a stand, popular in Latin-Caribbean dance music.

Timbre The characteristic sound quality of an individual voice or musical instrument; why a flute sounds different from a violin when they play the same note.

Tin whistle A small, six-holed, end-blown flute, popular in Irish music. Originally made of tin with a wooden mouthpiece, it is now more commonly made of brass with a plastic mouthpiece. Also called a "pennywhistle."

Tom-tom Generic term for African, Asian, or Latin American indigenous drums, of high but (usually) indefinite pitch. They may be played with the hands or sticks.

Tonic The first note of a scale and the pitch to which others in a composition gravitate.

Transcription A written version or notation of a musical composition.

Triangle A triangular piece of metal that makes a clanging sound when struck with a short metal stick.

Triple time/beat A rhythm with an accent every three beats.

***Tumbadoras*/Conga drums** Tall, cylindrical, single-headed drums based on African models but popularized in Cuban dance music. They are played with fingers and palms of the hands and come in three sizes: The larger drum is called the *tumba*; the *secundo* is medium-sized; and the smallest is called the *quinto*. Usually, the tumba and secundo play one rhythmic pattern, while the quinto plays a counterrhythm.

Two-finger (up-picking) style (banjo) A style in which the banjo player picks upwards with the index finger, alternating or coinciding with a rhythmic downward pick of the thumb.

Two-step A popular and simple couple dance, found throughout the United States. It can be performed to any duple-time melody.

U

Uilleann (bag)pipes Irish bagpipes; unlike the Scottish version, they are driven by a small bellows that is held under the elbow and pumped. In addition to drone and melody ("chanter") pipes, they feature so-called regulator pipes that play chords.

Undulating (contour) Melody lines that seem to meander or wander without any definite goal.

Unison Two or more vocalists (or instrumentalists) singing (or playing) the same melodic part at the same time.

V

Variation Slight changes in the melody line, often occurring on its second statement or repetition.

Veillée A house party; the Franco American equivalent of a kitchen racket.

Verse The changing text of a song that alternates with the chorus or refrain. Usually, the verse is sung to one melody and the refrain to another one.

Vibrato A trembling, "vibrating" pitch; a slight variation in intensity in pitch creating a sense of vibration or fluttering.

Vocables Untranslatable but not necessarily meaningless syllables (such as "fa-la-la") that are sung to a melodic line in place or instead of words.

W

Waila A type of social dance music with European roots that has been incorporated into Native American traditions.

Waltz A European couple dance in 3/4 time, introduced by immigrants to the United States in the mid–nineteenth century.

Washboard A metal board used to launder clothes, which, when adapted as a musical instrument, is vigorously "rubbed" by the player, who wears thimbles or other small pieces of metal on his or her fingers. Also called a "rubboard."

Water drum A small, skin-headed drum made of a crock or vessel that is filled with water to alter its tone.

Well-tempered (or **equal-tempered**) **scale** The modern Western scale with twelve equal steps. The piano is tuned to this scale.

Western swing A musical style that developed in the Texas-Oklahoma region during the 1930s, led by fiddler Bob Wills. A marriage of old-time string band music with big band jazz, Western swing bands performed popular songs and blues in jazzy, up-tempo arrangements. Typical bands included fiddle, guitar, electric steel guitar, piano, drums, and often a small brass section.

Whistle A short, single-note flute, often made of a short piece of hollowed-out cane. The player blows into one end of the instrument to create a sound.

Woodblocks Small, square blocks of wood that are used as percussion instruments; they are usually paired and struck with a small stick.

Work song A rhythmic, repeated song, often in call-and-response form, used to coordinate a group of workers.

X

Xylophone A wooden-keyed instrument played with two small mallets. The keys are of different lengths, mounted on a frame or connected with strings, so that they can freely vibrate.

Z

Zither A stringed instrument with strings that run parallel to the full length of the body of the instrument. The Chinese ch'in (or q'in) and the autoharp are both zithers.

Zydeco A dance music of southeastern Louisiana that combines African American and Cajun styles. Alternately spelled "zodico."

INDEX

Page references in bold refer to a main essay or sidebar on that topic. Page references in italics refer to illustrations.

H

I